# Legitimating the Law

# Legitimating the Law

## The Struggle for Judicial Competency in Early National New Hampshire

*John Phillip Reid*

NIU
PRESS
DeKalb, IL

Published by the Northern Illinois University Press, DeKalb, Illinois 60115



Design by Julia Fauci

Library of Congress Cataloging-in-Publication Data

Reid, John Phillip.

Legitimating the law: the struggle for judicial competency in early national New Hampshire / John Phillip Reid.

p. cm.

Includes bibliographical references and index.

ISBN 978-0-87580-451-4 (cloth: alk. paper) — ISBN 978-1-60909-059-3 (e-book)

1. Justice, Administration of—New Hampshire—History—19th century. 2. Courts—New Hampshire—History—19th century. 3. New Hampshire—Politics and government—1775–1865. I. Title.

KFN1278.R453 2012

347.742—dc23

2011047253

FOR THE BUDDS OF RIDGE ACRES

Macdonald and Elise

Alexandra, Vanessa, and Daphne

# Contents

# Legitimating the Law

*Chapter One*

# The Arena of the Giants

If the discipline of American legal history were as completely researched as scholars could wish, the judicial history of state-court systems would largely be a history of comparisons. To best trace the development and progress of the judiciary of a state, we would compare that development and progress to similar developments and progressions in neighboring states or in states of comparable importance in business, industry, or transportation, or in states of comparable size in area or population.

For the early years of British rule, comparative studies of the thirteen quite disparate colonial courts and judiciaries have only recently been commenced. The first volume of this unique research, covering events in the Chesapeake area and New England, has been published, and within a decade or so we may expect to have a comparative survey of at least the first century of colonial American legal history.[1]

For the years following the Civil War, we could now write comparative histories of our state courts, not because judicial histories of any of the individual jurisdictions are available, but because there are biographies of a few leading judges, and also because all states now publish, and for almost two hundred years have published, the decisions of their highest courts. Almost all states have law schools that publish journals that, over the years, have produced articles discussing legal questions, notes on locally promulgated judicial decisions, surveys of the law, and comments on judicial rulings, all of which allow investigations of the work of one state's courts to be compared to those of all other states.

What we do not as yet have is the scholarly research to make comparative studies of the state judiciaries between the colonial period and the

Civil War, a time that historians have labeled "the era of the early republic." There are comprehensive studies for some of those years in only two jurisdictions—from the Revolution to the year 1830 for Massachusetts,[2] and from 1790 to 1820 for New Hampshire.[3] But, aside from Massachusetts and New Hampshire, the judicial historical pickings are very slim for court systems of states during the early republic. There just are not any studies of other state judiciaries that concentrate on the jurisprudence of the judges rather than the politics of the courts.[4] Both Kentucky and Rhode Island have full-length works on their early federal trial courts but not their state high courts,[5] although Kentucky does have an excellent study of its county courts, that is, the justices of the peace, before the Civil War.[6] There are, of course, many valuable studies telling us much about the courts of a state but not what we need to know about the development of legal doctrine and the application of legal theory. The important state of Virginia has a fine book-length account of its lawyers and local courts up to 1810. It is impressive scholarship and certainly worth reading, but it is mainly concerned with colonial and social history—legal culture, not judicial happenings.[7] Yet that book is the best available for the judiciary in the American South at the turn of the nineteenth century, except for the various articles delineating the successful actions by Georgia Jeffersonian lawmakers to keep the courts and the judges of that state subordinate to the legislative branch of government.[8]

The state judiciary for which we have the most extensive historical writings for the early republic is the most interesting of all. It may also be the most important, although that is not something we can know until we have judicial histories of most of the states during that time. Until we have looked at the thirteen original states, plus Vermont, Kentucky, Tennessee, and Ohio, we will not be able to draw accurate comparisons. But from what little is known it seems evident that the most interesting jurisdiction will be Pennsylvania. That is the state where the Jeffersonian Republicans came the closest to enacting the most extreme reform programs, changes to the high-court system, that the more radical Jeffersonian Republicans of other states may not have come near to implementing. That is, they attempted to abolish the methodology of common-law litigation—jury trials, adversary proceedings—and curtail the monopoly of the legal profession by ending the right of litigants to counsel. They enacted the necessary legislation but were stymied by Governor Thomas McKean, a former chief justice, vetoing these attacks on the reception of English law and on the organized bar. He prevented the experiment of what would have been the most far-reaching series of judicial innovations in all of American law, an experiment, that is, that would have tested whether an American state could function and prosper without common law or the legal profession. Although there are excellent studies of both Governor McKean and the high court of Pennsylvania,[9] they concentrate on judicial politics and give less attention to jurisprudential maneuverings in noncriminal law.

This present book is the third in a series of three that seek to extend our knowledge about the judicial history of that era by recounting the development of courts, law, and legal theory in early republican New Hampshire. Because we have so little scholarship about the history of state courts during the early republic, it is difficult to know just how the Superior Court of New Hampshire related to other American judiciaries. By necessity, the story that the three books tell has to be one with little comparisons.

The first, *Controlling the Law,* is an account of how Chief Justice Jeremiah Smith transformed New Hampshire judicial theory from a static layman's law known as "common sense jurisprudence," taking it into the emerging American legal mainstream of receiving the methods and procedure of English common law (though not specific English doctrine or adjudications). It is not known how much Smith was moved by the example of jurists in other early American states to convert the jury from an instrument of rule by democracy into an instrument of rule by law. As far as can be told from extant evidence, he corresponded with only two of the great judges of his era, John Marshall and Theophilus Parsons. It may be that he knew no others except for the members of the Massachusetts Supreme Judicial Court. In fact, Smith did not meet or correspond with James Kent of New York until after retiring from the bench.

The second book, *Legislating the Courts*, tells how the legislature of New Hampshire asserted superiority over the judiciary, granting new trials to litigants who had lost duly adjudicated actions, that is, had lost certified jury verdicts, with judgments formally entered by the court and damages fully awarded. Without hesitation or expressing any doubts as to their authority, committees of the New Hampshire legislature summoned judges to answer for their judicial conduct and decisions, including why they had cancelled court sessions, or to explain why they had missed trial terms. There seem to be some legal scholars, notably judges, who assume that, from the time that state courts first were created, American constitutionalism balanced the powers of government then established by vesting in the judiciary, state as well as federal, supremacy over the legislature and the executive. It is even conceivable that some of these students of American law may think the subordination of the New Hampshire courts in the early republic was unique. The truth is that, although we have evidence that Massachusetts courts were generally independent of legislative and executive supervision, we know little of how strictly those of other states were regulated.

This book, the last of the three, recounts events that seem to be *sui generis* to early national New Hampshire. Again, however, we cannot be confident. Three occurrences took place between 1813 and 1818 that may have been New Hampshire novelties. One was a year during which New Hampshire experienced the embarrassment of having two rival high courts, each asserting jurisdiction and with one set of legitimate, constitutionally appointed judges forcing another set of legitimate, constitutionally appointed judges out of their courtroom. The confiscating judges not only occupied the bench but had the sheriffs serve them and not the members of the rival court.

Second, the New Hampshire executive and legislature several times addressed judges out of office—that is, the two legislative houses, the governor, and the Executive Council exercised the authority granted by the constitution to terminate the commissions of high court judges—in one year, 1816, even addressing out those who had since 1813 served on every state court except courts of probate. Kentucky lawmakers once used the authority of addressing out to clear from office some members of that state's court,[10] but little has been written of almost every other state except for the courts of Massachusetts, where the constitutional power to address from office was never employed against the judiciary.

Third, this book tells how New Hampshire's executive and legislature employed the tactic of legislating judges out of office at least five times to clear the high court of every member. Virginia did that once, which was more an unexpected outcome, a political mistake, which the assembly undertook to correct to the extent possible.[11] There were no such corrections in New Hampshire, no restoring of ousted judges to the bench. In New Hampshire legislating the courts out of office was always intentional, as it was for Thomas Jefferson when he had Congress legislate out of office the entire bench of a federal court.[12] It may be that legislating courts from office did not occur in most states. Indeed, it is possible that many state legislators did not even suspect the power existed. But this, too, is a question that remains to be researched.[13]

For many years historians knew more about the bar of New Hampshire than they knew about New Hampshire courts. Perhaps the one fact that was agreed upon among knowledgeable American lawyers during the nineteenth century was that the state of New Hampshire was generally known for having an outstanding judiciary. Indeed, the claim may be plausibly made and confidently defended that, among the small states of the Union, New Hampshire had the finest and most respected high court. Charles R. Corning made the point—or at least part of it—when he claimed in 1890 that "the judiciary of New Hampshire . . . have been men of learning and occasionally men of genius." Charles Henry Bell, a lawyer who had been governor of the state from 1881 to 1883, was more emphatic when observing that "New Hampshire has been adorned by a succession of jurists second to few—I had almost said, second to none—in point of learning and ability."[14]

It is not necessary to detail the evidence of New Hampshire's judicial distinctiveness during the nineteenth century. The story told in this book reveals some of the magisterial contributions to the growth of New Hampshire law made by the first two chief justices of the professional period, Jeremiah Smith and William Merchant Richardson. Their successor as chief justice was Joel Parker, one of the country's outstanding jurists before the Civil War. Louis D. Brandeis described him as "one of the ablest of American judges," and Oliver Wendell Holmes, using a slightly stronger adjective, said he was "one of the greatest of American judges."[15] Parker served fifteen years on the Superior Court of Judicature, ten of them as chief justice, and then went on to make an entirely different contribution to the development of American law as Royall Professor of Law at Harvard University. The move to Cambridge, Massachusetts, placed him onto a larger, more national stage, giving him an opportunity to have a wider influence. He ranks second only to United States Supreme Court Justice Joseph Story as the leader who gave Harvard Law School its direction during its earliest years.[16]

Ira Perley was New Hampshire's most prestigious and popular chief justice between the judgeships of Parker and Charles Doe. "No man in New England knows more law than Ira Perley of New Hampshire," Rufus Choate said of him, which was very high praise as Choate was universally regarded as New England's leading trial lawyer.[17] But it was the groundbreaking judicial career of Chief Justice Charles Doe that was the finest era of New Hampshire law and conferred on the judiciary its most lasting luster. He has been hailed as the leading judicial reformer on any American court, state or federal. Professor G. Edward White described him as "the most creative state judge of the late nineteenth century," and Harvard's Dean Roscoe Pound insisted that he was one "of the ten judges who must be ranked first in American judicial history."[18]

Charles Doe was chief justice when he died in 1896. His outstanding career marked the end of the nineteenth century for the New Hampshire judiciary. The greatness of the state's court system during the century has been outlined here to dramatize the contrast with some of the judges whose careers are described in this study. From 1809 to 1813, the state's high court, and its three judges—Arthur Livermore, Richard Evans, Clifton Claggett—were the opposite of the jurists that came before and after. They were the low point of the state's judiciary, the worst judicature in all of New Hampshire's history after 1800, not only the worst for the nineteenth century, but for the twentieth and twenty-first as well. Then for three years after that, 1813 to 1816, although two of the three judges were quite distinguished, they were hounded by one of the strangest episodes in all of American judicial history, a rival court of other judges who claimed to be the legitimate tribunal and who occupied their bench, forcing them to abandon their courtroom. It was a time of conflicting court systems that required the sheriffs, the clerk, and all the members of the bar to choose between them. It was an aberration when New Hampshire law seemingly lost much legitimacy, an illegitimate moment in the life of an otherwise remarkable judiciary.

There is another oddity making those years of judicial depths especially bizarre. During that era New Hampshire was home to what some of our early legal historians believed was the most distinguished rural bar that ever existed in America. It was, some scholars have said, the most memorable small-town bar in United States history. They meant the bars of two small towns, Portsmouth and Exeter, which were the half-shire towns or county seats of Rockingham County, New Hampshire.

At the turn of the eighteenth into the nineteenth century, the geographical area of Rockingham County was larger than it would be in the twentieth or twenty-first centuries. Stretching the full length of New Hampshire's seacoast, it was the center of the state's commercial, political, and intellectual life. Embracing the old Yankee settlements from the Piscataqua River almost to the Merrimack, and extending beyond the Scotch-Irish country around Londonderry and Chester to the future state capital at Concord, it was anchored by those two "half-shire towns," Portsmouth and Exeter. The legal profession that practiced in Rockingham County during the years between the 1790s and the 1820s was sometimes referred to as "the arena of the giants."[19]

"Consider who they were that fixed the standard of talent at the New-Hampshire bar in the first quarter of the nineteenth century," Robert Rantoul, Jr., Boston's leading political reformer, recalled in 1852. "There were giants in the land in those days."[20] He did not mean all of the New Hampshire bar. He meant the lawyers of one county, the Rockingham County bar. Daniel Webster often remembered with awe the years he had spent arguing cases at that bar. He told the great Boston attorney Rufus Choate that "he had never met anywhere else abler men than some of those who initiated him in the rugged discipline of the New Hampshire Courts."[21] On another occasion he remarked that he had practiced law, commencing before an old justice of the peace in Boscawen, a man who had received his commission during the reign of George II, and had conducted litigations all the way up to John Marshall, presiding over the Supreme Court in Washington, and "had never found any place where the law was administered with so much precision and exactness as in the County of Rockingham."[22]

Because the number of remarkable lawyers was so large and the number of important cases so small, the trials that were conducted in Rockingham County's two courtrooms were often more than contests, they were tournaments. Sometimes there were two or three attorneys on each side of a litigation. Frequently one of the attorneys for the defense was William Plumer, one of the two main protagonists of the story told by this book. A political genius with a daedal mind, Plumer will be traced in the following chapters as a governmental office holder, first as a Federalist, then as a Republican. Like his friend by correspondence, Jeremy Bentham, he distrusted oaths and never took one, making affirmations instead, a peculiarity that did not trouble the orthodox, God-fearing people of New Hampshire, who rather admired his obstinate individualism. As a correspondent of Jefferson, Bentham, and a half dozen of America's statesmen, he had a reputation that extended far beyond the physical limits of the world in which he lived. At another time or place he might have been regarded as the leader of the local bar, yet so notable were his rivals in the Rockingham County legal profession that, to his neighbors, he seemed to be a better-than-average attorney practicing among titans.

It might be said that the salience of the Rockingham County bar began in 1797 when Jeremiah Smith and Jeremiah Mason moved from the more rural inland counties to southern New Hampshire and began to try cases in Exeter, a town that previously had been the private legal-practice bailiwick of George Sullivan. He was the son of General John Sullivan, the state's Revolutionary War leader, and heir to all the Sullivan name meant to New Hampshire people. He was a good deal inferior to Smith and Mason in legal scholarship, but not even Webster could surpass Sullivan's power to sway juries. He was one of the most accomplished orators ever to practice law in New Hampshire, and this was both his strength and his undoing. As the state's nineteenth-century legal historian, John Shirley, observed, "He relied too little on his preparation, and too much upon his oratory, his power of illustration and argument. But neither the court, the jury, nor the people ever grew weary of listening to his silver tones or his arguments, that fell like music on the ear."[23] The courthouse was sometimes crowded when Sullivan appeared, for it was a pleasure to hear the rich resonance of his voice as the sentences came rolling out with their full, regular, and sonorous cadences.

Sullivan's extraordinary eloquence and charm along with his father's name gave him such a hold on the people's imagination that he was the only arch-Federalist whom Isaac Hill, the Republican "Director" of the state, was never able to disparage. He had been an anti-Madison congressman during the opening days of the War of 1812 and had supported the aims and spirit of the Hartford Convention, which had been convened to provide a unified voice for New England's opposition to the war. Such a record would have been enough to damage the public career of other lawyers during the patriotic reaction that followed Jackson's victory at New Orleans. While greater attorneys such as Webster, Mason, Smith, and Ichabod Bartlett were voted out of office or even quit the state in disgust, Sullivan remained New Hampshire's attorney general for twenty-one years, well into the heyday of Hill's reign as the leader of the Democrats, the dominant political party in the state. Yet despite his popularity and his unusual sense of professional and personal honor, Sullivan was regarded by his contemporaries as only a great advocate, not a great lawyer.

Jeremiah Smith, by contrast, had a highly cultivated legal mind. As will be discussed in the following chapters, Smith's two terms as chief justice were extraordinary contributions to the development of New Hampshire jurisprudence, for it was he who guided the law of the state away from the shifting "common sense" legal theory, expounded in the days when farmers, clergymen, and physicians constituted the judiciary, and prepared the lawyers to receive the common law.[24] As a legal philosopher, only Charles Doe equaled him in the nineteenth-century history of the New Hampshire judiciary. Almost as important to his neighbors in Rockingham County, he was a master of the wisecrack in a day when wit was a valuable courtroom weapon. He had a high originality and true genius in his humor throughout which ran a rare vein of satire and raillery, always sprightly and amusing although sometimes a bit offensive. In this respect he differed from Jeremiah Mason, who, though often humorous, was never offensive.

The inimitable Mason was the central figure of that prodigious group of lawyers who made Rockingham County during the first three decades of the nineteenth century so memorable. He had no peer. Six-foot-six, of powerful frame and striking features, he was one of those extremely rare individuals who become living legends before middle age and retain their reputations throughout their lives. He had few interests except practicing law, and he shunned public affairs. He served less than one term in the United States Senate, resigning his seat to hasten back to Portsmouth and his law office. Cool, wary, and devoted to his clients, he had, in legal acumen and power of reasoning, no equal at the bar or on the bench. He has often been described as America's greatest common-law lawyer, and probably he was, at least during the early nineteenth century. "I regard Jeremiah Mason as eminently superior to any other lawyer whom I have ever met," Webster once said. "I would rather, with my own experience (and I have had some pretty tough experience with him), meet them all combined in a case than to meet him alone and single-handed."[25] Mason, Webster added, always put him up to all he knew.

Mason did not have a good speaking voice or a graceful manner. He made no pretense toward oratory and sneered at all appearances of feeling or emotion as mere affections unsuited for a court of law. It has been said that the jury was not so much persuaded as compelled to go along with his argument, so irresistible was the force with which he focused attention on the conclusion he sought, "a conclusion which the hearer felt, long before it was reached, that he could, by no possibility, avoid, or stop short of, or turn aside from."[26]

In direct contrast to Sullivan, Mason despised eloquence, addressing juries without rhetoric, polish, or artificiality of manner, bearing down always on the issues pertaining to the case at bar. If he had any weakness as a trial advocate, this may have been it because at times he was thought to be too cautious and refined, and his distinctions could be too minute. Yet he had a remarkable way with juries that can be partly explained, as Harvard law professor John Chipman Gray pointed out, by "a knowledge of human nature amounting almost to genius."[27] He would associate himself with rural jurors by affecting country speech, a tactic that has sometimes proved disastrous for lesser litigators. The only passion he seemed to feel was contempt, especially toward paid testimony. Once approaching a particularly damaging professional witness dressed in Quaker garb, he asked, "Where did you get your clothes?" The man was so shaken by Mason's scorn he admitted that they had been furnished to him for the trial.[28] Yet Mason's power of sarcasm was not, as Webster pointed out, "frothy or petulant, but cool and vitriolic,"[29] and it was in this respect that his humor differed from Smith's. For with his trenchant wit and brusque manner, Mason had a style peculiarly his own, growing out of a severely practical turn of mind that shunned all affectation.

Whenever Jeremiah Mason contested Jeremiah Smith in court, lawyers anticipated shrewd, witty, often rough retorts during the course of the trial, although, when it came to the pure art of wisecracking, the acrid humor of Ichabod Bartlett, the "Little Giant," frequently outdid them both. A contemporary, writing of the Rockingham County bar, "described him as 'the Randolph of the North,'" a nickname he had earned while a member of Congress, and said that "the brilliant flashes of whose wit, keen sarcasm, and pungent irony, gave life and spirit to the dry juridical discussions, whose logical congruity they were allowed to relieve, but not to impair."[30]

Bartlett had a reputation for employing the choicest and fittest phrases to put across his point. Although not an orator like Sullivan, it was his fashion, when he wished to place particular emphasis upon a word, to hesitate an instant before pronouncing it. One lawyer said he was "*poising* his word before he launched it."[31] A small, buoyant man, he was physically the opposite of the elephantine Mason.

He was full of mischief. It was seldom that he was out-jested, but whenever it occurred it was sure to be told throughout Rockingham County. Once he offered an affidavit during a trial, and Mason, who was opposing counsel, began to comment on it with a good deal of severity. Hoping to soften the strictures, Bartlett announced that the affiant was reported to be dead. Mason stood silent for a moment and appeared to be so deeply moved that Bartlett, fearing he had carried the joke too far, added, "But there is some reason to suppose that it is a mistake." "Thank God for that!" Mason responded. "The man who gave that affidavit ought to have time for repentance."[32]

After Mason had been practicing for a short while in Portsmouth, he heard rumors of a wonderfully clever country attorney from Boscawen said to be "as black as the ace of spades."[33] The rumors persisted and Mason became quite eager to meet the new lawyer, especially when Jeremiah Smith returned from a trial term in Hillsborough County to report that he had never before met such a young man as this. A story once popularly told in Rockingham County, but surely somewhat overblown, told of Mason's being in Exeter to defend a client accused of forgery. Attorney General William King Atkinson, who had been scheduled to prosecute, failed to appear, and the judge was about to dismiss the indictment when a young stranger arose in the back of the courtroom and asked permission to argue the government's case. Mason anticipated little difficulty and was inclined to relax at first, but so brilliant was the newcomer's presentation of the state's evidence that Mason soon found himself forced to exert all his efforts before he won an acquittal.

"He broke upon me like a thunder storm in July," Mason later recalled, "sudden, portentous, sweeping all before it."[34] And now began the most epic rivalry in the legal history of New England: Jeremiah Mason versus Daniel Webster. Long after they had left Rockingham County, until at least the end of the nineteenth century, if not into the twentieth, the question as to who was the greatest was hotly debated by lawyers in hotel rooms and courthouses from Hartford to Bangor. Few accepted the compromise offered by one of Mason's biographers, who suggested that "Mr. Mason was a great lawyer, but Mr. Webster was a great man practicing the law."[35]

Unquestionably the most competent judge of their legal and forensic talents was their friend, United States Supreme Court Justice Joseph Story. There were few days in the year, Story said, that he enjoyed more than when holding court in Rockingham County, and he freely expressed his pleasure with what he called "the vast law learning, and the prodigious intellectual power of the New Hampshire bar."[36] There is one bit of evidence that, even though he and Webster were greater friends than he and Mason, he regarded Mason as the greater lawyer. At the 1812 term of the United States Circuit Court held at Portsmouth, Story held a ceremony, vesting Jeremiah Smith and Jeremiah Mason with the "honorable degree of serjeant-at-law," while he bestowed the lesser title of barrister-at-law upon George Sullivan and Daniel Webster.[37]

Students of the early nineteenth-century New Hampshire bar emphasize the mastery of sarcasm because it was a powerful weapon for a lawyer under the rules of court then prevailing. Rudeness in court while conducting jury trials was permitted among members of the bar. The practice may explain in small part why many lawyers were unsuccessful competing against Mason, Webster, Smith, Bartlett, Sullivan, and Plumer—they could not match the bullying. This truth, however, by no means tells the whole story. To appreciate how much these men stood above their fellow lawyers we need only note some lesser members of the Rockingham County bar. Consider Levi Woodbury. He was a lesser practitioner, but except for Webster, he was not of lesser importance in American history than any of the giants. He began his public career at twenty-six, as the youngest judge ever to sit on New Hampshire's highest court and then went on to be governor, senator, Secretary of the Navy, Secretary of the Treasury, and after declining the ambassadorship to the Court of St. James's, became the only nineteenth-century New Hampshire lawyer appointed to the United States Supreme Court. He might have become the only New Hampshire president, too, but for his untimely death. As it was, Franklin Pierce received the honor, partly because he came from the same state as Woodbury and had been Woodbury's law student.

Another lawyer worth noting is Richard Fletcher. One evening while serving as principal of the academy in Salisbury, the home town of Webster and Bartlett, he took a walk, and as he was ascending a hill his gaze turned westward and he noticed a young man approaching out of the blazing red of the mountain twilight. "It was the most majestic figure and noblest countenance on which I ever gazed," Fletcher later recalled. "It seemed almost like an angel standing in the sun." Fletcher followed Webster to Portsmouth and became a student in his office. While practicing among the giants at the Rockingham County bar he made little headway. Only after he moved to Boston was he able to establish a worthy reputation, becoming a congressman and arguing many important actions before the Massachusetts and federal Supreme Courts, the most memorable of which was the *Charles River Bridge Case*, which he won in the high court of Massachusetts in opposition to Webster.[38]

It is fair to say that there were four tiers of lawyers who practiced at the Rockingham County bar during the first quarter of the nineteenth century. At the bottom were the average, run-of-the-mill attorneys. Some, like Congressman Nathaniel Appleton Haven, might enjoy national political or literary reputations, but at home they were mere pygmies among the giants pursuing their profession, some even seeking other means of livelihood, as Haven did when he established a Portsmouth newspaper.[39] A little higher up were Woodbury, Fletcher, and Samuel Bell,[40] who might have been the leaders of any other bar. Next were Sullivan, Bartlett, and Plumer, exceptional lawyers by any standard. And finally the giants, Webster, Mason, and Smith. Even so loyal a son as William Plumer, Jr., did not suggest that his father belonged in the class of the latter, admitting him to be "[u]nequal in mere law learning to Smith, with less acuteness of metaphysical discrimination than Mason, and yielding, as all others have done, to the massive intellect of Webster."[41]

Some may quarrel with the notion of placing two forgotten country lawyers in the same category as Webster, but he himself placed them there. With the exception of Fisher Ames, he considered Smith the most brilliant man he had ever met. "I entertain for him the highest regard," he wrote Chancellor James Kent of New York. "He knows everything about New England, . . . and as to the law, he knows so much more of it than I do or ever shall, that I forbear to speak on that point."[42] He had even greater reverence for Jeremiah Mason. He once said that if you were to ask him "who is the greatest lawyer I have known, I should say 'Chief-Justice [John] Marshall,' but if you took me by the throat and pushed me to the wall, I should say 'Jeremiah Mason.'"[43] In fact, Webster put Mason not just first among lawyers but perhaps first among men. "If there be in the country a stronger intellect," he reflected in his autobiography, "if there be a mind of more native resources, if there be a vision that sees quicker or sees deeper into whatever is intricate or whatsoever is profound, I must confess I have not known it."[44] These were no mean compliments from a man who had studied under Christopher Gore, argued before John Marshall, Joseph Story, and Lemuel Shaw, and against William Pickney, John Holmes, William Wirt, and Franklin Dexter. This was no hometown boy speaking with patronizing nostalgia of one who had made good. This was the measured verdict of a lawyer who mulled as a judge of lawyers.

The men who argued at the Rockingham County bar during the first and second decades of the nineteenth century would be but legends to the boys of the next three New Hampshire generations who trained in the small-town law offices of the state, such as that of Daniel Christie at Dover. Among the students that Christie guided to the law were Ira Perley, John Parker Hale, one of America's finest advocates and the first free-soil senator, the younger Jeremiah Smith, who later followed his father onto New Hampshire's highest court and went on to be professor of tort law in Harvard, and Charles Doe. Though none of those studying with Christie would see or hear the old giants of the seacoast towns, their strengths and weaknesses were as closely studied as if they were still litigating in the courtrooms of Exeter and Portsmouth. The contemptuous power of Mason, the withering scorn of Webster, the flashing anger of Sullivan came back to life in their imaginations. To William Plumer, Jr., who witnessed all of them in court contests, they were worthy of comparison with Grecian heroes. He saw his father, Governor Plumer, as "the Nestor or Ulysses of this assembly," Chief Justice Smith as "the Menelaus, with a touch of the Thersites humor," Mason as "the Ajax or Agamemnon, towering head and shoulders above the rest," and Webster as "the Achilles, *impiger, iracundus, inexorabilis, acer.*"[45] "To strangers, such language may seem extravagant," he admitted. "Perhaps it is so. But one who witnessed, always with admiration, sometimes with awe and reverence, the encounters of these extraordinary men, cannot speak of them in language appropriate to the ordinary routine of practice in an obscure country court."[46]

It can plausibly be contended that Jeremiah Smith was the most successful practitioner of the great Rockingham County lawyers. As will be discussed below, at one time he had the largest law practice, exceeding that of Jeremiah Mason, perhaps doubling that of George Sullivan and Daniel Webster. But it is as a judge, not as an attorney that Smith is remembered. He had been elected to the Second Congress in 1790, when thirty years old, and had resigned seven years later to accept appointment as United States district attorney for New Hampshire. In 1800 he became probate judge for Rockingham County, and the next year, nominated by John Marshall and appointed by John Adams, he took his seat as a United States circuit judge, only to be legislated out of office in 1802, making him one of the men famed in history as the "midnight judges."[47] In May of that year, however, he was named chief justice of New Hampshire's highest judicial bench, the Superior Court.

The chief justiceship of New Hampshire was the vocation for which Smith had been born, in which he was most comfortable, and where he excelled. Supported and advised by his then best friend, William Plumer, he set about to change completely New Hampshire law. It had been shaped by the common sense of laymen, serving not only on juries but also on the courts themselves, and epitomized by Chief Justice John Dudley, a farmer by occupation, who told juries: "It is not law we want, but justice. They [the lawyers] would govern us by the common law of England. Trust me, gentlemen, common sense is a much safer guide for us,—the common sense of Raymond, Epping, Exeter and the other towns which have sent us here to try this case between two of our neighbors. A clear head and a honest heart are worth more than all the law of all the lawyers."[48]

Chief Justice Dudley's laymen law has been entitled "the jurisprudence of common sense." Commonsense legal theory has not been studied in the detail that it merits,[49] but basically it can be described as law without principles, without a system, and uncontrolled by any rules of procedure. "The consequence," Jeremiah Mason explained, "was that the practice and proceedings of the courts were crude and inartificial; and the final determination of causes depended more on the discretion and arbitrary opinion of the [lay] judges and jurors. . . . This, of course, rendered judicial decisions vague and uncertain, the most intolerable evil of a bad administration of justice."[50]

As chief justice of the state's highest court, Jeremiah Smith dedicated himself to professionalizing New Hampshire law. We might think it an easy task. After all, considering the caliber of the Rockingham County bar, it was unlikely that the lawyers then in practice could long tolerate a law that was mostly arbitration and largely unpredictable. Moreover, although they did not know it, that generation was on the brink of the Industrial Revolution and the state, with its numerous waterfalls, would soon have cotton, woolen, and paper mills stretching from Dover up to the mountains beyond the river uplands, and the law would have to become more instrumental and certain if the emerging manufacturing community was to be served. But reform was not as readily effected as we might expect. In truth, when Smith left the bench to become governor in 1809 he had accomplished very little except for educating the bar about goals and objectives. It was not because he had failed to introduce reforms. It was, rather, due to a dedicated, united, and well-organized opposition. New Hampshire was not only bitterly divided between two political parties, but the extremities of politics perpetuated a jurisprudential dichotomy. Against Smith was a school of legal thought that held that the law was not to be found in the taught traditions of the trained legal profession or even in the rulings of a professional judiciary. Rather, the law was, in practice, the spontaneous value judgments of juries, and, in theory, the ever-changing and ever-practical command of the sovereign, republican people legislating through their elected representatives. For the school of legal thought espoused by Smith, the law is not willed by a sovereign but autonomous. The obligation of contract and rights of property exist independently of civil law or of any government authority. Law is custom, but custom can originate as much from the democratic people as from the taught traditions of the professional bar.[51]

Today the strength of the opposition surprises us, but during the first decade of the nineteenth century, it was strong enough to put Chief Justice Smith's reforms on hold. He introduced one change after another, only to have the Republican majority in the two houses of the legislature overturn each one—courts presided over by a single judge, law terms, instructions binding on juries, reporting and publishing judicial decisions, all of which will be elaborated below.[52] What may be even more surprising to us today is that these events were known to the informed sections of the public. Correspondents to the newspapers of that day gave detailed attention to matters we might expect would not interest anyone but lawyers—issues such as single judges presiding at jury trials or whether difficult legal questions should be resolved at special law terms rather than at jury terms. It was not that people thought him a failure as chief justice. He was too admired as a jurist for that conclusion, the most respected judge to have sat on a New Hampshire bench up to that time. Even so, we can assume that some of his prestige was not judicial but came from his standing at the Rockingham County bar. After all, he was one of the two leaders of that outstanding assemblage of lawyers—he and Jeremiah Mason. He was simply known as just about the best legal mind in the state, the best judge, and perhaps the best practitioner.

For the remainder of the nineteenth century, New Hampshire lawyers marveled at the memory of the arena of the giants that had once flourished at the Rockingham County bar. The influence of those practitioners upon future generations may be partly judged by the fact that, throughout the remainder of the nineteenth century, New Hampshire attorneys never ceased to repeat stories about them and that among the papers Chief Justice Charles Doe was carrying at the time of his death in 1896 was an old brief in Mason's handwriting and a picture of Chief Justice Jeremiah Smith. The lessons that those lawyers learned from the giants of the Rockingham County bar was that great advocates win cases not by emulating the strengths of their rivals but by developing their own strong points: Smith, his greater knowledge of the law; Webster, his greater intellect; Mason, his greater understanding of human nature. If they wished, they might try to copy the graceful actions of Bartlett or the industry of Woodbury. But who could hope to imitate Sullivan, the charmer and the orator? Or the elaborate learning and quaint humor of Smith? Or Mason, with his original mind and proud superiority? Who could hope to emulate Webster, the most ambitious and successful?

The epitaph of the Rockingham County bar was written by the younger Plumer. "It, indeed, often witnessed the strife of Titans; weak men did not mingle in it; strong men felt the need of all their strength."[53]

Not all the men were strong, however. At a time when the Rockingham County bar was at the height of its strength—when Smith, Plumer, Mason, Webster, and Sullivan were all competing, one against the other, impaneling juries, filing motions, and trying cases—the New Hampshire judiciary was at its weakest. The sitting Supreme Court did not measure up to the courts of Smith, Richardson, Parker, Perley, or Doe. From 1809 to 1813, it hardly measured up at all. In fact, briefly, during part of 1813 and 1814, there was judicial comedy, with two high "courts" contesting each other. The tale of those "courts" is told in the following chapters. And during all of the times while these events unfolded, the Rockingham County bar continued to flourish. Our main interest focuses on but two of the Rockingham lawyers, William Plumer and Jeremiah Smith. From the day each was admitted to law practice, they worked to improve the courts of New Hampshire, primarily by upgrading the quality of the judges. Though they started their program of change as young men, as soon as they had been admitted to the bar, other lawyers acknowledged that they were New Hampshire's leading judicial reformers; they were the lawyers to be followed.[54]

## *Chapter Two*

# An Unschooled Judge

During the year that the eighteenth century turned into the nineteenth, William Plumer, Jeremiah Smith, and other New Hampshire lawyers working to reform the state's judicial system thought that the main difficulty they faced was the low compensation that the state paid to its judges. Next, perhaps not quite as serious, but nevertheless quite troublesome, a number of state officials shared a public-policy theory that some high-court judges should be nonlawyers. It was not just a matter of New Hampshire politics but a frequently articulated principle of New Hampshire jurisprudence that the state should have laymen on the bench.

Jeremiah Smith might have become chief justice as early as 1795 had New Hampshire paid judges reasonably decent salaries. He was then a congressman, and of course he would have had to leave Congress, but there are convincing grounds for believing he would have done so had he been named chief justice. But, planning to get married and expecting to raise a family, he could not have accepted the office at the salary it paid. When he did leave Congress and set up practice in Exeter, his net income for his first year, ending on 1 September 1799, was $2,351. For the next two years his net annual incomes were $3,018.69 and $3,077.60. In 1797 the compensation for the chief justice of the Superior Court was raised to $850, and for the associate justices to $800. That was up from $600 annually for the chief and $466.67 a year for each associate. Yet, even that small amount was not a judge's take-home pay. While on circuit he had to absorb all of his expenses, not being reimbursed by the state. And these costs—transportation, bed and board, livery stable—were expected to rise substantially in the next two decades as New Hampshire would surely be adding at least four new counties and, therefore, more courts and more shire towns, further from the coast, to which he would have to travel.[1]

The better lawyers with successful law practices simply could not afford to become state judges unless they had other sources of income. That fact was especially true for judges of the court of Common Pleas. Their pay was lower than that of Superior Court justices. "The Legislature have virtually said, by the small salaries allowed them," A FRIEND TO TRUTH concluded, "that it is not expected that they should be lawyers by profession."[2]

It might be thought that the two problems were related. Had New Hampshire paid adequate salaries, more attorneys surely would have been willing to join the judiciary, and there would have been no need to appoint nonlawyers to the bench. But cause-and-effect was not that simple. The fact that good lawyers were unwilling to serve was not the only reason that laymen were appointed. There was a prevalent theory in turn-of-the-century New Hampshire, shared by many important state officials and not just by agrestic members of the general public, that not every judge should come from the ranks of the practicing legal profession. In fact, there was an argument quite often articulated politically that it would be a better court if some of the judges were not legal practitioners but had the experience of a more practical line of work. It was a theory of judicial governance that Lynn Turner did not credit. Turner will be often mentioned in this study, for he is the scholar of political events during this era, having written both the best biography of Plumer and the most detailed account of the state's governance during New Hampshire's formative years.[3] He thought the policy of appointing lay judges was due to antilawyer bias. "The two factors that seemed most influential in guiding legislative and executive policy towards the judiciary," he observed, "were niggardliness and a prejudice against lawyers," adding that "[n]either of these was confined to one party." Turner is certainly right if all he meant was that there was a very strong strand of antilawyer sentiment in turn-of-the-century New Hampshire. But there was also a political theory, perhaps not peculiar to New Hampshire, yet widely shared within the state, that there were other experiences besides legal training that fitted a man to be a judge.[4]

A measure of just how strongly some officials felt that nonlawyers should be appointed to the state's highest bench surfaced in 1798, when a vacancy occurred on the superior court. Jeremiah Smith said he would have become a candidate, except that the salary was just too low for his needs, and besides, he realized he did not have sufficient political backing. He supported Arthur Livermore, perhaps the only young lawyer in the state with sufficient income to serve on the bench. "Judge Edward St. Loe Livermore consents to sit this week at Dover, and then leave the bench,"

Smith observed. "I shall use all my endeavors that Arthur Livermore succeed his brother."[5]

Edward St. Loe Livermore and Arthur Livermore were sons of Samuel Livermore, who had been attorney general and chief justice of New Hampshire and currently was representing the state in the United States Senate. A well-trained, competent, and successful lawyer from a politically powerful family, Arthur Livermore was, for Smith and Plumer, the logical person to be appointed to the court. He was not such an obvious choice to the governor, and one reason was prejudice against lawyers. Both of New Hampshire's chief executives of the 1790s, Josiah Bartlett and John Taylor Gilman, did not favor placing lawyers on the bench. They preferred, as one historian put it, "to select judges on the basis of their military or genealogical records rather than their legal attainments."[6]

"The governor and council have just dispersed, and monstrous to relate, have appointed Paine Wingate and Ebenezer Smith," Jeremiah Smith wrote to an acquaintance. "If you are curious to know why it was that Arthur Livermore was not appointed I will tell you what they say. That Arthur Livermore was too young; that there have been two of that name and family on the court before, and that the bar were universally for him, and therefore they could not appoint him." Plumer was more blunt. "Previous to this," he observed, "the governor had been considered by lawyers as being hostile to the bar; these appointments confirmed that opinion."[7]

It would be impossible to measure the depths of antilawyer feeling in New Hampshire when Plumer and Smith were at the bar. It is, however, telling that the governor about whom they complained was a Federalist, the leader of what was correctly known as the lawyers' party. It was their opponents, the Republicans, who were vocally antilawyer. "Much of this opposition to the Barr proceeds from a few restless antifederal men," Plumer had written a few months earlier, referring to Republicans. "They think, & justly, that the Barr are opposed to their measures & that we have much influence in the State." Another reason, Turner pointed out, was that lawyers "played an important part in giving the Federalist party that intellectual superiority which it enjoyed almost to the end of its existence." As New Hampshire turned more and more Republican, the leadership by lawyers among the Federalists made them "the more unpopular with the mass of the people."[8]

In retaliation, Federalist newspapers regularly counted the number of lawyers that Republicans nominated for public office, but inevitably the Federalists ran more. "Are not four lawyers out of five candidates rather too many to have on one list?" QUERIST asked of the Federal congressional slate in 1808. "Would it not be *republican* to have some merchants and farmers, as well as *lawyers*?" Three months later Jeremiah Smith was a Federalist candidate for presidential elector along with six other lawyers. There were no lawyers among the Republican nominees, but there were "five substantial, honest Farmers." "Men of Newhampshire," ROCKINGHAM asked, "will you choose Lawyers or Farmers?" The "men of Newhampshire" answered two years later by electing Smith as governor and filled other state offices, RATTLE thought, with too many lawyers. "Behold at the head of our government is a lawyer, the secretary is a lawyer, the treasurer of the state is a lawyer, and some say a speculator, the speaker of the house of representatives a lawyer, the president of the senate a lawyer, and a great proportion of the justices of the peace in the state are lawyers," RATTLE pointed out. "Now is it not high time that the people should awake from their slumber and prevent themselves from being trodden under foot by lawyers who are mostly educated in the jurisprudence of Great Britain?" He added that he was only referring to Federalist lawyers. "With pleasure we recognize a number of republican lawyers attending our bar who treat the court with respect and their clients with decency and who are ornaments to their country."[9]

There were few sins that Republican writers did not lay on lawyers. "[A]s a profession or society of men, a more intolerant and persecuting is not to be found," a Concord newspaper complained. "The business of nearly one half of our attornies is made up of unprincipled speculation and persecution." "Lawyers in this State," a Portsmouth newspaper lamented in 1805, "a few years since, were very scarce, and poor, for want of business, and since they have increased, and are increasing, like the locust in Egypt, their business has become very lucrative, (what is that a sign of?) now all the youth, are studying law, instead of divinity—what is that a sign of?"[10]

During the years after Jeremiah Smith left Congress and was practicing law in Exeter, the Republican newspapers in the state became more politically vocal, which meant criticism of attorneys became even more public and partisan. One complaint they frequently voiced was that lawyers were a profession, and any profession, by being an exclusive, separate class, was out of place in a republican society. Because of their education, their professionalism, and the fact that they did not work with their hands, they stood out with clergymen and merchants, apart from the remainder of the population. "There are three classes of people, *viz.* The *priests*, the *lawyers*, and the *merchants*, who complain of our low salaries," a Republican newspaper explained. "The most of these, somehow or other, create to themselves great estates; but how much does any of them, who follows his profession exclusively, add to the wealth of the community? The first is a tax on the vices, the second lives on the distresses, and the third piles up wealth by pampering the luxuries, as well as supplying some of the necessities of the people."[11]

Lawyers and clergy were always linked as two parts of the nonproductive trio, although sometimes the third group was physicians, rather than merchants. A toast at a Fourth of July celebration at Plainsfield in 1809 explained that connection: "*Professional characters, Clergymen, Lawyers and Physicians.* May they never forget that their main support is from independent farmers, mechanics, and laborers." Five years later, in another Fourth of July toast, the three were still together. "*Professional Characters.* Clergymen, Physicians and Lawyers—May they not inter meddle in cases where their knowledge does not extend." It was a Republican Fourth of July celebration, and people in attendance knew what was meant. It would not have been offered at the Federalist celebration.[12]

A Republican complaint that had much substance was that lawyers were pro-British. Republicans said it was due to lawyers' training, and they may have been partly right. "[T]he profession of the law, considered as a body, is devoted, heart and head, to the support of British principles and British politics in the United States," Decius asserted. "The causes of this attachment to England will be found in the *nature of their studies* and the *objects of their pursuit.* These studies are the laws of Great Britain. . . . The praise of British jurists, consistently sounding on their tongues, soon finds its way into their hearts. Immured in these pursuits, and seeing nothing beyond, they contract by degrees, a habit of admiration for the celebrated men whose opinions they adopt; and of attachment for the country where those laws were first enacted, from the explanation of which, their own respectability and importance have arisen."[13]

Identified with the Federal party, lawyers were tarred with all the evils that the Republican press visited upon the Federalists, especially the claim that they were conspiring to create a monarchy and introduce a hereditary aristocracy. Rockingham demonstrated how easily one favorite argument—that education in English law made lawyers pro-British—led to the conclusion that lawyers were plotting the downfall of republicanism. "The men of the law, whether Judges or practitioners, are early habituated to receive information and instruction from British authorities; they study British law; quote British writers; imbibe British personalities; and fancy the British form of government, the most stupendous fabric of human wisdom," Rockingham supposed. "From ideas and opinions such as these, the transition to anti-republican sentiments is natural and easy. *Men of this description* . . . wish to assimilate the political institutions of our Country with those of Great Britain."[14]

It is difficult today to imagine that the Republican writers were serious, but they repeated the accusation so often it is likely they thought there were people who believed it. The contention was most concisely summed up by A DOVER FARMER: "The RIGHTS and LIBERTIES of this happy country, are a nuisance and an eye sore to the Judges and Lawyers. They wish to remove them, to overthrow them, to trample them under foot, and on their ruins to establish a monarchy and an aristocracy." After Plumer converted from the Federal party to the Republicans, VERITAS, writing in the *Concord Gazette*, accused him and his eldest son of repeating the same charge of conspiracy against his former friends that he would have dismissed as a lie just three years earlier. "Lawyers seem to be particularly obnoxious to them," VERITAS wrote of Republican propagandists. "No class of men (*old tories* only excepted) are pointed out as irreconcilable enemies to the union and the liberty and rights of the people. The Epping lawyer and his son, previous to the March election, trimmed the mid-night lamp to persuade the good people of this State that lawyers were conspiring with British agents to overthrow our government, and they must not be trusted with any office."[15]

Anyone sifting through New Hampshire newspapers, Federal as well as Republican, for the first two decades of the nineteenth century, is surely struck with how much antilawyerism was part of the political culture. When, for example, PHILO criticized the writing style of JUSTITIA, he felt he did not have to explain his criticism. Rather, he took for granted that his readers disliked the way in which lawyers constructed their arguments.

> As a writer you possess the merit of ingenuity and the astuteness of legal science. You have seized with avidity upon every artifice and circumstance to turn the weapons of our "correspondent" . . . against himself, and attempted to screen your friend from public odium by attributing all his unpopular acts to the "best intentions." Your liberally bestowing terms of reproach upon our "correspondent," was the natural result of your indignant feelings at the attack upon your friend. And to denounce our "correspondent" as a disappointed office-seeker, was certainly an ingenious method to refute "facts."
>
> Despairing of vindicating your friend against most of the charges alledged against him, you discover the cunning of the shuffling lawyer, by selecting the most favorable points in your defence, while you declare it "needless to notice all the *trivial* items objected against our chief magistrate."[16]

Writers simply assumed that newspaper readers had internalized a distrust of lawyers and introduced remarks disparaging lawyers without any attempt to explain why they were doing so. They expected readers both to know what they meant and to agree with them. Urging voters to elect George Sullivan to Congress, the *Concord Gazette* claimed, "He is a lawyer, who studied the profession as a noble science . . . not as an art, that he might more easily pray on his fellow man." A law student was reported by the *New Hampshire Gazette* to have told his father he was ready to practice law because his studies "had initiated him in all the sophistical chicaneries of the Lawyers, and that he now perfectly knew how to make right wrong, and wrong right." Some writers utilized the anti-lawyer culture to create interest. An example is Lucius, a Portsmouth commentator, who tossed out the following remark in a newspaper article when making a point that had nothing to do with lawyers: "Who ever heard of a client looking for a new lawyer to transact his business because he found from experience (if such a thing is possible) that his present attorney was honest and faithful."[17]

The antilawyer culture was not based on unreasoning bias. There were many people in New Hampshire who could recite a list of reasons for mistrusting lawyers. Consider Circular, who thought lawyers a class apart, spending their professional hours "misleading the people of this State, and making their fortunes, on the sins of the people." "[C]an a free government possibly exist, where any one class of citizens are commissioned, or tolerated by authority, to lord it over, or mislead, any other class?" Circular asked. "Can it be consistent with a free government, to tolerate any class of citizens, to excite law-suits among the ignorant people, and be the real cause of, perhaps, two thirds of the actions that are commenced in the State yearly, . . . can it be consistent, for them to be active, in making laws, to govern a free people, and to make them lengthy and mysterious, and then to take the lead, in the bar, and on the bench, to explain those laws, their own way, to deceive the Jury."[18]

Circular's chief complaint, that lawyers formed an exclusive group, socially and politically out of place in a republican society, was perhaps the aspersion most frequently voiced against attorneys during the years that Plumer and Smith were in practice. "That *Lawyers* esteem themselves a privileged order—an *Aristocracy!* admits of no dispute," the *American Patriot* complained. A few months after printing those words, the owner sold the *American Patriot* to Isaac Hill, who would take the newspaper to new heights of partisan journalism, making it, in only two to three years, the most influential Republican organ in the state. He changed the name to the *New-Hampshire Patriot* and began thrashing lawyers, constantly and relentlessly. His favorite word for describing a political enemy was "pettifogger." One major theme Hill reiterated continually was that "the interests and rights of the people are adverse to the interests and prosperity of the lawyers." Many New Hampshire citizens seem to have agreed, especially after being served with papers in a lawsuit. Defendants assumed they never would have been sued if a lawyer or two had not moved into the vicinity where they and the plaintiffs lived. It was an assumption that Hill readily turned into a certainty. "Towns which before they [lawyers] were introduced lived in peace and quietness, without quarrelling or litigation of any kind, are now kept in a continued scene of uproar and confusion, without any other visible means than the introduction of a lawyer."[19]

There were, to be sure, other commentators who complained about New Hampshire lawyers as forcefully as Hill. Perhaps no other republican commentator stated the case against them as an economic class apart more forcefully than did A Dover Farmer. "What interest have the Lawyers in common with the rest of the community?" Farmer asked. "None," he answered. "If the merchants lose their property by capture or shipwreck; what harm does the Lawyer suffer? None. If by frost, by drought, by blast or mildew, the fruits of the earth are destroyed and the Farmer is disappointed in his expected harvest; what injury does the Lawyer sustain? None.—He is totally unconnected with the rest of the community. His views, his wishes and interests are distinct and separate from theirs."[20]

A Dover Farmer lay bare the heart of the case against lawyers in the early republic. Lawyers were a breed apart from the general New Hampshire population. That was a key complaint of people fearful of outside economic forces they could not control or nostalgic for the more communal, less individualistic society they recalled from their youth. They remembered a colonial past when, in town meetings, their votes determined the route along which the local turnpike would be laid out, set tolls on bridges and ferries, and when serving as members of juries, they decided the law for the enforcement of agreements to deliver crops to market after the harvest. If there were a drought, or blast, or mildew, so crops had failed or somehow did not meet the contracting parties' expectations and could not be delivered as promised, jurors had applied rules of fairness, sometimes not enforcing the agreement or enforcing it differently from the parties' intentions. Now the turnpikes over which they sent their produce to market had most likely been financed by a partnership in faraway Portsmouth or Boston, and moneymen never seen in town, unknown strangers, laid out the routes, determined the quality of repairs, and set the tolls. Judges were now beginning a "reform" effort to take questions of law away from jurors and, when crops failed, attempting to enforce contracts by the "will" of the contractors, that is, as the parties had intended, not by community values of what was fair or what was just, as had been the rule before the American Revolution.[21] People living in rural areas or in small towns knew they could blame lawyers for serving these outsiders who were reshaping, remaking, and taking over their lives and livelihoods. It was the lawyers who were the local agents for these new manipulative economic forces that they could not control. It was lawyers, as A DOVER FARMER said, "totally unconnected with the rest of the community."

Bad economic times made such fears even more acute and complaints even more frequent, as when New Hampshire suffered greatly from the twin blows of the national embargo and the War of 1812. "The whole-sale merchant called upon his debtors, the petty traders in the country, and they in turn upon their customers," a column in the *Patriot* explained, "and, on failure of prompt payment, recourse was had immediately to a lawyer, or more properly a collector, for the knowledge of many who assume the name of lawyers, extends no further, than to commence a suit on a note of hand or account, prosecute the same to judgment, collect a few dollars from some unfortunate or negligent man, pay it over to their employer, and tax an exorbitant fee for their services. If any fault is found with one of them for extortion, the reply is—'I gave two thousand dollars for my *knowledge*, and I cannot afford to do business for nothing.'"[22]

At a time when the population of New Hampshire was 214,000, and there were 130 lawyers in the state, the *Patriot* lamented that that number was far too many. "If lawyers multiply as fast in the years to come as in the few years past," it complained, "farewell to the prosperity and peace of our citizens—farewell to industry and enterprise. Simple justice is requisite to the happiness of the State; and so far as lawyers are instrumental in facilitating this, so far they are beneficial to society. More than simple justice is oppression, and less than this, is injustice."[23]

So many lawyers, Republican printers feared, not only meant that a multitude of lawsuits would be filed, but also that there would be too many poorly paid, yet greedy attorneys, causing the bar to degenerate into mere bill collectors. "The Courts of law would never be so constantly crowded with petty, vexatious and disgraceful suits," PUBLICOLA complained, "were it not for the herds of pettifogging Lawyers that infest them. . . . They are in law what quacks are in medicine; exciting the malady for the purpose of profiting by the cure, and retarding the cure for the purpose of augmenting the fees." William Plumer blamed "a class" of lawyers, "the third and fourth ranks" of the profession. "These men assume the names of lawyers, though they are profoundly ignorant of the first principles of law and government. Their knowledge is confined to a few technical terms, to the forms of declarations and pleas in plain simple cases, and the taxing of bills of cost. They are, in fact, mere *collectors of debts*." "They have an interest directly opposed to that of the people, that of multiplying suits and increasing fees: this interest conflicts with that of the public, excites their opposition against every system which tends to render laws plain and simple, the collection of debts prompt and easy, or reduce the fees of collection," Plumer wrote as CINCINNATUS. "Too many of them take much pains to promote litigation and increase the number of suits, by purchasing demands and urging the people to sue, by engaging to carry on suits without fees if their clients should not recover, or by making the amount of their fees altogether dependent upon the result of the suit."[24]

Plumer did not say so, but others charged that lawyers made litigation more expensive than it should have been. One popular accusation, which many people believed, was that lawyers had formed a conspiracy to keep the law complicated, known only to themselves. "Their interest, as a profession," PHOCION alleged, "requires that laws should be obscure, tautological, contradictory and uncertain, so that to understand them should be a labor of a life—that the path which leads to the temple of Justice should be crossed and indented, so winding, perplexed and involved, that none but themselves should be able to find their way through it."[25]

There is little evidence as to what New Hampshire attorneys thought about their bad press. It is not discussed in extant letters written by Plumer, Smith, or other members of the bar. Nor is it mentioned in Daniel Webster's published correspondence, and of course there were as yet no bar association publications to defend the profession or criticize its disparagers. Lawyers may not have felt harassed, but they could have been annoyed, especially if they felt that antilawyer sentiment hurt their law practice. Just as on one hand it was charged that the only reforms that lawyers permitted were those that increased the "glorious uncertainty of the law" and, of course, increased their fees, so on the other hand the only legal reforms that Republicans supported were those that suppressed the practice of law, such as allowing defendants to avoid trial by jury by electing arbitration, at which neither side could be represented by an attorney. Writing to Smith in 1797, Plumer attributed the enactment of some reforms he had sponsored in the House of Representatives to the fact that country legislators assumed they "would lessen the business & influence of lawyers." And of course, as in all the other states, there was strong opposition to efforts by the bar to form associations and to set standards for admission to law practice. "The rule and regulations of the practitioners at our judicial courts, and called '*bar rules*' are oppressive and unconstitutional," JUNIUS objected. Because, as they had been "made by a class of men, whose interest is to create a monopoly of practice," they violated the right of the people to equality.[26]

Although it cannot be measured, not even for purposes of speculative history, the antilawyer press surely had a negative effect on Plumer and Smith's program of juridical reforms. Consider, for instance, how mistrust of the bar made it difficult to persuade the public that only trained lawyers who were leaders of the profession should be appointed to either the Superior or Common Pleas courts. There is no need to trace the controversy through every appointment of a layman to the bench. The debate whether judges should be lawyers received its most extensive public airing in 1809, when Governor John Langdon appointed Richard Evans to the state's high court. Jeremiah Smith, who had been chief justice of the Superior Court since May 1802, had just been elected governor, defeating Langdon (who had stood for reelection), and was due to be sworn into office the day after Evans's appointment. He was annoyed, not only because Langdon had made an appointment that Smith had expected to make but because Evans was a nonlawyer. In his gubernatorial address to the General Court the next day, Smith asserted that the time had come when only lawyers should be appointed judges. Some Republicans were furious. "If the late Chief Justice thinks *himself* the only correct standard of justice—if he supposes law was never properly dispensed except when he was on the bench—then may he justify himself in saying that only lawyers ought to be judges," the *New-Hampshire Patriot* replied.[27]

Evans had been a Portsmouth merchant, a dealer "in muffs, tippits, blankets and other merchandise." He first gained public notice when he undertook the management of a lawsuit on a commercial contract worth several thousand dollars. "He stood alone," the *New Hampshire Gazette* reported. "Opposed to him was a very wealthy house in Philadelphia, ably supported by several great lawyers and by a partial court. His efforts upon this occasion—efforts embracing much legal learning and the most complicated mercantile transactions, commanded universal admiration, and ensured a verdict in the whole amount for which he sued." William Plumer said that Evans actually lost the case but agreed that "he gained the applause of a large concourse of people who were present at the trial." Win or lose, Evans's efforts as an amateur lawyer made his reputation in New Hampshire.[28]

He almost immediately went into politics, taking the Portsmouth seat in the legislature that had been filled by John Langdon. Langdon became governor that year, and Evans made himself useful to the winning party. He became one of the chief organizers of Republican political campaigns in New Hampshire and was a frequent contributor to the newspapers, especially the *New-Hampshire Patriot*. He was, quite frankly, a Republican party hack, perhaps the first individual in New Hampshire history who was known among the general public as a political hatchet man, ever ready to write scurrilous articles for the *Patriot*. His appointment to the Superior Court was Langdon's reward for his service to the party.[29]

For the New Hampshire public Evans's appointment dramatically clarified the issue of what the standards of judicial qualifications should be and got the more politically conscious portion of the population asking anew what attributes made a fit judge. As mentioned, Smith introduced the topic in his gubernatorial address to the General Court, the day after Evans's appointment. He focused most of his attention on the judiciary, touching only briefly on the issue of judicial qualifications. He was not even as direct as he probably wanted to be. Apparently hoping to avoid arousing opposition, he spoke of a need for competence rather than of legal education. "It is vain," he argued, "that the legislative body frame and adopt the wisest and best system of laws, if the interpretation of them be entrusted to incompetent or unskilled hands." Immediately coming to Smith's support, the Federalist majority in the House of Representatives praised the merits of formal legal training. "A long and diligent study of jurisprudence, with a competent knowledge of the practice of law," the lower house replied to the governor's address, "can alone enable a person to fill the responsible office of judge in our first and highest judicial tribunal with honor to himself, or safety to the community."[30]

The *Patriot* pretended to be outraged. "[W]e were still more surprised, that a deliberate body, selected from among the best citizens of the State, should reverberate the [idea] that none but lawyers, none but those who had studied or practiced law for a 'long' time, were qualified for a seat on the bench of justice. Experience has shown that our very best judges have been among those who never practiced in the courts of law." In fact, the *Patriot* added, lawyers "are oftentimes improper persons for judges" because of their training and unsavory practice. "Even federalists (federal lawyers aside) in their more sober moments, would spurn at the idea of our benches being exclusively filled with lawyers." And so, the *Patriot* concluded, "[i]f judges who dispense law must be lawyers, we think the necessity still greater, that legislators who frame laws should be exclusively lawyers."[31]

The *Patriot* was arguing from New Hampshire's homegrown school of legal theory, the jurisprudence of common sense. It was, of course, a legal philosophy that Smith and his colleagues were struggling to replace with English common law. It exalted equity over law, intuition instead of research, snap judgment above precedent, and the emotional politics of the fair-minded layman in place of the trained, acquired, taught traditions of the studious legal scholar. Republicans often sought to depict Evans as the ideal commonsense practitioner. A good example of their praise was an obituary published in party newspapers recalling his adept handling of the litigation against the Philadelphia commercial house. The description of his forensic skills summarized the mental strengths most admired in the commonsense jurist. "His genius here had an opportunity to display itself," the obituary related. "In logic, in detail, in retort, none of his antagonists could stand before him. Taught by nature, he proved himself superior in art, and humbled those whose collegiate degrees were the principal evidence of their genius. He did not aspire to be learned in the common acceptance of the term, because his first impressions were beyond the bounds of learning." That, indeed, was the essence of commonsense jurisprudence. Spur-of-the-moment judgments, decreeing a neighborly, commonsense solution to a dispute—that is, the "first impressions"—were not only preferred, they were expected to be superior to the conclusions of a lawyer needing hours to find an answer in some musty precedent or inscrutable treatise.[32]

In his gubernatorial address Smith mentioned his own experience of "[t]wenty years' attendance on courts of justice." The *Patriot* twisted the governor's meaning, telling its readers that he said no one should be appointed to the bench without first studying law for at least twenty years. Smith had not said that, but the Republicans, by continually repeating that he had, created a charge that was devastating to his reputation. Moreover, it was claimed, Smith had been thinking of Evans when "he undertook to say what *ought to be* the qualifications of a judge of the superior court—he ought to have studied law 'twenty years.'" Again, Smith had not said this, but it is doubtful whether many Republicans realized how he was misquoted. His "pointed and personal illusions" to Evans, the public was told, "was as immodest and vain in the Governor as it was degrading to the Judge."[33]

It is a safe guess that Smith would have been more cautious in criticizing Evans's appointment had he realized how much he was thrusting the judiciary into contemporary politics. He was partly responsible for making Evans's appointment a major political issue, although it never became as important as the *Portsmouth Oracle* professed to think. "The appointment of RICHARD EVANS to be judge of the Superior Court has filled the State with astonishment," the Federalist *Oracle* claimed with much exaggeration. "Without respect to political party, it has made a deeper impression on the public mind, than any domestic occurrence since the Revolution. No man supposed, that Governor LANGDON would reward an electioneering partizan by such an appointment. Indeed to regard politics in appointing a Judge, is unheard of." The argument was hyperbole, of course, but it has influenced some historians, Lynn Turner, for example. "It could fairly be said that, until the appointment of Evans, the Republican revolution had not affected the judiciary," he asserted. "From 1809 until 1816, however, the judiciary was to become the most battered football in state politics."[34]

The Federalist press did what Smith surely did not want it to do. By harping on Evans's work for the Republican party, those newspapers kept the judiciary smack in the middle of New Hampshire politics. "[W]as Mr. Evans' personal merit and indefatigable industry what induced Governor Langdon to nominate him?" CITIZEN asked. No, he answered. "It was in spending weeks before the State election in writing pamphlets, and the most scandalous and abusive falsehoods that ever disgraced the black columns of the New-Hampshire Patriot." Federalists charged that Evans had moved from Portsmouth to Concord to write for Isaac Hill's newspaper. "He was there, I believe for some months, the *hireling editor* of a twopenny newspaper, conspicuous for virulence and vulgarity, through which Mr. Even's [*sic*] talents, if he has any, never peered out. The principal burden of his song at that time was, that the *judges were corrupt; the courts were nuisances; the law was an evil.* Where there were courts and laws, and judges he seemed to think there could be no liberty." That assertion was more than another exaggeration, it was false. Even Hill did not say such things about the courts or the law. He disliked lawyers, not the judiciary. But there was a political point that Federalist writers succeeded in getting across. "We hope," the *Portsmouth Oracle* summarized, "the people see sufficiently the folly of choosing *such* rulers, as appoint an electioneering partizan Judge to the Superior Court, as a reward for his party services, though destitute of every qualification of a Judge."[35]

That last point was what interested newspaper correspondents most, Evans's "qualification." Legal education briefly became a political topic. Although deliberately opaque, Jeremiah Smith had been understood by most observers to have been referring to professional training when he told the two houses of the General Court, "I am not conscious of a wish more sincere than that of seeing the place I now leave on the bench, filled by a person every way better qualified for this station than I could have pretended to be." He did not have to mention legal education directly; everyone in the legislature and most people in the state knew what he meant by a "better qualified" judge. The Federalist press took the issue from there.[36]

"The people of Newhampshire will not soon forget, that a man without education, study or experience, without reputation or public confidence . . . was foisted into a seat in the highest judicial tribunal in the State," AN IMPARTIAL CITIZEN wrote, reflecting the tone of the debate. "[D]oes he possess those indispensable acquisitions necessary for a Judge of the Superior Court of the State?" RESTORATOR asked Governor John Langdon, who had appointed Evans. "Is he well read in the intricate science of the Law? Has he made it his profession, his study and his pursuit? Would you Sir, if so unfortunate as to be engaged in a suit at law, apply to him for advice and information, although at that time he had an office in the town in which you resided?" The Federalist newspaper published in Evans's hometown answered no to each question. Evans was "a man unlearned in the law," the *Portsmouth Oracle* pointed out and, being uneducated, was "destitute of most of the qualifications necessary to render the Judiciary respectable in the eyes of ourselves and of the world." It was an argument new to the state. For the first time New Hampshirites were being told that legal education was significant but, even more, that an educated judge was a better judge. It would have been surprising should people heed the message, but if they did the judicial future of the state could be changed.[37]

Republicans answered by falling back on the old New Hampshire saw that the practical experience of an intelligent layman's common sense was as good, if not better preparation for the making of a judge as was education in the common law. "Though he may not have pored over Coke on Littleton, or any other law author, 'twenty years,'" the *Patriot* said of Evans, "though he may not be acquainted with all the manoeuvres of *green bag* errantry, nor guilty of the mal-practice of many of our federal lawyers; yet few men in the state are so well read in the jurisprudence of their country." It was, to be sure, a forced argument, and even Isaac Hill must have known it could not be supported. Today, looking back on the law treatises then available in New Hampshire, it seems unlikely that Evans could have borrowed enough books to "become well read in the jurisprudence" of his country. From what some of his critics said, it is possible that he could not even spell the word "jurisprudence."[38]

The Republican press was consistent in its defense of Evans. It presented him to the public as a judge vilified for no other reason than for being a nonlawyer who had the procacity to accept appointment to the Superior Court. "When federalists are asked to their objections to Judge E. they shrink, or assign the peurile [*sic*] one that he has not *studied law* so long as *their* champion, viz *twenty* years," the *New Hampshire Gazette* contended. "What evil has he done?" the *Gazette* asked, suggesting that the individual only was important, not his legal experience. The judge was respected by everyone except for those "previously pledged to cavil at his appointment," who, of course, were Federalists. Politics was the reason they were against him. It was not his qualifications.[39]

The Republican printers contended that, thanks to the books he had read, Evans knew "the law." It is difficult to believe, but William Plumer came close to saying the same, that Evans's reading was sufficient to qualify him for the bench. By the time that Evans's judicial competency became a topic of public debate, Plumer had changed political parties. More surprising, he had also changed a few of his ideas about the judiciary and did not hesitate to rush to Evans's defense. "Evans for some years, previous to this appointment, had devoted a considerable portion of his time to the study of the law," Plumer explained. "This he did, not with a view to be a judge, but to practise law, and the better to qualify himself for the political life." When Evans lived in Portsmouth, Plumer pointed out, "*Law books* were at his command, and he obtained and read them with fixt attention." Federalists writing to newspapers effectively conveyed the impression that they were amazed at the very suggestion that reading a few books could make a lawyer. PHIL LAOS made an argument that read as if it had been written by Governor Smith. "You certainly must know from *sad experience*," he said in an open letter to Evans, "that no man can obtain a competent knowledge of the law in a few months, else you are more profoundly ignorant than *your friends* are willing to allow. You must know that twenty years close application will scarcely qualify any person for the important office of Judge, and even the most profound with this preparation meet almost insurmountable difficulties."[40]

Governor Charles H. Bell, a generation later writing judicial biographies in his study, *Bench and Bar of New Hampshire*, claimed to know as a fact that Evans had done a substantial amount of reading. "But rather unwisely," Bell admitted, "he determined to do his studying by himself, and not to enter the office of a practicing lawyer." Answering that contention some years earlier, Plumer turned rather viciously against his former friends at the Rockingham County bar. Unable to deny that Evans did not study with a lawyer, Plumer said it was not his fault. It was rather that the "*associated* bar" refused him permission to study in an office. It was an amazing claim and perhaps untrue. "And without that *permission* how could he *read*, how could he understand them," Plumer asked, meaning how could Evans understand law books. "I am not for passing indiscriminate censure on lawyers—some of them are honest and useful members of society; but they arrogate too much to themselves if they say no man is qualified for judge who has not read law in one of their offices."[41]

RESTORATOR scored points against those who said Evans had read enough law to qualify for the bench when he observed that "[n]o man is a Lawyer by intuition—the midnight lamp must be trimmed," but Isaac Hill of the *Patriot* was not convinced. It was not important whether Evans knew any law or not, he insisted. Legal education was not only unnecessary for a judge, it might, in fact, be a detriment. The real issue, Hill contended, was whether the study and practice of law made a lawyer "more unfit for the dignified impartiality of a judge, than the practice of a man of science and learning in any other profession or situation whatever." Referring, of course, to Jeremiah Smith, Hill asserted that "the characteristic industry and intense application of Mr. Evans would better qualify him for a judge, than the 'twenty years study at law' of him who knows little of the principles of natural justice, of business, or whatever is out of the immediate line of his profession." This was fast becoming the Republicans' principal contention. "Nothing in our opinion, so well qualifies a man for this office as being conversant in the common concerns of life, in the business of traffic, barter or merchandize—the management of the police of towns—the frequent attendance on courts as jurors, or a continuance in the legislature for a time," the *Patriot* argued. "[H]e is not searching continually in the books of the days of barbarism for precedents to excuse the palliate villany, or omit to bring the deserved punishment on the head of the offender. He knows enough of *common law* to know it ought to be founded in right opposed to wrong; and his judgment extends far enough not to make an unjust decision."[42]

Today there is a tendency to brush aside the *Patriot*'s words as quaint, too agrestic in spirit, or even hopelessly anachronistic. It is too easy to forget, however, that, only a few years before Jeremiah Smith became chief justice, Hill's view had been the political and social philosophy that determined the course of judicial appointments in New Hampshire. The better judge, it was held, could make the just decision by drawing more on his own social, business, and civic experience than he could by reading law books or by searching for precedent long forgotten by all but a few lawyers. It may no longer have been the dominant judicial theory in 1809 when Isaac Hill wrote this editorial, but he obviously thought it still persuasive and so would many Republicans in New Hampshire, at least for the next decade. After all, it was jurisprudential theory directly drawn from commonsense jurisprudence, and commonsense jurisprudence still had a following in the state. Evans must have thought the following was quite substantial, for he made the *Patriot*'s thesis his own, adopting it as his chief argument when defending his right to be on the Superior Court. His lifetime of practical experience in nonlegal affairs, especially in trade, he claimed, qualified him for a judgeship. Evans even said that was why he had been put on the bench. The people, he asserted, did not want a judiciary made up only of lawyers. He had, he told the two houses of the legislature, "accepted the appointment in a great measure, to gratify the wishes of many, who believed it important to have upon the bench of the Superior Court one member at least, who should possess some practical knowledge of commercial affairs, and the ordinary pursuits of life; and who, not having engaged in the active practice of law, although possessing some knowledge of its general principles, acquired by a course of private study, might be free from those prejudices, which too often attach to those whose pursuits are confined to the practical part of professional life."[43]

Evans was speaking to the past, not to the future. Nevertheless, there were many people in New Hampshire, mostly Republicans, who agreed with what he said. There might have been even more who supported him, except for Evans's political ineptness. He just did not belong among the leadership of the state. The day after he was appointed to the Superior Court, he surprised even Republicans by taking the seat to which he had been elected in the lower house as one of the representatives for Portsmouth. Already he was being addressed as "Judge Evans" and, having accepted his judicial appointment, was disqualified by a provision in the Constitution of 1792 from sitting in the House, but no one is on record protesting, and Evans may not have realized that there was a problem with his being in the legislature. As a result, he was in the House when the members debated the text of their reply to Smith's gubernatorial address. When the draft of a proposed official "answer" was first read, Republicans moved that the words, "long and" be struck from the sentence, "a long and diligent study of jurisprudence . . . can alone enable a person to fill the responsible office of judge. . . ." The movers hoped the amendments would "screen" Evans, or so a newspaper explained. They wanted to spare him the embarrassment of being marked by a majority of the House for not measuring up to its judicial standards, that is, of not being qualified for his appointment. It goes without saying that the three representatives who had drafted the "answer" told the House they were not referring to Evans, or to anyone else's lack of legal education. The words "long and diligent," they claimed, were "no more than a general truth, a maxim founded on the experience of ages." No one was persuaded, certainly not Evans, who knew the words were aimed at him. Undoubtedly, everyone expected him to keep out of the debate, but lacking self-restraint, he could not remain silent. "At length," one account of the proceedings indicates, "*Judge* Evans rose. He said, some perhaps, would consider it indecorous in him to rise on that occasion." However, he "considered it his duty" to enter the debate. The words that "a long and diligent study of jurisprudence" was necessary before anyone should be appointed to the high bench, were "*personal, illiberal* and *unjust.*" He was not speaking for himself, for he cared nothing about the insult. "But it reflected on many Judges in the State, who were not Lawyers. He would not allow the principle to be correct. He thought other qualifications necessary for a Judge—An acquaintance with the common affairs of life, with trade, with the principles of insurance. Judge [John] Lowell of Massachusetts had said, that in the best constituted judicial tribunal, ONE at least of the judges, should be acquainted with merchandizing."[44]

There are two striking aspects to Evans's defense of his appointment that deserve emphasis. First, he did not countenance the jurisprudence of common sense. It may not have become quite the "anachronism" that one historian says it was,[45] but with ever more competent lawyers coming to the New Hampshire bar, especially to the Rockingham County bar, and with the rising economic importance of commercialism and the first stirring of manufacturing, Evans was shrewd to plead the need to have someone with business experience on the bench, rather than a need for men with good common sense and the democratic values of small-town neighborliness. The second feature is how Evans utilized one of the elements of antibar politics being disseminated by the *New-Hampshire Patriot*. Note what he did not say. He did not claim that lawyers had no place on the bench or that homespun common sense produced better judges than did years spent in legal practice. Rather, Evans picked up the *Patriot*'s persistent theme, that legal education and law practice developed professional "prejudices," that the bench could not help but be intellectually broadened by balancing the narrowly focused lawyer-judge with associates of more "practical knowledge."

That was the theme the *Patriot* continued to trumpet. After Evans had completed his first circuit as a member of the Superior Court, the *Patriot* marveled at how successful he had been. Evans had not only proven that a layman could survive and even succeed on the bench, he had proven that laymen were needed there. "[T]he people can now decide whether our bench ought to be filled exclusively by lawyers—by those who have spent *twenty years* in the study and practice of law," Isaac Hill argued. "[T]hey can now say whether reason and experience in the common affairs of the world be not as necessary ingredients in a judge, as the exclusive application of the barbarous precedents, and musty books of other countries." A Federalist writing in the *Concord Gazette* was amused. "I do not recollect," Citizen pointed out, "at any former period, after a new Judge had completed his first circuit, of seeing the whole column of a news-paper devoted to his praise—telling of his wonderful capacity, candor, patience, assiduity, and admirable wisdom."[46]

Evans needed all the candor, patience, and wisdom he could muster. During the four years he served on the Superior Court, it is safe to say that he became the judge most despised by New Hampshire lawyers in the entire history of the organized bar. No other member of the high court has been treated with such disrespect, not to mention outright hostility. Evans, as Lynn Turner points out, "had to deal with some of the most brilliant and ruthless attorneys in New England and they delighted in publicly exposing his ignorance of the law." Plumer had predicted what would happen when he told the public that "the arts and talents of *the host of federal lawyers* will, more perplex and embarrass, than aid" Evans. In private he had warned Evans not to accept the appointment. "[H]e will be embarrassed & Perplexed," Plumer wrote in his autobiography. "I frankly appraised him of the opposition he would have to encounter, & assured him it would require talents & prudence to support him in office."[47]

The *New Hampshire Gazette* hoped that the campaign of stigma and reproach would backfire and cause people to think sympathetically of Evans, persecuted by the state's one group of professional browbeaters. "The unrelenting malignity with which Judge Evans is pursued by the blood hounds of federalism, their unceasing exertions to hunt him down, are the best evidence in his favor," it opined. Even RESTORATOR, who despised Evans, admitted that he "must have often experienced inconveniences in his situation as a Judge, and found himself unable to decide many questions of law, which have been submitted to his decision—which were familiar and easy to his learned Brethren on the bench, and who could untie those knotty points, *as easy as their garter*."[48]

Years later Governor Bell, himself a lawyer, wrote a one-sentence description of the tactics employed by the Federalist bar against Evans. "A plentiful crop of pleas in abatement, special demurrers, and other like refinements came suddenly before him, and made his life a burden," Bell explained. He also seemed to say that Evans deserved the harassment. "His political friends regarded the treatment which he received from a large portion of the bar as simple persecution," Bell recalled, "but the more impartial could not fail to see that he had undertaken duties which neither his training nor his delicacy of constitution enabled him to perform to complete satisfaction."[49]

It is possible that Bell is right. Some of Evans's supporters may have realized that he was in over his head. Certainly William Plumer did. Publicly he supported Evans, expressing no reservations. Republicans, he wrote for publication, "*universally approve*" of Evans's appointment. "They consider him a man of talents, information, and integrity—that he will administer impartial justice, and *pronounce*, not *make* the law." By "information" he meant knowledge of law. Privately, Plumer had an entirely different attitude. "As a partizan politician," he wrote of Evans, "he has been industrious, persevering & decided. But as a judge he will be deficient in legal science, judgment, accuracy & decision of character." Many years later, Plumer looked back on the four years when Evans was on the bench and decided that he had not been up to the job. During his first two years on the Superior Court, he recalled, Evans "gave proof of decent talents and close application to business; but it was apparent to every well informed man, that he was deficient in legal science, and that his judgment was not so accurate and discriminating as the office required."[50]

Evans was more than deficient in legal science, he was judicially incompetent, and his tenure on the court may have taught New Hampshire that an untrained level of commonsense competency or years of experience in commercial or political affairs alone would no longer do. Although laymen would continue to serve as judges on the Court of Common Pleas, Evans was the last nonlawyer to sit on the Superior Court. He remained on the court for four years, becoming more and more ineffective, until 1813, when the General Court legislated him out of office.

*Chapter Three*

# Federalist Indian Summer

We must go back to the decade before Jeremiah Smith first became a judge, to the first week of 1793, and a moment when William Plumer pretended to be annoyed. "My patience is exhausted," he wrote Smith. "Every week, for near two months, when the post called at my door, I have in vain anxiously expected a letter from you. This was not the case last winter. 'Tis true, I was then Speaker of the house of Representatives, & I am now a private citizen. I could then perhaps more effectually have served your interests than at present. But I am still your friend & my wishes are warmly interested in your favor." Plumer meant what he said and what he said was the truth. No one would work harder in Smith's interests than would he, and no one would deserve greater credit when Smith was first appointed chief justice of the Superior Court. He was sworn into his judicial office in the summer of 1802, on a day that Daniel Webster recalled as a memorable date in New Hampshire history. "[W]hen Jeremiah Smith became chief justice," he would exclaim, "it was a day of the gladsome light of jurisprudence."[1]

Smith had become "chief" of a court system in turmoil. In an eight-year period during the previous decade, Lynn Turner noted, the Superior Court "had suffered seven resignations, one impeachment, and innumerable threats [from the legislature] of removal." Turner listed several causes, but an old one alone told most of the story: money. New Hampshire still would not pay salaries sufficient to attract lawyers to the bench. Not as serious but still damaging were the divisive politics of that day. "The spirit of party ran high," Plumer recalled a quarter century later. Politics, he explained, "divided families, neighborhoods, towns & states; &, blind to public interest, embittered the sweets of social life, & hazarded the rights of the nation." Even an apolitical judiciary had to be affected by the bitterness, and at the turn of the nineteenth century, the New Hampshire judiciary was anything but apolitical.[2]

At the time Smith became chief justice, New Hampshire had been a solidly Federalist state for over a decade. John Taylor Gilman had been governor since 1794, but the political configuration that kept him in office was most unusual, and the Republicans only needed competent electoral leadership and a vote-getting gubernatorial candidate to challenge Federal ascendency. Portsmouth, the largest town and only center of shipping, ship building, and mercantile interests, was also the center of Republicanism, and it was the merchants and traders who furnished the leadership of the Jeffersonian party. The Federalists' strength lay inland where nine-tenths of the population were farmers. Elsewhere they were the people who furnished the base of Jefferson's strength, but fear and hatred of France, driven and preached by the Congregational clergy, had kept the agricultural yeomen of New Hampshire voting for the Federalists and incidentally keeping Governor Gilman in the gubernatorial chair so that he had been able to appoint Smith as chief justice.[3] The politics of New Hampshire were ripe for drastic change. In no other state did Republicans have so much opportunity for growth. Soon the Federalists would learn that Jeffersonian gains and Federal decline were unavoidable.

Chief Justice Smith and his closest political friend, William Plumer, were disciples of Alexander Hamilton in legal theory,[4] but they were less Hamiltonian in politics. Although both were nationalists, they were primarily New England Federalists, thoroughly narrow in their regional loyalties and completely distrustful of all political activity south of Delaware. As the Republicans in the 1790s became more and more pro-French and anti-British, Plumer's apprehension of southern Republican politics increased in proportion. "I fear more [from] our Democrats, our frenchified Americans, than from the French themselves," he told the congressman from New Hampshire's Hillsborough County. "The time is come when our country's *foes are those in our own household*." Smith was more harsh. Republicans, he suggested, were "lawless," both because they were men who "dread the whip of the law" and because they were enemies of law—"the enemies of the rights of property," "the enemies of order and good government, the enemies of peace, and, in my opinion, the independence of the country." That was an extremely condemnatory statement, and Plumer would not have gone that far, but he did claim there was a difference of intellectual and moral substance dividing the two political parties. The men of one were unquestionably superior to the men of the other. "[Y]ou may rely upon it," he wrote a brother, after serving a few months as a United States senator, "though the federalists are the minority yet in point of talents, industry & respectability they are superior to the Democrats."[5]

New England Federalists owed a very peculiar debt to France. Nothing else so united them into an effective political movement and so defined their program as the shock they felt in what they perceived as French betrayal of republican principles and their fear of French militarism. "We must consider France as an ambitious & perfidious nation," Plumer urged a fellow Federalist. Again Smith agreed. "I almost hate the name of a Frenchman," he mused. "They have opened some leaves in the volume of human nature, that I never believed were in the book. They have done the cause of liberty an irreparable injury. . . . Their principles are hostile to all government, even to ours." What he meant is explained by his belief that the French were "endeavouring to spread their principles (hostile to all Government & subordination) in all directions wishing to overturn the Governments of their neighbours inviting them to humane work of murdering their Priests & magistrates." Plumer might have been attracted to the Republican party earlier than he was but for its French policy. "I could not approve of men who deliberately condemned our government, & justified that of France," he recalled thirty years later.[6]

Republican opposition to President John Adams's foreign policy had shocked Plumer. Adams almost singlehandedly kept the country from going to war with France, Plumer believed, yet Republicans gave the president no credit. "Some think that after the injuries & insults that we have received from the *terrible republic* it would be dishonorable to attempt negotiations further," he explained to Congressman William Gordon. "I am not one of them. I never would sacrifice the peace & prosperity of my country to resentment or the etiquette of State." Smith concurred. "I am glad to learn by your letter that our people are generally averse to War," he had written from Philadelphia three years earlier. "I confess when I find any man in a public capacity in favour of a War or which is the same thing, of measures which lead to War, I cant help suspecting that he has some private views, because I am sure that it would be the most dreadful calamity that could befall our Country."[7]

Some Federalists perceived another menace threatening New England that was almost as dangerous as was France. It was Virginia, not only the ganglion of Republicanism after Thomas Jefferson became president but the most influential, dynamic, and powerful governmental and political entity in the country. Virginia's dominance grew so steadily that New England, which had always thought itself the nation's intellectual, moral, and even political center, was, Plumer suspected, facing marginality. He could not resist comparing Virginia's growing strength and its southern arrogance to that of France. "This state resembles, in one point of view, France, in [that] it is anxious to preserve its own *aristocracy*, but zealous to promote *democracy* in other states."[8]

"The southern gentry do not please me," Smith wrote a brother when first arriving at Congress and meeting his new colleagues from around the country. He meant all southerners did not please him, but Virginians more than others. "I am clearly of opinion that the people southward of Pennsylvania are in a State of barbarity when compared with the New England States," he told Plumer the next month. "The Members [of Congress] of the south ward seem much more dependent on the Will of the people than the northern members by which I would be understood to mean a servile dependence—slavish. Even the great Madison is said to be discouraged on many occasions from speaking & acting his sentiments if they happen to be unpopular in the *ancient dominion*." Plumer found a new complaint once he had been elected a United States senator and had arrived in Washington, a decade after Smith first joined the Congress. "I assure you all the principal measures of administration have a direct & powerful tendency to encrease the power of Virginia," he concluded, meaning that Jefferson and his Republican subordinates shaped national policy for Virginia's enhancement.[9]

To prevail against the political weight of slave-holding Virginia, Plumer and Smith put their faith in New England as a region. "The good sense & steady habits of those States will be the mean[s] of preserving our liberties, if they are to survive the violence of party," Plumer wrote on first arriving in Washington and encountering the South's influence. Looking back on those times some years later, he recalled that he then believed that "if the federalism of New England could be maintained, it would preserve our liberties & our free government. My fears were alarmed with the idea, that the measures of the president & of congress, would eventually endanger the rights of property, & morals of the community." Now that Thomas Jefferson's southern party was triumphant in the nation, the virtues of New England represented the last barrier defending the northern states. "I consider the steady habits & federalism of the eastern States as the sheet anchor & political salvation of the nation," Plumer wrote an acquaintance on reaching Washington.[10]

The month that Plumer was sworn in as a member of the United States Senate, the political fortunes of New Hampshire Federalism began to crumble. A few weeks before Plumer arrived in Washington, John Langdon, then the only Republican senator from New England, left the capital. He had been the first New Hampshirite to serve the full term of six years and the first to be elected to a second term. His reelection had been opposed by most Federalists but not by Jeremiah Smith. Langdon,

Smith thought, would be much less dangerous to Federalism staying in Philadelphia than returning to New Hampshire, where he would furnish Republicans with leadership they had been lacking. Smith wrote Robert Fletcher, soon to obtain notoriety as the plaintiff in the famous litigation of *Fletcher v. Peck*, that if he had the choice he would have returned Langdon to the Senate and left him in Washington where he could do less harm to New Hampshire Federalism. "If he is not elected, he will, I fear, be soured, and rear up an anti-federal party in the state; set up democratic clubs, poison the pure principles of our virtuous citizens," Smith warned. "Let our people fall into the hands of the devil, but let them not fall into the hands of these men; famine, the plague, and pestilence are nothing to it.[11] Smith was apocalyptic. Langdon returned to his home in Portsmouth and in just four years led the Republican Party to triumph.

It is important to keep in mind just how extreme were Plumer's anti-Republican, anti-Virginia prejudices before his election to the United States Senate. His six years in Washington changed his political perspectives. While serving his only term as a senator, Plumer overcame his fear of Virginia's dominance and, much to his surprise, became personally friendly with Jefferson. Several times the president invited him for dinner, and he not only accepted, but he found what Jefferson had to say impressive enough to be quoted, often favorably, in his journals and letters. At first, his opinion of the Virginian remained much what it had been before he left New Hampshire. Jefferson, he continued to believe, intended "to build up & aggrandize Virginia in particular & the states south of the Potomac in general." New Englanders, he complained to Smith, were living "under the feeble, nerveless administration of a dry-dock & indissoluble salt mountain philosopher," and we may wonder if Smith understood what he was being told. What Smith surely did understand was that his friend was changing his perception of Jefferson. It was, however, a slow, if steady process. "I may be blinded by the partiality of party," Plumer had explained earlier that same year, "but I declare, almost every new measure he recommends, recalls to my view Ezekiel's vision, & the declaration made to him by the angel—Turn, & thou shall behold yet greater abominations."[12]

We no longer can poll them, but it is a reasonable guess that had New Hampshire Federalists been asked what aspect or event of Jefferson's administration they thought most objectionable, many would have said the Louisiana Purchase. Plumer feared New England's influence could now be easily destroyed. "Admit this western world into the union," he told himself, "& you destroy in a single operation the whole weight & importance of the eastern states in the scale of politics." He meant that there soon would be new southern states supporting Virginia or, more specifically, new slave states to outvote the free states of New England.[13]

During the early months of 1804, Plumer was at the low point of his public life. If it were permissible to invent a mental condition, it would be said that he was in a state of political depression or, considering his suspicions of Virginia and the South, a state of political paraphrenia. "What is to be done?" he asked the leading Federalist of the Merrimack Valley. "Do you wish this State of things to continue?—a state, if it progresses, in which the rights of persons & property cannot be secure; a situation which every year will add power & influence to the south & to the west at the expence of the east." The government seated at Washington may have governed, but it was not a national government, a United States government, it was a Virginia government. "The general government is Virginian, its views & tendencies center there," he told Smith. "I think New England must soon feel its degraded condition; & I hope will have energy to assert & maintain its rights." There had to be "necessary changes," he added, and then asked: "What think you of this, must the inheritance be severed?"[14]

The impeachment of Judge John Pickering of Portsmouth was almost the last straw. It "very much alarmed my apprehensions," Plumer later recalled. Now he knew that Jefferson planned to replace not just administrative and lower-level Federalist officeholders but that he had "a settled determination to displace the judges." "In this state of mind, I th[ough]t Virginia . . . had engrossed nearly all authority into their hands, & that the eastern states bore an undue proportion of the public burdens, but had little or no influence in the government." He was willing to consider secession. "I fondly hope I shall live to see the righteous separated from the wicked by a geographical line," he told Smith. "If New England will not *come out & be separate* from this mass of southern corruption," he wrote Thomas W. Thompson, "*she must partake of their plagues.*"[15]

It would be well to pause for a moment. There is a perspective that is very difficult to understand. The words of Plumer quoted in the last two paragraphs are worth our close attention, not only for revealing the depths of Federalist New England's apprehension and narrow intolerance of southern political power. What is hard to comprehend is that these attitudes were expressed by a Federalist who soon would convert to Republicanism and in eight years would succeed John Langdon as the leader of the party in New Hampshire and as governor. The conversion was so extreme it defies understanding. Perhaps most startling is the realization of the extent to which Plumer had been prepared to be taken by his Federalist principles. He was one of the very few New Hampshire Federalists who actively joined in the secessionist plot led by Timothy Pickering of Massachusetts, even writing over four hundred letters "to discern the extent of public support for disunion."[16] His participation did not become public knowledge, however, and his reputation was not tainted by the charge of misprision of treason. Even so, he would eventually admit that it had been the greatest error of his life. As time passed he realized that he was being motivated not by his own common sense but by extremist Federalist politics. Federalism meant plotting secession, not building nationalism, and he drew away from the party, separating himself from colleagues with whom he had worked closely for years, ending all contact with some of his oldest friends, never speaking again to a few of them, at least not in the relaxed, informal, familiar manner of personal, confidential friendship. Slowly but progressively he came to understand Jefferson in new ways. "The more critically & impartially I examine the character & conduct of Mr. Jefferson the more favorably I think of his integrity," he decided in 1806. "I am really inclined to think I have done him injustice in not allowing more credit for the integrity of heart he possesses. . . . He has too much cunning. Still I repeat the errors of his administration proceed more from the head than the heart."[17]

When William Plumer was a young man and first ran for the New Hampshire House of Representatives, the Federalist party had been as much an intellectual as a political movement, an association of committed nationalists that had guided the United States Constitution through the ratification process to the triumph of adoption in Concord on 21 June 1788. By 1805 it was no longer the dynamic, optimistic political organization that had elected the first two presidents and sent Jeremiah Smith to Congress; it had narrowed into a defense of New England regionalism, a decline that soon would push Plumer into the eager political embrace of Thomas Jefferson. He would not be the first New Hampshire leader to abandon Federalism. Others had crossed over to Republicanism before him. John Langdon had been one of the Federalist leaders who, against the political odds, persuaded New Hampshire voters to make the United States Constitution the law of the land. During his first years in the United States Senate, he had supported the financial program of Alexander Hamilton, but a number of political incentives, primarily distrust of Great Britain and his Francophile penchants, pushed him toward the Jeffersonian party. Jay's Treaty, the Franco-British wars, and political opportunism carried him the remainder of the way. Following his failure to be reelected to the Senate, he returned to Portsmouth, and soon the political landscape of New Hampshire underwent dramatic alteration. By November of the next year, the *Gazette* was able to boast that the state had experienced a "revival of Republican principles." In 1801 the Federalist governor had won by over a thousand votes. In 1802, with Langdon opposing him, the plurality decreased markedly. "Republicanism notwithstanding federal success, increases in New Hampshire beyond example," a Baltimore newspaper noted. "There is every reason to believe that in one year the state of New-Hampshire will be completely republicanised."[18]

"The Demos are taking unwearied pains to revolutionized the State," a Federalist newspaper reported in February 1803. Most political observers anticipated the coming "revolution," but no one foresaw how swiftly it would sweep across New Hampshire. In the gubernatorial election of March 1804, Federalist John Taylor Gilman lost only seventeen votes from his total of the year before, but Langdon picked up so many new voters that the outcome was in doubt until the last town had reported. He lacked only 208 from becoming governor. In June, when the first Republican House of Representatives in New Hampshire's history met, he was elected speaker. Gilman was so stunned that he sent the General Court a message, indicating that he did not understand what was happening. "There are undoubtedly solid reasons which might induce many of my fellow citizens to prefer some other person for this Office," he told the lawmakers. "In addition to these, extraordinary exertions have been made, not only within, but from without the State, to prevent my election."[19]

The governor may have been surprised by the surge of Republican votes, but the man he had appointed chief justice was not. Unlike Gilman, Smith had been impressed by the statewide organization that the Republicans had created to coordinate their election efforts for 1804. It had been a level of political activity, Lynn Turner believed, unprecedented in New Hampshire. It had been directed by Philip Carrigan, a "hotheaded young Concord lawyer," whom Smith and Plumer seem to have thought somewhat inept, and Daniel French, a Chester attorney, whom Plumer, when governor in 1812, would appoint as attorney general. They gathered what Smith called "a general convention of the Republican members of the General Court," who selected candidates to run for every state and local office and agreed to support them actively, creating "a grand committee of election & correspondence" that reached into every town in the state. When Smith learned that Carrigan's scheme was to "promote peace, order, law, and pure and undefiled religion," he was so amused that he hastened to tell Plumer. "What think you of pure & undefiled religion under the care of Carigain & French," he asked. "[A]re you willing to confide your temporal concerns to these worthy citizens? They have leisure and I presume inclination to superintend the management of *your* property—neither of them are much embarrassed or cumbered with any of their own."[20]

Federalist newspaper writers pretended to be outraged, depicting Carrigan's convention as a secret conspiracy or illegal plot to steal the election. In fact, as every Federalist leader knew, Plumer had organized their party into an even more effective machine. Historians of New Hampshire politics generally agree that the program he put together was what gave Gilman his small margin of victory in the gubernatorial election that year. A key element of Plumer's plan had been that he and Smith "should write an address to the freemen of the State"; 6,000 copies would be printed, and the committee would have a representative in every town to distribute them. "I applied to judge Smith," Plumer recorded, "he approved the measure, but said as he was chief Justice of the Superior Court of Judicature, he thought he ought not to write, as he could not disguise his composition." Plumer was bitter. "He was always too much inclined to hunt with the fox & run with the hare," he remarked, a comment that may have been his first criticism of Smith, whom he would soon no longer think of as his friend. Plumer wrote the pamphlet by himself.[21]

There is one documented cause that may explain Plumer's angry words. He suspected that Smith was being the hypocrite. If his information was correct, just before election day the chief justice published an item in a Federalist newspaper that was as partisan as the pamphlet Plumer had asked him to co-write. Carrigan, on behalf of the Republican convention, had written a secret report to a party member in each New Hampshire town. In one Rockingham County village there were two men of the same name, one a Republican, the other a Federalist. Carrigan's letter was given by mistake to the Federalist, who immediately turned it over to the printer of the *Portsmouth Oracle*. The *Oracle* published the letter and with it a comment that is so uninteresting it would not be worth mentioning if we did not know who was said to be its author. Plumer was told the author's name by his oldest son, writing him from Portsmouth where the son lived. The comment or letter to the *Oracle*, the son reported, was written by Chief Justice Smith. If the younger Plumer had his facts correct, Smith had given Plumer an excuse for not co-writing with him that may not have been truthful. It is most likely the son was mistaken, for the editorial comment is too unimaginative and says too little to have been written by Smith. But then, Smith may have meant what he had told Plumer, that "he could not disguise his composition"; perhaps he wrote the editorial comment with so much "disguise" that, even if we had proof that he had written it, we would be hard pressed to recognize it as his work. But there is little doubt about what Plumer thought. Both his reaction and subsequent criticism of Smith are evidence that he believed his son.[22]

The election campaign of 1804 was Plumer's last significant service to Federalism and the greatest contribution he made to the party as a political operator, rather than in public office. "I consider New Hampshire in fact as revolutionized," he concluded before the year was over. Smith agreed. "Let the event of the election be as it may . . . federalism is done over in this state." Both men foretold a bleak future. "Democracy has obtained its long expected triumph in New Hampshire," Plumer explained to one of his Senate colleagues, "and [its] success is not owing to snow, rain, hail, or bad roads. It is an incontrovertible fact that federalists in this State do not compose the majority."[23]

The election of 1805 was the last political contest fought along the old issues with familiar Federalist arguments, now quite worn out. "We acknowledge then, with pleasure and with pride, that GOVERNOR GILMAN is a FEDERALIST OF THE WASHINGTON SCHOOL, true to the principles and to the policies of his master," Daniel Webster wrote in a pamphlet addressed to the people of New Hampshire. "Opposition to the adoption of the Federal Constitution, opposition to Washington and Adams, opposition to every important measure of the Federal Administration, has invariably been made by one and the same Party, under different names. Shew me the man who persevered in hostility to the Federal Constitution, and I will shew you a friend of Mr. Jefferson and his administration."[24]

Webster was a young man, only twenty-three years old, yet he spoke the language of past politics and for the moment appeared not to understand the political present, let alone the political future. He wrote as if the political issues of 1805 were the same as they had been in the 1790s and as if the slogans were also the same. At one time Federalists could win elections by tarring Republicans with hostility to the United States Constitution and to the ideals, values, and virtues of George Washington. That fact was no longer true by 1805, as Plumer well understood. Ever since Washington had died, the Federalists in Congress had celebrated his birthday. This year Plumer talked them out of doing so. The party, he feared, was too buried in a past to which fewer and fewer New Englanders looked for guidance. The next month New Hampshire voted, and his predictions were fulfilled. The Republicans won everything: the governorship, the executive Council, a fifty-member majority in the House of Representatives, and they outnumbered the Federalists two to one in the Senate. Langdon was elected governor with the amazing total of 16,000 votes. Gilman got 12,000. The next year the state's congressional delegation, all Federalist, was voted out, and the new representatives were Republican to the last man.[25]

William Plumer and Jeremiah Smith then waited for the inevitable to occur. For surely Langdon would legislate Smith out of his chief justiceship, just as Thomas Jefferson in 1802 had legislated him from the United States Circuit Court.[26]

*Chapter Four*

# Federalist Apostate

The uniqueness of Jeremiah Smith's service as chief justice was one of the very few aspects of New Hampshire governance about which the Federalists and Republicans were able to agree during the first decade of the nineteenth century. When it was believed that he would resign because of the low compensation, the extraordinarily parsimonious legislators of both parties, not just the Federalists, granted him a salary at least a third higher than that received by any other state official. The lawmakers intended the money as a tribute to him, not as an insult to his colleagues on the bench, Arthur Livermore and William Atkinson, who were angry that they received no raise at all. It was a matter of respecting Smith, not of disparaging the other justices, acknowledging New Hampshire's good fortune to have a legal scholar serve on her high court, not putting down talent that was by comparison ordinary and average, though competent and honest. The increase in salary was incredible by the standards of contemporary politics. Both branches of the legislature had been Republican, and Smith was not just a Federalist jurist, he was an active Federalist partisan. He was voted an extra 500 dollars a year, and it was truly "extra," for it was voted to him and to him alone as long as he remained chief justice. It was not to be paid to his successor after he retired. It had "passed the House 101 to 54," A VOTER later recalled, "and in the Senate but *one* in *twelve* lifted his hand against it." Many of the leading Republicans supported the bill, a remarkable tribute to the chief justice in those highly partisan times. One Republican legislator supporting the measure was Samuel Bell, an outstanding lawyer. "MR. BELL stated on the floor of the House, *that Judge Smith, by his assiduity in business and correct decisions,* had saved to the county [Hillsborough] in which he [Bell] lived, more than TWO THOUSAND DOLLARS a year."[1] It was a very generous statement for a Republican, although we cannot be sure just what it means. Possibly Bell was saying that Smith moved business so swiftly through the court that judicial fees amounted to an additional $2,000 more than they had been before he became chief justice. More likely Bell meant that Smith managed judicial proceedings so effectually that the county's expenses were as much as $2,000 less than they had been. Or he could have meant a combination of both explanations. In any event, that the boast was made by Samuel Bell is what should impress us. For he was destined in time to succeed Smith in two of his offices. Bell became a justice of the Superior Court just when Smith left the bench. And then, like Smith, he would resign from the court to become governor.

It is our misfortune, but we in the twenty-first century can never hope to appreciate Smith as his contemporaries saw him; we cannot know what particular personal attributes and intellectual traits so completely captured their admiration. Except for William Plumer, no contemporaries commented extensively about his capabilities; there were then no legal scholars evaluating the state judiciary in law-review articles; and New Hampshire newspapers of that day seldom reported on the courts. We can know the words he wrote, understand the work he did, and appreciate the reforms he planned, but we cannot experience the sense of pride that New Hampshire people took in their chief justice, whether they realized what he meant for the future, whether they comprehended the professionalism he was introducing into their law, or whether they had just been told there was now a special judge on the Superior Court who was well trained, hardworking, and knowledgeable in the law. All we can know is that during his first years on the bench Smith overcame the great political animosity that dominated public affairs in the early republic and produced the unprecedented civic moment of Republicans joining Federalists to keep him on the bench as a judge.

Whatever public criticism existed toward the judiciary during Chief Justice Smith's first term was directed against his colleagues, not aimed at him. At least two of the judges deserved censure, tarnishing the reputation of the two courts—the Superior Court and the Common Pleas—by accepting or retaining other offices while on the bench.

Nahum Parker who had succeeded Plumer in the United States Senate had been appointed chief justice of the Court of Common Pleas for Cheshire County the same year that he was elected senator. People had expected him to decline one post but he did not, asserting "his ability to perform the duties of both offices," despite the fact that those duties were separated by 500 miles. Worse for Smith, his colleague on the Superior

Court, William Atkinson, retained his position as register of probate for Strafford County even though the constitution forbade judges from holding other public offices. One day in court, Jeremiah Mason, then the attorney general, claimed that by accepting his commission as judge, Atkinson had constructively resigned as register and that all probate records certified by Atkinson in the interim were invalid; Mason threatened to conduct no criminal trials if Atkinson continued to retain both positions. It is not certain, but Mason had probably challenged the validity of some certificates that had been offered in evidence, requiring the court to rule on the issue, for the question was put to the four judges. Livermore was the most emphatic of the four judges sitting on the court, ruling that the two offices could not be held by one person, surely meaning that all Atkinson's probate certificates since becoming a judge were null and void. Paine Wingate was much more vague, saying that certificates of the register were valid *de facto* but not *de jure*, "& therefore [he] was for admitting" them into evidence. Atkinson remained silent. With the court evenly divided the question was left to the chief justice who ordered the matter continued, saying it was too important to be resolved without study for "if decided one way [it] nullified all the probate proceedings in the county for nearly a year past." People with probate cases pending, Smith reported, "turned pale & trembled." It was a very embarrassing situation, the first scandal of Smith's tenure as chief justice. Despite the fact that he had tolerated the situation for almost a year, it did not reflect on him, and it never reached beyond Strafford County. The remainder of the state paid it little heed.[2]

Smith had a second reason for being upset with Atkinson. In addition to being register, he was county solicitor of Strafford. That is, he was occupying three offices when constitutionally a member of the Superior Court was allowed to hold only his judgeship. "The love of money" was at the root of the problem, Smith concluded, adding that he also "could say something about the rage for office."[3] Even without constitutional, statutory, or ethical issues, Atkinson's behavior would have troubled Smith. It was not just the multiple offices that he faulted but any nonjudicial business. "There is a dictum in one of the books of reports," he had written some years before becoming chief justice, "which, I suppose, will pass for very good law in this court—'Ye cannot serve God and Mammon'—you cannot be a judge and a merchant. 'Tis easy to guess, in the context, which will get the mastery. I fear, if we look into human nature, we will find it written in page the first, in very legible characters, that interest will prevail, and that our judge will be more solicitous about fitting out his brig, than about settling a knotty point of law."[4]

While Jeremiah Smith was basking in the prestige of his first term as chief justice of the Superior Court, his personal life sustained a radical change. Smith probably had no idea that his friendship with William Plumer might be ending, even though Plumer gave him remarkably clear warning. When he had been a senator for less than a year, Plumer wrote Smith that he had a better opinion of Thomas Jefferson now that he had gotten to know him personally. "I think I have been deceived as to the character of the President," he confessed. "I am willing to acknowledge my error with as much frankness as if you were my *father confessor*."[5]

Smith may not have been disturbed, realizing that his friend was speaking of Jefferson's person, not his politics. Plumer was still complaining that the "office of the President, is filled by an *Infidel*, & that of the Vice President by a *Murderer*." His increasingly friendly attitude was due to what his biographer called Jefferson's "social graces." "The more initially I examined the character & conduct of Mr. Jefferson, the more favorably I thot of him," Plumer recalled in his autobiography. "That he was a man of science & literature; that as to what is called *revealed religion* he was an *infidel*, but on all other subjects too credulous."[6]

Plumer had begun to question his own Federalism as early as 1804. "Perhaps I have been in error," he reflected just a few months after leading the party to its narrow gubernatorial victory of that year. "I feel less interest in politics than I did last year," he told his oldest son. "The decline of federalism in the east [i.e., New England] induces me to believe that democracy must over run us." Although continuing to reassure himself that he would always be a Federalist, he realized that he was unquestionably changing politically. What was especially surprising to his friends, he was growing much less partisan. "I live on friendly terms with all parties," he noted during the second week of 1807, his last year in Washington. "My credit as a *party-man* with the federalists is gone. They know I will do nothing with them for the sake of making opposition to the administration, or supporting their party." On returning to New Hampshire, he avoided politics. "Visited several of my friends & acquaintances of both political parties," he wrote after three days spent in Portsmouth. "Was received by all with much cordiality & treated with great attention." He was neither disappointed nor surprised when not reelected to the United States Senate. "I am too much of a federalist to have republican votes, & too much of a Republican deeply to interest federalists in my favor."[7]

There were many reasons why Plumer had been a committed Federalist before going to Washington, but primarily it had been because he was a strong nationalist and a New Englander who feared the political hegemony of the American South and the instability of republican France. By the time he left the Senate, he realized that the Republicans had usurped many Federalist values, while the Federal party had become increasingly regional and was no longer a force for nationalism. Moreover—and on this point Smith strongly disagreed with Plumer—the Federalists were too pro-British, unwilling to criticize Great Britain's high-seas tyranny. After extensive study Plumer concluded that too much was made in New England newspapers of American seamen being impressed into the British service. "I have no doubt that nin[e]teen out of twenty whom they have taken were in fact British subjects—& according to the laws of that country were lawfully impressed."[8] By defending the national interest against the encroachments of *both* the French and British, he believed, Jefferson and his secretary of state, James Madison, pursued a more evenhanded foreign policy than a Federalist administration would. The public first received notice of Plumer's new political bearings when he asserted that "the embargo was a necessary and prudent measure."[9] With that announcement, Turner claimed, the Federalists "declared him apostate and cast him into outer darkness."[10]

The always suspicious Isaac Hill may not have acknowledged Plumer's political conversion until 1810, the year the Republicans elected him to the first of two terms in the state senate. Yet, since 1808 under the name VERITAS, he had been contributing party polemics to Hill's newspaper, the *New-Hampshire Patriot*.[11] Writing for the *Patriot* in 1810, Plumer revealed not only how much his apostasy was due to the Federalist pro-British policy but how viciously he had turned against Jeremiah Smith, who then was running on the Federalist ticket for a second term as governor. Plumer urged New Hampshirites not to support Smith since a vote for Smith was a vote for Great Britain and against the United States. Smith, he charged, supported London against Washington and never spoke on behalf of Washington against London. "But," he concluded, "if it is your object to dissolve the Union, to destroy its government, and expose your country to foreign domination, than boldly avow the fact, and as a means to attain that end, give your suffrages to Mr. Smith."[12]

Plumer turned against his friend as early as 1805 and used various ways to let people know about the estrangement. In December of that year, he was trying to locate someone and told Jeremiah Mason that he had recently learned the whereabouts of the individual. "This information I have principally from Samuel Smith of the Senate," he explained. "I am inclined to think that *Smith* is correct, though I have less confidence in that *name* (but more in Samuel) than I formerly had."[13] There is no reason to ask if Mason understood Plumer's meaning. Of course he did. What we cannot know is how saddened it made him and other Rockingham County attorneys that the two members of the bar to whom everyone else looked for intellectual leadership—to bring the law, the judiciary, and even themselves as lawyers to new heights of professionalism—were no longer a team. The greatest shock, however, may have occurred when they realized how bitter Plumer had become. For Mason and other friends of both men, the realization probably arrived when they read Plumer faulting Smith for actions and policies that he had not only supported but had urged Smith to take. Every lawyer in Rockingham and Strafford counties would have remembered how Plumer had rejoiced when Smith became a midnight judge and how he had thought the United States circuit judgeship was an office both valuable to the country and worthy of Smith's talents.[14] Now he said that the circuit court had been created only "to give big, protected salaries to friends of [President] Adams," and even hinted corruption, suggesting that Smith had been overpaid, in "[a]n office that required only a portion of his time—that gave him a large salary—but yielded little if any benefit to the nation."[15] Friends like Mason must have been astonished that Plumer could become so openly hypocritical.

Mason may have been even more puzzled when told that Plumer's break with Smith had been triggered by a lawsuit presided over by the chief justice. Plumer's brother had been the plaintiff and Mason counsel for the defendant. It was an unexceptionable litigation, and the main faults that could be charged against Smith were that he allowed the suit to be dragged out longer than necessary and that he was too inclined to give Mason's apparently meritless motions the benefit of the doubt. Plumer thought the court's delays were costly to his brother. After Plumer spoke to Smith about the litigation, he decided that Smith had been so unresponsive as to have insulted him.[16] Twenty-two years later, Plumer still retained much of the resentment he had experienced at the time. "The rudeness & passionate manner in which Jeremiah Smith . . . treated me—his pride, vanity, selfsufficiency—his inordinate love of popularity—& his apparent partiality in several cases he decided, particularly one of my brother Samuel's, induced me to come to the resolution not to visit him, & to that I have long adhered."[17] He meant that he resolved never to visit Smith again. He not only adhered to the resolve, but the two never again spoke to one another as friends.

The chief justice never understood what had occurred. Ending the friendship was entirely Plumer's doing. Smith begged him not to. "He said he wished to live friendly with me," Plumer recorded, "he thot that men of science & liberality were so few in the state that they were bound to visit each other—that our separation was a grief to him—& he had no objection to converse upon our disagreement alone or in company of mutual friends."[18] But Plumer was a much different individual than was Smith. He was angry about a number of events he blamed on Smith, the most significant being his brother's lawsuit, which he believed the chief justice continued without good legal cause for over two years while the defendant, in possession of disputed land, was cutting timber that Smith eventually ruled had belonged to Samuel Plumer.[19] Plumer never questioned Smith's integrity, but he did get quite close to questioning his judicial competence, as when criticizing a strikingly similar cause of action with remarkably similar facts and rulings. It was a litigation "in which the title of land was drawn in question," Plumer recalled. Smith "allowed one of the *parties in interest* to be sworn as a witness to shew that the deed he had given to the *other party* was obtained through fraud, and therefore void; and he directed the jury to find a verdict accordingly, against the testimony of *disinterested witnesses*, who testified the deed was given for *a good and valuable consideration*!"[20]

A second event that annoyed Plumer more than it should have was Smith's agreeing to run as a Federalist presidential elector in 1808. Writing as VERITAS, Plumer told the public how four years earlier Smith, on the excuse that he was a judge and should not engage in politics, refused a Plumer request that he run as a presidential elector against Jefferson. "I stated with great freedom the impropriety of electing Smith," he later recalled in his autobiography. "Previous to the last Presidential election, this same man was nominated by the *federalists*, for an Elector;" he told the readers of the *New Hampshire Gazette*, "but as federalism was then in rapid decline, he refused standing as a candidate—alledging that *he held an office by which he was bound to administer equal justice to men of both parties—it was therefore improper to suffer himself to be a candidate for an Elector supported by one party, as it would impair the confidence of the other in his adjudications*. . . . But *now*, when federalism, in his opinion, is gaining the ascendant, this man can see no impropriety in being a *party* candidate for the electoral office, or intimate a wish to decline its honors."[21]

There was more behind Smith's decision than Plumer allowed. In 1804 Smith had been a new judge, just beginning to establish his political reputation anew. By 1808 he was the most respected official in state government and was being urged by many Federalist leaders to run the next year for governor. By agreeing to stand for presidential elector, he tested his popularity, for in New Hampshire during the era of the early republic, people voted for the elector, not for the presidential candidate. Smith did so well in 1808 that he may have proven Plumer right: had he run in 1804 his candidacy could have made a difference in the outcome. In that year, when he and his colleague Arthur Livermore refused to stand for election, the party lost, and there were Federalists, Plumer claimed, "who impute the failure of their list [of electors] to that circumstance."[22]

Four years later, when he agreed to be a candidate, some of the Republican press congratulated the Federalists for nominating him. "The Hon. Judge Smith, with an enlightened mind and conciliating manners, is calculated to command respect and attention on all sides," the Dover *Sun* exclaimed. And he not only was elected, but with 14,006 votes he had the highest number of votes of all the candidates on both the Federalist and Republican slates.[23] Plumer, of course, drew a different lesson: "To guard against the alarming and numerous evils arising from *seekers after popularity*," he wrote as ARISTIDES, "would it not be an additional security to the rights of the people, if your constitution precluded an acting judge from being a *candidate* for an elective office?"[24] This proposal may have been Plumer's first public call for restrictions on the judiciary. Despite his conversion to Jeffersonian politics, there would not be many others.

Plumer also had jurisprudential complaints against Smith. He thought the chief justice too readily went off the judicial deep end and that he too often failed to rein in his decisions, legislating when most judges would have limited themselves to adjudication. "It is the duty of judges to *administer,* not *make* the law," he complained. "Indeed, the very principles, as well as the form of our government, explicitly prohibit our judicial officers from being *law makers*." Plumer had become a Jeffersonian in politics, but as the story in this book develops, it will become evident that he would not become a republicanist legal theorist. Yet he became such a committed Republican leader as well as office holder that he could not help but internalize some Jeffersonian legal principles, prejudices, and oddities. One of the least controversial was that the methodology of the common law invested judges with more discretion than is compatible with republican government. Plumer's criticism of Smith—that "[t]here should be no more discretionary power invested in judges than what is absolutely necessary"—was certainly not what he would have said before switching political parties. But now he was addressing the discomfort that Republicans felt when realizing that lawyers, not the legislature, were making law, and worse, that it was being made not only by appellate decision but also in litigation.[25]

There was a time when Plumer's theorics of judicial restraint were less well known to the general population, and they may have seemed to some New Hampshire people to have been original principles that he concocted to use against Smith. It may be difficult to believe today, but it has been only since the last half of the twentieth century that newspaper readers in the United States have been saturated with arguments as to why judges should not make law. Today judicial legislation is so extreme as to make the legislating of Chief Justice Smith almost nonexistent by comparison. We have become conditioned to government by the black robe. Plumer was writing at a time when republicanism was in vogue, and the people—not judges—were supposed to be the rulers. "From the nature and principles of the government established in our country, where the people themselves elect their law-makers," he explained during 1823, in what was just about his strongest acceptance of some judicial law-making, "it would seem to be the duty of the judges to pronounce the law, but not make it, and yet the fact is that the *unwritten or common law*, which has been adopted and made by the decisions and adjudications of our judicial tribunals, is more voluminous than our statute laws."[26] On reading these words we must keep in mind that they can easily mislead. It is necessary to reiterate, therefore, that Plumer had always been and in 1823 still was a proponent of receiving the common law in both New Hampshire and the federal jurisdictions. He believed in both the common law's utility and its necessity. He also wanted American courts to receive the common law's methodology as his words just quoted clearly state. But after his political apostasy he developed several Republican reservations to receptionist jurisprudence. "I cannot approve of our judges extending its [common law's] limits, and virtually making, instead of explaining and pronouncing law," he told New Hampshire newspaper readers. "If the state of society require[s] further improvements in our common law, let these improvements be made by the legislature."[27] Although not a surprising statement, it owed less to the common lawyer than to Jeffersonian jurisprudence.

It should be reiterated that Plumer was being pulled from two directions. On one hand his training as a lawyer and his early adherence to the common-law methodology made judges not just finders but determiners of what the law is. On the other hand his recent conversion to both the Republican Party and to Jeffersonian republicanism almost persuaded him that judges must not make law. The struggle to strike a balance would be a dominant factor in his politics for the remainder of his professional and political life, and it would have a profound influence on New Hampshire judicial history. It will be Plumer, as governor in 1816, who will give the state's highest court its defining mystique. It is therefore important to understand that Plumer was doing more than saying that judges should confine themselves to finding the law, not making it. There is every reason to believe that he truly thought that the distinction could be drawn in practice and that it was one to which judges could be held. He showed the strength of his belief when objecting to common-law judges plugging holes and filling gaps in the law, whether the holes and gaps were found in inadequate legislation or were due to judicial rulings being unreported. "If case[s] occur where the law affords no remedy to a plaintiff or defence to a defendant, where in equity and good conscience both may have claims, the judges have no authority to supply the deficiency," he explained. "They cannot, with propriety, provide a remedy, by making law to suit those cases."[28] Chief Justice Smith thought differently, for he knew he could provide the remedy, though he would never have admitted publicly that he was making law. Of course he understood what Plumer was saying, but the line that Plumer drew was too fine for him. It was a line to guide the unimaginative judge, not for a judge like Smith, ever ready to push the law in the directions he wanted it to go, making it independent of juries, more controlled by rules of procedure, and therefore more predictable. Smith was a realist and appreciated that he was unable to bring about innovations in other areas, even if he wanted to do so. Restricting juries and instructing New Hampshire lawyers to file cases by uniform rules of process were enough, however, for Plumer to complain that some of Smith's rulings were "not only *novel*, but *unprecedented*."[29]

Because criticism of judicial legislation became so familiar during the latter decades of the twentieth century, it is easy for us in the twenty-first century to overlook how difficult it was to adhere to Plumer's newly formulated republican theory of law during the terms when Smith was a judge. There were so few published judicial opinions and even fewer precedents to follow that judges had little choice. They had to make law, and surely Plumer knew it. His conversion to the politics of Republicanism had been entirely sincere, and that sincerity surely helped him to adopt a few Jeffersonian jurisprudential tenets. And the urge to criticize Smith made it convenient for him to fashion antijudicial platitudes more suitable for legal discourse in Virginia than in New England. But Plumer never embraced the extremes of Jeffersonian legal philosophy, though there were times when he surely thought he did. As the events that took place during his last two years as governor will show, he never abandoned the core receptionist legal principles. Despite his public rhetoric he remained almost as much a receptionist jurisprudent as did Jeremiah Smith. And it is that reality that would shape the future of the judiciary in New Hampshire.

Although Smith would have said that his judicial decisions were not legislative, he did make law in some of the ways to which Plumer objected. He did so by acting as he understood a common-law judge should act, in part because it would have been difficult not to. With scant volumes of published reports available in the state, and with manuscript opinions scattered and unannotated, there were few New Hampshire or American precedents to direct him. Many questions arose for which there was no guidance, except for possible English or Irish reporters, which were not available in most shire towns; certainly there was no guidance in New Hampshire law. Smith had no choice, he had to "legislate" and write law in the manner of a common-law judge. He would have appeared even more to be legislating had he been able to publish his appellate decisions. From a practical perspective legislating jurists were judges like Smith, in courts of the early republic, when there were few judicial precedents and even fewer published reports. With hardly any precedents to guide them and no reports to read or cite, of course the members of the judiciary wrote policy in creative strokes. They had to create when there were no previously pronounced judgments to follow. The general theory explaining the difference between them and the judges of the next era, the period of so-called "formalist law," is not that they were broad visionaries and the formalists were unimaginative, narrow technicians. The difference is that the legislating jurists of the first two decades of the nineteenth century had less law that they could follow, and the formalist jurists of the post–Civil War era had the benefit of law written and reported by their predecessors of the generation or two before.

In fact, that was Smith's most difficult judicial challenge: to bring New Hampshire law to the ideal stage where judges would have enough legal precedent to be formalistic. Or, as Plumer suggested, where New Hampshire courts could apply the maxims of rule-of-law. "The decisions of Courts of Justice," Plumer contended, "should be publickly known, & carefully presented, that justice may always [be] administered this day as it was the day before." Jeremiah Smith was the first New Hampshire judge to write law of this standard. He was not on the bench for much time, yet when he left the court after his second term, New Hampshire law was pointed toward the standards of rule of law.[30]

Rule of law was not an applied judicial concept in New Hampshire even after Smith became chief justice, but everything he did as a judge was intended to establish the doctrine, although he did not know it would be called "rule of law." Plumer also did not know the term "rule of law," even though he was referring to it when writing about commonsense jurisprudence as it had been expounded before Smith became a judge. "No axiom," he said, "is more dangerous than that the spirit of the law ought to be considered, & not the letter; if this is adopted, the same laws that condemn to day, will acquit tomorrow, according to the different opinions which different judges may form of its spirit." That criticism could not be charged against Smith, who not only looked for the letter and the spirit of a law, but also for its intent, its purpose, and its history. Of course, in that era before decisions were officially published, it was the "intent," the "purpose," and the "history" of those prior litigations that were well enough remembered so that their procedure, rulings, and holdings still could be recalled and even recited by members of the bar. Smith was cautious as a judge, yet bold enough to change his mind when he concluded that a previous interpretation of the law was faulty or could be improved. It was a distinctive part of his legal philosophy that Plumer refused to credit once he and Smith no longer were friends. "In a number of suits brought by individuals against the selectmen of a certain town on account of ministerial taxes, though the suits depended on the *same principles*," Plumer complained, "yet Mr. Smith at the winter term charged the jury clearly in favor of the *defendants*; but at the next autumn circuit in the *same suits* he charged as fully in favor of the *plaintiff*. This diversity might proceed from a real change of opinion, occasioned by reflections in the vacation, or from a conviction that the *rights of conscience* had become *more popular with the* people."[31]

Although Plumer's harangues against judicial legislation were generally effective in damaging Smith's reputation as a judge, he was not always consistent in some of his attacks against his former friend. A point already made is so essential that it deserves repeating: Plumer often censured the very reforms that before their estrangement he had urged Smith to implement and which he had once publicly endorsed. The most striking turnabout, a flip-flop that surely struck some New Hampshire lawyers as extreme hypocrisy, was his reversal of positions on Smith's efforts to end the jury's right to determine law as well as fact. Next to his campaign to get laymen off the bench, few other reforms meant more to Smith than his rulings limiting the role of lay jurors to fact finding and establishing the authority of the court to correct what New Hampshire lawyers were beginning to call "errors" by juries. Plumer did an intellectual about-face, not only reversing himself and abandoning the jurisprudence he had actively and openly championed since his admission to the bar, but also putting his approval on some of the most discrepant Jeffersonian legal demagoguery. He said, for example, that Smith was servile to English law and that he was undermining American democracy by destroying the main prop of American liberty, trial by jury—at least as republican-leaning legal theorists wanted trial by jury to remain, that is, trial by a jury of laymen who not only decided questions of law as well as fact, but who were mandated by the state constitution to maintain autonomy from the judiciary. Many lawyers surely thought Plumer shameless when he published an attack on Smith addressed to "the freeman of New Hampshire." "Indeed," Plumer scolded, "the great number of verdicts of juries that he sat [*sic*] aside, . . . but too fully proves, the little value in which he considered what your Constitution declares to be an *inestimable privilege*, TRIAL BY JURY. He seemed to consider, like the English system, which he servilely attempted to copy, that the duty of juries, was that of *simple triers of the fact only*, and not according to their oath to give 'a true verdict according to the *law* and evidence.'"[32]

Jeremiah Smith never answered William Plumer. Though he had as sharp a pen and as caustic a bite, he never tried to meet Plumer's vindictiveness or to match him attack for attack. During the fifteen years following their breakup, Plumer would rack up spectacular accomplishments in New Hampshire government. Readers may well come away from this book thinking him one of the state's greatest nineteenth-century governors, if not the greatest. He was not only a political leader, he was basically a very decent human being, one of those steady, upright, and forward-looking officials who, during the early years of the republic, pointed the United States on the road to its future greatness. Yet he can unquestionably be faulted in one respect, the manner in which he treated the man who had been his best friend. This is so difficult to understand that it may be best not to probe his reasons. They are as unfathomable as are Smith's reasons for never revealing what he thought or how much he was hurt.

Promising to send the *New-Hampshire Patriot* the first of his ARISTIDES articles, which he described as "*an examination of governor Smith's pretensions*," Plumer told the newspaper's printer, Isaac Hill, "I shall write of him with the freedom & boldness which truth & republicanism demand from their advocates. I wish you to give them publicity in the Patriot, & I will, if your interest should render it necessary, avow myself the author, & defend you." Plumer meant everything he said. Although he wanted to disguise his authorship with the pen name, ARISTIDES, he was not hiding from a lawsuit. "Though I will indemnify a printer against a suit brought against him for what he publishes of my writing," he explained, "yet I should be unwilling to have my name known as the writer, for it would unnecessarily expose me to the ill will and resentment of individuals, that I should otherwise avoid."[33]

We can only wonder what can be made of Plumer's assurance to Hill that, if "necessary," he would "avow" himself "the author" of the ARISTIDES articles and "defend" Hill. Did he think there was a chance that Smith would sue the *New-Hampshire Patriot* and Hill, its printer? If so, he did not know his former friend as well as he should have. Suing either Plumer or Hill was so far beneath Smith's priorities, he may not even have contemplated it.

During August 1814 Plumer was informed that he had been elected a member of the American Antiquarian Society. He was asked to propose other people he knew, worthy of membership. He recommended six men, four of them Federalists and two Republicans. "One of the gentlemen whom I recommend," Plumer explained, "Jeremiah Smith, is my personal & political enemy; but I thot him capable of offering aid to the society."[34] It is doubtful whether Smith would have told a stranger that Plumer was an "enemy."

*Chapter Five*

# A "Law" Governor

Jeremiah Smith had been chief justice for less than a year when the Republicans spread stories that he was slated to replace John Taylor Gilman as the next Federalists' gubernatorial candidate. Instead Gilman was replaced as governor by Republican John Langdon who was so popular that his reelections in 1806, 1807, and 1808 were foregone conclusions.[1] Then, late in 1808, New Hampshire politics underwent a drastic change. Opposition to the embargo energized and reunited the Federalist party. In March Langdon was reelected by an overwhelming majority of 9,383 votes, but by the time of the congressional elections in August, a political revolution had occurred. The Federalist ticket was swept into office by an average plurality of 1,300. "I fear our governor & legislature will be changed," William Plumer predicted to one of the defeated congressmen. He expected the election of 1809 might result in a Federalist sweep.[2]

For three years, according to Lynn Turner, the Federalists "had seemed to be a dead party." Then, in 1808, they came back to life: "the caucus suddenly agreed upon candidates for all state and national offices." For the November election the caucus abandoned Gilman as its candidate for presidential elector and substituted Chief Justice Smith in his place.[3] Then, the next February, Federalists again substituted Smith for Gilman, abandoning a man whom they had elected governor eleven times. The Republicans had expected the change, but feigned surprise. "The pioneers of the Federal party," STRAFFORD commented, "have exhibited Judge SMITH as candidate for the office of governor at the ensuing election. In announcing this nomination, they are aware of the scrutiny to which their motives will be exposed."[4]

It was not the Federalists' motives, but Smith's that have puzzled historians. "For some unaccountable reason," Turner noted, "Jeremiah Smith was persuaded in 1809 to resign his seat on the superior court, where by patient and indefatigable labor he had been reforming the jurisprudence of the state. . . . It is difficult to understand . . . why Smith left a secure, nonpolitical position which was congenial and peculiarly honorable to him to hazard his career for a political bombshell which offered three hundred dollars less salary and infinitely more trouble."[5]

Declining health was the only explanation reported by the newspapers of both parties. "[T]he labourious duties of his office," UNION claimed, "are found to have operated injuriously." His friends, the *Farmer's Museum* agreed, urged him to change offices, fearing "his health may be impaired" if he remained on the bench. AN ELECTOR made the very dubious assertion "that physicians of eminence had declared he cannot live long, and labour as he has done." Consequently, according to the *Dartmouth Gazette*, "by the advice of his friends and physicians," he probably would have resigned anyway as chief justice.[6]

There is no direct evidence that Smith was in failing health or that any physicians warned him that he should not continue as chief justice. That his health was declining may be a tale the Federalists concocted. The *New-Hampshire Patriot* said it was lawyers, not doctors, who pushed him to leave the court. "He was becoming unpopular as a judge among those of his own political profession," the Republican editor Isaac Hill fantasized, "and many lawyers within our own personal knowledge exerted themselves to the utmost to effect his election . . . , to replace him from the more important office of judge." "[L]awyers," AN INJURED PEOPLE wrote, "thought him too *arbitrary* and too *partial* in his decisions for a Judge; and that he would make a better Governor."[7]

New Hampshire Republicans had never before staged an election campaign quite like the one in 1809. Considering the extreme bitter politics of that decade, it was hard for many people to believe, but just about the most strenuous anti-Smith argument was that he should not be elected governor because he was too valuable to the state as chief justice. "[S]*ome* of his friends, though *more* of his enemies will say, We cannot spare him from his present office; he is too useful as a Judge, to be made Governor," THOUSANDS told the *Farmer's Cabinet*. "This, we are sensible, will be the grand weapon made use of by the friends of Mr. Langdon—Mr. Smith is too good a man to be lost as a Judge." The Republicans, PHILO later recalled, said "that the State of New Hampshire could not furnish a man, capable of filling his place upon the Bench, with equal ability and usefulness, in short, that he was *too good* for the office of Governor!"[8]

The chief justice himself left no extant explanation why he was willing to run for public office.[9] It was not until he delivered his gubernatorial address to the General Court that Smith publicly offered a token explanation for giving up his judgeship. He had not wanted to, he claimed. "I have consulted neither my interest nor inclination" by becoming governor, he asserted. "In the office of chief justice," Smith went on to explain, "I began to indulge the hope, if my life should be spared and health restored, that I might realize in some small degree, the wish always nearest my heart, of being useful to my fellow-citizens. But it has always been my belief, and I am not sensible that my practice has been at variance with it, in a government like ours, every citizen is at the disposal of his country; and though no wise man will ever aspire to office, yet no dutiful citizen will feel himself at liberty to decline its labors and its cares, at the call of his country."[10]

It is doubtful whether many in the audience listening to the address were either impressed or persuaded by Smith's explanation. It is somewhat surprising that his biographer, who knew him well, claimed that there was evidence supporting Smith's assertion that "his fellow-citizens [were] the best judges in what way he can best serve them." What John H. Morison may have been referring to was that Smith had been passive during the entire political process. "I cannot learn that he ever consented to be a candidate except by not formally declining," the biographer pointed out. "He went steadily on in the performance of his judicial duties, taking no part in the election, and probably as indifferent to the result as any man in the state."[11]

A sounder explanation is that Smith realized that the governorship could be an opportunity to take his work as chief justice into areas he could not reach on the court. "[T]he laws themselves were exceedingly defective, and he considered that it was only by establishing the judiciary on a more liberal foundation, and reforming the whole body of statute laws, that the jurisprudence of the state could be made as perfect as the lot of humanity would admit." Once governor, he could "give his whole strength to the improvement of the laws, and thus introduce into the executive and legislative, what he had already accomplished with such remarkable success in the judiciary department." That last statement paraphrased Smith's own answer to a friend who pleaded with him not to run for governor. He knew what his friend meant but he had been a success as chief justice, a success he and most people attributed to his education, intelligence, and work habits. He would have the same intelligence as governor and the office required much less work. Why should he not do as well? He soon learned that intelligence and application were not enough. Success in politics required quite different talents and instincts than success on the bench or at the bar. "[I]n each and every respect," Morison summed up, "he found himself disappointed."[12]

The gubernatorial election of 1809 became a referendum on the Embargo Act. The Federalists made the embargo the issue, and little wonder, for it was after all the reason the party had made such a spectacular comeback, a fact the Republicans understood even better than did the Federalists.[13] The Republicans, of course, told voters that the embargo was irrelevant for, after all, even if he were elected governor Smith could do nothing to end or modify it.[14] Not so, the Federalists replied, Smith's election would do substantial political good just by letting Washington know how deeply New England rejected the embargo.[15] There is no way to prove it, but it seems probable that voters thought the campaign was more about the embargo than about Langdon and Smith. The election had little of the bitterness or abuse that dominated other political contests in New Hampshire during the era of the early republic. The Republicans did not criticize Smith personally,[16] even though the Federalists made much of his qualities as a good man, a dedicated public servant, and a jurist of great learning.[17] Hardly any mention was made of the judiciary, except for the praise heaped on Smith for his work as chief justice and the disparagement of the Republicans for their perceived national policy of subjecting courts to legislative supervision.[18] It was understood on all sides that the very popular Langdon was handicapped by running in a year when anti-Jeffersonian sentiment was extremely high in New Hampshire, and Smith benefited from the fact that voters could express dislike of the national government by changing the state's chief executive.[19] "The strength of [the] political parties were never more equal in this state," Plumer observed, "but the embargo gave the ascendency to the federalists."[20]

"The HONOURABLE JEREMIAH SMITH is Governour elect of New Hampshire," the *Portsmouth Oracle* announced on the first of April. The year before Langdon had obtained four-fifths of the votes, and his fellow Republicans had elected nine of the twelve state senators and a majority of the House of Representatives. Now, in 1809, Langdon had 15,241 votes to Smith's 15,610, with a Federalist majority in both branches, seven to five in the Senate and ninety-three to seventy-eight in the lower house.[21] William Plumer came very close to saying the Federalists had stolen the election. "The returns from some of the towns were illegal, but there being a majority of federalists in the legislature they received all the votes," he explained to New Hampshire's junior United States senator.[22] He was so upset at the election that he accused Smith of misleading the Republicans, if not all the people of New Hampshire, by running for governor. "His life has been devoted to the *love of money* & *vulgar popularity*; but he is now placed in a situation in which neither his personal or political enemies ought to envy him," Plumer wrote. Just a few years before Smith had told the legislators that he wished to remain a judge, and they had raised the salary of the chief justice to $1500, as long as he remained in that office. "Some of the republican representatives, tho they thot the grant improper, yet trusting to his declaration he would remain on the bench if the salary was raised, & to prevent his being candidate for governor, they voted for it. Their course was crooked & Smith has deceived."[23]

It is unlikely that Smith had promised any legislators that he would remain on the bench for his entire constitutional term, that is, until he was seventy. If anything was implied to the General Court when he had asked that his salary be raised, it was that he would resign if he did not receive at least $1500 a year. Of course he knew that should he resign most Republicans expected him to become a candidate for the governorship. But again it is unlikely that he intended, or that he even understood that, by accepting the pay raise, he was promising never to be a gubernatorial candidate. There is good evidence, however, that many Republicans thought that he had, and a few even voted for his raise, which they refused to the other judges, as the price for keeping him from becoming a gubernatorial candidate. His prestige and the public's respect for him had never been higher than when the two houses had granted him the largest salary ever paid to a New Hampshire public official. Now both were in sharp decline and would never recover their former luster. For the same reason the reputation of the Superior Court was extensively damaged. Plumer concluded that Smith's public career was just about finished. "Governor Smith's prospect is unpleasant," he told a fellow Republican. "[A] majority of the people . . . are opposed to him. And while he was professing himself *poor*, he abandoned a permanent office with a salary of fifteen hundred dollars, for a temporary office of twelve hundred dollars, with reason to expect that will terminate with the year, which I hope will be verified."[24]

Smith enjoyed no triumphs and suffered numerous setbacks as governor. The first disappointment occurred before he was even sworn in. While the General Court was convening for its June 1809 session, Governor Langdon met his Council for the last time. There were at the moment only four councilors, yet on the very day when their commissions expired, they appointed two of their number as sheriffs of Hillsborough and Grafton counties, one as a judge of the Common Pleas for Rockingham County, and, in a direct blow against Smith, they also appointed a justice of the Superior Court.[25] The appointee was Richard Evans, whose judicial difficulties as the last nonlawyer to sit on New Hampshire's highest court were discussed in chapter two. The Republicans could make the appointment because a statute, enacted the previous December for the purpose of ousting Paine Wingate from the court, authorized the governor to terminate the commission of any judge reaching seventy years of age, and Langdon had told Wingate he was off the court.[26] Evans took his place, upsetting Smith both because he had counted on making the appointment, hoping to use it to show how the judiciary could be improved by placing the right type of lawyer on the bench, and because Evans was the epitome of everything he wanted kept off the court. The Federalists instantly pounced on the appointment, disparaging Evans's lack of professional qualifications.[27] To the surprise of many New Hampshirites and the annoyance of lawyers, Plumer defended the appointment, even though at the time that it was voted he had warned Evans not to accept. "I am willing to admit that this appointment has *astonished*, even in Newhampshire, certain lawyers and suitors, whose hopes of success and gain depended more on sophistry, sqirks [*sic*] and quibbles, than on *substantial justice*," he wrote, an argument that must have shocked his colleagues at the Rockingham County bar. "I see no reason why a merchant or shop-keeper cannot carry on the business of trade, and yet acquire a competent knowledge of jurisprudence. The business of trade and a knowledge of law are not incompatible."[28] Plumer did not say, but he may have defended Evans because he wrongly thought the attacks against the judge that he was answering had been written by Daniel Webster, and so a defense had to be made. To his twentieth-century biographer it was a low point in his hypocrisy . "These articles reflect no credit on Plumer," Lynn Turner concluded. "In attempting a defense of what he himself believed to be indefensible, Plumer was forced to resort to evasion and insinuation rather than rebuttal. The removal of his former zeal for a trained judiciary which these articles denote should be interpreted, probably, as a reaction against Judge Smith's presumed tendency to sacrifice the 'merits of suits . . . to *forms*, to quirks, & to the subtleties of nice distinctions.' Plumer's flattery of Langdon and Evans, however, cannot be excused by a genuine change in his earlier sentiments, for he later criticized both men in private for the part they played in the affair."[29]

After swearing in the members of the two houses of the General Court, Smith's first duty on his inauguration day was to address them, laying out his program or his hopes and plans for the year. It turned out to be the most important event of his governorship, though not for reasons he intended. He had expected to use the governor's office to enhance the judiciary, and, given the short legislative sessions in New Hampshire, his best opportunity to do that was to use his gubernatorial address. The governor's speech to the two houses was the major event opening every session of the legislature, and moreover it was published in just about every newspaper in the state. With the session likely to last two weeks at the most, if he wanted the legislature to enact his reforms, there was little time to lobby for them or to meet with legislators either individually or in small groups. He was aware that at least for the last ten years no governor had mentioned judicial issues in an annual address. He not only had the opportunity to do so now, but he surely knew it was a topic to which many members of his audience had given little or no thought.

Smith began by acknowledging the obvious: the judiciary's welfare depended on the legislature's good will. "I cannot forbear calling your attention," he told the assembled lawmakers, "to the administration of justice, and recommending this most important branch of civil polity to your protecting and fostering care." He then raised three topics that surprised no one who knew him. He wanted judges to be professional lawyers, not laymen, to be well compensated, and to be independent of party politics. He went on to make a statement that later he must have wished he had worded differently. "Adequate provision must be made by the legislature for its [judiciary's] support. Twenty years' attendance on courts of justice has taught me something of the importance to the community of an able, upright and independent judiciary, and nearly nine years' experience on the bench has given me some knowledge of the perplexities, labor and great responsibility incident to the office of a judge." What he had learned, he explained, was that "Judges will generally bear an exact proportion to the provisions made for the office. . . . When the office is made as respectable as it ought to be, the emoluments adequate to its arduous duties and high responsibility, men will always be found who will cheerfully devote twenty years of their lives in preparation for the office, and the residue in the laborious and faithful discharge of its arduous duties."[30]

Few in the audience of lawmakers could miss how much Smith was talking of his own experience, and some were surely amused thinking of how they had refused to raise the salaries of his colleagues, including Judge Atkinson who had resigned when his own pay was not increased. What they may not have noticed is how careful he was not to criticize them, at least not openly. He probably had felt the urge to do so for, after all, from his perspective the sorry state of the judiciary was the fault of the legislators. They treated the courts as an inferior branch of government, overturning verdicts by restoring litigants to their law and summoning the judges to explain why they missed circuits or did not attend sessions of the court.[31] These factors were indicative of the judiciary's inferior rank in relation to the legislature but were not what troubled Federalist lawyers most about how the New Hampshire legislators treated the courts. From the point of view of Governor Smith and his fellow attorneys, the legislators were even more at fault for not paying salaries needed to attract professionally competent judges. Lawyers would have thought Smith justified telling his audience that the incompetent judges were their responsibility. He could have made the argument without calling attention to or saying anything at all about how Evans lacked judicial competency. All he had to do was point out that there were well-qualified lawyers who might accept appointment if the compensation was adequate. Instead, Smith was so cautious that he was banal. He had the opportunity in the most important part of the most important speech of his life to admonish the legislators, to try to shame them into raising judicial salaries. Instead, he dared nothing bolder than to change the word "impartial" to "perfect" when paraphrasing a well-known sentence from the state constitution's bill of rights, that "[i]t is the right of every citizen to be tried by judges as impartial as the lot of humanity will admit." "With the legislature, then, it rests to determine what shall be the character of our judiciary," he contended. "The constitution requires and enjoins that it shall be as perfect as the lot of humanity will admit. Will our citizens be content with one less perfect, because they can have it for a less price?" the governor asked. "It is in vain that the executive possess the power of appointment. It is but the power of inviting to a seat on the bench those whose learning, ability and integrity qualify them for the employment. But will such obey the call if the provision for the office is deemed inadequate?"[32]

It was a long speech, longer than the addresses of his two most recent predecessors. Smith ended by pleading with both parties to keep the courts free of "popular clamor and popular prejudices," pledging that politics would not have "the smallest influence" on his appointments of judges. He knew he had tried the patience of the legislators by spending so long on one topic to the exclusion of almost every other. "I trust you will excuse my earnestness on this subject," he concluded. "I feel its importance. It lies near my heart. I urge my sentiments with the greater freedom, because I cannot, I shall not, receive the smallest benefit from the best judicial establishment, except in common with my fellow-citizens. I can have no other inducement for what I recommend, than a full conviction of its utility and indispensable necessity to the honor and well-being of the state. I am not conscious of a wish more sincere than that of seeing the place I now leave on the bench, filled by a person every way better qualified for his station than I could pretend to be."[33]

This speech was Jeremiah Smith's one chance to make a memorable public impression, the best opportunity he ever was likely to have to promote the well-being of the judiciary, the institution to which he had been devoting his life. Yet, as New Hampshire's most acute political historian observed, "he made but a poor exposition of it to the legislature." He may have been a first-rate lawyer and a distinguished judge, but in that era of oratory, he was only a decent speaker and he was not a politician. He just did not know how to promote his cause; he did not merit the hearing that he so keenly sought. "It is true he painted a glowing picture of the importance of a good judiciary," Lynn Turner has observed. "'Next to the power of religion,' he said, 'a strict, able and impartial administration of justice is the best security of morals. It is indispensable to the peace, happiness, and good order of society.' But to obtain this object, Governor Smith recommended no change in the judicial system, no reforms of procedure, no clarification of the laws. His sole suggestion . . . was the provision of larger salaries for the judges as a means of securing the best-qualified incumbents."[34] Turner's criticism is justified, but he overlooked the fact that Smith's argument needed to be made in New Hampshire in 1809. It was important and almost any lawyer could have made it with effect. But compensation should not have been the main theme of Smith's address. Republicans did not want to hear about the need for higher judicial salaries, and probably many of the Federalist lawmakers who were not lawyers were unwilling to raise them as well. Surely, as they listened they could not help but think of Smith's own recent record of incessant importunity. The Federalists had a majority in both houses, and in their reply the senators told Smith they agreed with what he had said. They appreciated that only adequate pay would persuade the best lawyers to consider becoming judges. They even carried the argument beyond what Smith had contended, pointing out that better judges would save public money, because they would "decide causes with much greater dispatch and uniformity and of course with much less trouble and expence to the parties concerned." Joining the lower house, the senators appointed members of a joint committee to report on salaries and then, when the committee submitted its report, both houses slashed by more than half the increases recommended.[35]

Smith had had great expectations for his gubernatorial address, knowing that, unless reelected for another term, he never again would have so splendid an opportunity to strengthen the prestige of the judiciary and increase its public support. It did not take long to discover that the speech had been a failure. Perhaps as discouraging, it exposed Smith to criticism, or, more precisely, to abuse. Nothing else in his public life so much damaged his public standing. He had predicted that he would be hurt: "In any times, a person called to this station [the governorship] might expect to have his actions misrepresented, and the purity of his motives called in question."[36] Smith very quickly learned that it was not his actions but his words that were misrepresented and not his motives but his ideals that were questioned.

The *New-Hampshire Patriot* and its printer, Isaac Hill, led the vituperation. The speech, Hill complained, was a "piece of studied egotism, personality and hypocrisy," "the ebullition of vanity . . . strongly tinctured by sentiments unbecoming a chief magistrate."[37] Even for that political age, these are harsh words, seemingly too mean and bitter to be comments on Smith's gubernatorial address. They were, rather, directed at only one small part of the speech. Smith had faulted his predecessor, Governor Langdon, for his lame-duck appointment of Richard Evans to the Superior Court. That was what the *Patriot* meant by "studied egotism"—Smith had wanted to make the appointment himself, and having won the election, he believed himself legally entitled to do so. But publically to assert the claim was to voice "sentiments unbecoming a chief magistrate," as it was unseemly for an incoming governor to fault his outgoing predecessor. But to be fair, Smith had to bring up Evans. Nothing meant more to him than judicial reform, and the reform that mattered most was getting competent judges, which meant keeping nonlawyers off the court. Even so, he had tried to be circumspect. He gave the appointment only two sentences and did not mention Evans's name. But mere allusion, the *Patriot* said, "was as immodest and vain in the Governor as it was degrading to the Judge."[38]

Smith had promised that he would throw aside party spirit. He did the opposite, the *Patriot* claimed, for he "evinced all its rancor—the personal reflections cast on his predecessor, a patriot of the revolution—on a late appointment, which tended to throw disrespect upon, and destroy confidence in the decisions of the Judiciary."[39] That was exactly what Smith had not done. He had not mentioned Langdon by name, and a person listening to the address or reading it had to be well versed in the politics of the day to know he was criticizing the appointment of Evans to the Superior Court. But if these allusions were all that Republicans could fault, Smith would have been relatively unscathed. What hurt him were comments he had never made and never intended to make.

In the speech Smith asked the General Court to support the judiciary adequately and then began the next sentence by saying, "Twenty years' attendance on courts of justice has taught me something of the importance to the community of an able, upright and independent judiciary. . . ." The one other time that he mentioned the words "twenty years," occurred six sentences later, where he was discussing the appointment of judges. "When the office is made as respectable as it ought to be," he suggested, "men will always be found who will cheerfully devote twenty years of their lives in preparation for the office. . . ."[40] He surely intended these words to be politically neutral and personally inoffensive. Republican newspapers, however, pretended to take offense and the words "twenty years" became attached to him for as long as he remained in public office. "Gov. Smith," Isaac Hill editorialized, "as if endued with some power paramount to every other, undertook to say what *ought to be* the qualifications of a judge of the superior court—he ought to have studied law 'twenty years' (for no other reason, perhaps, than because he himself had been in the practice about that time)."[41] This sentence was just about the mildest use the *Patriot* made of "twenty years," yet it was a deliberate misrepresentation. Smith did not say twenty years "ought" to be the test of a judge, but soon many New Hampshire voters would think that he did. His biographer summed up: "The expression, 'twenty years' attendance in courts of justice,'" John Morison summed up, "was tortured from its true meaning, and made in the democratic papers a hissing and a by-word against him. In a series of articles written with much adroitness and ability, . . . the changes were rung upon them with a disingenuousness which nothing but the malevolence of party rage could palliate or excuse."[42]

There are so many examples of Republican political sarcasms spurned about the words "twenty years" that nothing would be gained by reciting them or even repeating just a few. The use of "twenty years" can be summed up by considering what William Plumer had to say. After all, "twenty years" was used to disparage Smith, and no one would be more disparaging toward Smith or his speech than Plumer. He even tried to dismiss the governor's address by tagging Smith with a put-down name. He called him "a law governor." Isaac Hill used the same description in a letter to Plumer, referring to Smith as "the 'law governor.'"[43] The term fitted Hill's prejudices. He detested lawyers and fastened on them the most disparaging word in the Republican vocabulary, "aristocracy." Plumer, by contrast, was irresponsible. He was not only a lawyer, he was pro-lawyer and to call Smith "a law governor" was, for him, pure demagoguery, except that he had become so obsessed with his dislike of Smith that he probably felt that anything he said was permissible.

Plumer evaluated the words "twenty years" as no other person could have done—he recited facts from Smith's life, facts that hardly anyone else could have known, and did so to question whether Smith had ever studied law for twenty years. No matter that Smith never said he had studied for twenty years. It became Republican dogma that he had said so, and Plumer readily adopted the party's stratagems. He reached back to his original contacts with Smith, when he had asked for advice about obtaining admission to the bar and Smith had responded with his friendship. He recalled that when Smith applied to the Hillsborough County court for admission to practice, he was opposed by members of the bar who claimed that, while he had been a law student, "he had spent more of his time in teaching school than in reading of law." After admission Smith served three terms in the General Court. "In the years 1790 and 1791, he was employed in revising your laws," Plumer calculated. "[T]his must have taken up to a year more of his time. From October 27, 1791, to July 10, 1797, he attended seven sessions of Congress, which including the time of his travel to and from Congress, was equal to two years and eleven months. He was for about two and a half years judge of Probate; this engaged two months more of his *actual* time. And he was judge of the Circuit Court of the United States something more than a year and a third; this including the time of travel to and from the court, employed five months more of his time, making in all more than *five years*, and to this you must add the time devoted to *clients*, for he had *some*. Where then is his boasted *twenty years of preparation*?" The answer was obvious, at least to Plumer. "If *twenty years devoted to the study of law* is requisite to *prepare a man for that office*, he himself was guilty of accepting the office at a time when he was *unqualified to perform its arduous duties and bear its high responsibility*."[44]

Never was Plumer more petty than when he scolded Smith for "twenty years," and it is very likely that no other of his political writings did more harm to the bar and the legal institutions about which he cared deeply. After all, Smith alone was not being ridiculed over "twenty years." The disparagement had to rub off on the law and the judiciary as well, neither of which Plumer wanted to damage. Plumer became so obsessed with striking at Smith that he was carried to arguments he surely did not want to make and which he did not believe. It must have been painful for Smith to read conclusions that he knew Plumer did not mean and which were written only to hurt him. "[I]t is not true," Plumer went on, "that it is necessary for a man to *devote twenty years* of his short life to the study of law, to be prepared for the office of a judge. A term much shorter is amply sufficient, if a man possesses talents and industry that places him above mediocrity." Plumer meant the first sentence, twenty years of study were not necessary to prepare for a judgeship, but not the second. A "much shorter" term of study may have been enough for talented candidates, but not for anyone whose abilities were only above mediocrity.[45]

Smith must be judged not only by what he accomplished but by what he hoped to accomplish, and if we evaluate Smith's governorship by what he hoped to do for the judiciary, there is no other conclusion but that it was a failure. More than that, it was a failure almost before it had begun. Its opening moment, his address to the General Court, and the reaction to that address, cost him some of the personal esteem he had enjoyed among the public. It might not have had such a negative impact on his reputation had he outlined a legislative program of judicial reforms in the address.

After the speech was concluded, his failure to do so left little chance that he could successfully introduce reform later. In fact, there was little prospect for passing legislation during his one term as governor, for the General Court voted not to hold a December session that year. He had only one other opportunity to salvage anything from his sacrifice of the chief justiceship. It was to raise the quality of judicial appointments to a high level of respectability. Yet on this policy too Smith experienced disappointment and, even worse, outright failure.

Smith was only interested in the Superior Court. Salaries were so low on the Court of Common Pleas that he knew he had slight chance of naming his level of candidate to that tribunal, and if he did make appointments, he might have to select nonlawyers, a distasteful prospect. He was, therefore, left with little opportunity to make the impact he had hoped. With Arthur Livermore remaining on the court, Smith had expected to have two Superior Court appointments. A small number, perhaps, but two judges were two-thirds of the court's membership, giving Smith the chance to make a substantial contribution if he could find the right candidates. The appointment of Richard Evans after Smith's election, during the lame-duck period of Langdon's administration, deprived him of half the opportunity he had anticipated. To protect his one remaining appointment, Smith did not resign as chief justice, remaining in that position until Langdon, returning home to Portsmouth, had left the state capital. It was, therefore, his former office, the chief justiceship, that was vacant and the only Superior Court judgeship he would be able to fill.

Smith knew whom he wanted to appoint, and he undoubtedly knew that he would not be able to persuade the man to become chief justice. He asked Jeremiah Mason. It would have been an extraordinary appointment, returning instantly to the court much of the prestige it had lost when Smith resigned. But Mason would not accept. He could not afford to; the compensation was too low. He had served as attorney general, but that was not a full-time position, and he had maintained an extensive law practice while performing his official duties. We can never know for certain, but it is unlikely that Mason would have joined a three-member court when one colleague was Richard Evans and the other Arthur Livermore. He might have tolerated the eccentric, irascible Livermore for his credible ability as a lawyer, but Evans?

Unable to persuade Mason, Smith was confronted by the dynamics of New Hampshire constitutionalism as they existed whenever the two political parties shared power. In New Hampshire the governor together with his appointees did not constitute the entire executive department, as was the case in most states. He was not even the only executive official who was elected by the people. There were five others, the members of the Council, which had as much authority as the governor to make appointments. In the election of 1809, the Federalists had won the governorship and small majorities in both houses of the General Court. But the Republicans had captured the Council, three Republicans to two Federalists, and therefore in the matter of appointments Smith was outvoted. The mechanics of Council politics were not complicated. Neither the governor nor the Council was exclusively vested with authority to nominate candidates for office. The governor could suggest names, and so also could each councilor. As Plumer would later explain, "No nomination is of any avail, unless the governor and a majority of the council agree to it: nor can any appointment be made without the consent of the governor and three of the council." As the law operated regarding both nominations and appointments, it is accurate to think of the governor and the Council as having a veto on each other.[46]

Once Mason turned him down, Smith faced two problems: the Republican majority on the Council, and the fact that the Council was difficult to convene. It could meet only if sessions were scheduled with much notice. When the Council met for its second session, Smith nominated in succession two of the Council's own members, one a Federalist, the other a Republican. They both were superb choices. The Federalist was Caleb Ellis, who would become an associate justice during Smith's second term as chief justice and, Smith would say, was the most competent and most professional judge he would sit with on a New Hampshire bench. The Republican was Samuel Bell, whom Plumer, as governor, would appoint to the court in 1816 and who would be one of the judges to return professionalism to the New Hampshire bench in the post-Smith era. In 1809 both Ellis and Bell refused appointment. Next Smith asked George Sullivan, Exeter's leading trial lawyer, who had the advantage of the Sullivan name, being the son of General John Sullivan. He too refused. As the state now had been without a chief justice since Smith resigned, a choice had to be made before the Council adjourned. Reluctantly, but necessarily, Smith nominated Arthur Livermore to be chief justice. The Council concurred.[47]

Between sessions of the Council, the three Republican councilors settled on a candidate for the associate justiceship vacated by Livermore when he became chief. They nominated Clifton Claggett, and they insisted on him. He would go on the court when the Republicans returned to power, and so his lack of any merit is discussed below. It is enough now to note that he was unfit for the position. Smith knew that if he put him on a court with Livermore and Evans, every reform he had worked for could be lost. He refused to agree.[48]

The governor and the Council next met in December, only to find the impasse was complete. Three councilors continued to insist on Claggett, whom Smith could never accept. He asked them to nominate an alternative, but they could not agree on a candidate. Then, at the February 1810 session of the Council, after Smith had nominated three lawyers unacceptable to the Republicans, the majority changed its strategy and named William Plumer. Surely Smith took the proposal as a personal insult and vetoed Plumer for lacking sufficient legal education, which must have been intended as a counter insult. But the mutual insults, if that is what they were, broke the stalemate. A majority of the Council agreed on Jonathan Steele, whom the governor had to accept, "it being," he explained to Chief Justice Livermore, "deemed (by the Council) more important that the court should have right opinions in everything else than of law."[49]

That Steele was the best appointee he could obtain from the Council shows how completely Jeremiah Smith was defeated by the politics of judicial appointment. The selection of Steele made a mockery of the hopes and expectations he had possessed when entering his governorship. Steele had been the clerk of the United States District Court in Portsmouth who, together with John Samuel Sherburne, the United States district attorney, had gone to Washington to testify against their mentor, John Pickering, at Pickering's impeachment trial. He had expected to be rewarded by President Jefferson with appointment to Pickering's place on the bench, and when the judgeship went to Sherburne, Steele was so angry he declined appointment as United States district attorney and, after running that year as a presidential elector pledged to Jefferson, ended his support of Republicanism. He did not, however, become an active Federalist, and as a result, Plumer noted, "Steele was claimed by some partizans of both parties." The politically neutral newspaper, *Farmer's Cabinet*, said that Smith could not be accused of partisanship, for he had appointed a Republican to the court. But Plumer thought Steele a "violent Federalist."[50]

Steele's appointment brought credit to no one, least of all Governor Smith. Plumer, who had been admitted to the bar with Steele and "long practised at the same courts," said that as a lawyer he was "above mediocrity," that is, of "decent talents" and considerable legal education. But, aside from his "energy, promptness, & decision of character," there was not much positive to be said for him.[51]

Steele, Smith had told Plumer when the two were still friends, was a man "of violent prejudices, & of a malevolent temper." His one term in the State House of Representatives had not been "distinguished for prudence or moderation," Plumer believed, and as a judge "[h]is passions and prejudices, his irritable temper and haughty unaccommodating manner, rendered him unpopular."[52] Certainly he was not a person that Smith would have wanted on the same bench with Arthur Livermore. They were very much alike. Steele "was unacquainted with human nature, and the ways of the world," and so, to a lesser extent, was Livermore. It may be that they did not get along, for soon Steele "was dissatisfied with the judges with whom he was associated, disgusted with the duties of the office, and vexed with his own unpopularity."[53]

Smith should not be faulted for accepting the appointment of Steele. His political position could not have been weaker. He had been elected on an issue, the embargo, that was politically dead by the time he took office; he had been chosen by a plurality so small that any policy he recommended did not have behind it the weight of public opinion; and, what Lynn Turner described as "most trying" of all detriments, three of his five councilors were Republicans.[54] Had Smith vetoed the appointment of Steele, the Superior Court would not have been able to function. Yet that was his only excuse for making Steele a judge—that he had been politically helpless. During the remaining months of his term as governor, Smith must have been discouraged and dispirited as he contemplated the Superior Court. Livermore, Evans, and Steele were the judges. The court that he had so much helped to remodel was far weaker than the one over which he had presided just a year ago.

Smith was the most inefficient governor of New Hampshire during the era of the early republic. The leading political historian of the period has concluded that only one "notable" piece of legislation was enacted during Smith's term in office. It was a "generous grant" to Dartmouth College, enabling Dr. Nathan Smith to commence a medical school. Called the "Smith grant," it had the support of both political parties, yet during the election of 1810, the Republicans made the legislation an issue against Smith. "The act itself was grossly misrepresented, and made the innocent subject of a thousand electioneering false hoods," the *Constitutionalist* complained. "The people will recollect that the *Governor* is *ex-officio* trustee of Dartmouth College," the *New Hampshire Gazette* pointed out. "No wonder he wishes to increase the number of buildings at Hanover on the expence of public money." Silly as that claim was, there was one even sillier that may have been more effective with some of New Hampshire's more inerudite voters. "Does his grant of 3450 dollars to erect a brick building at Hanover to cut up human bodies in, deserve the approbation of a christian, civilized people," the *Gazette* asked of Smith. These items would not be worth quoting if they were not indicative of how low Smith's prestige had sunk in the public esteem. It was, however, a gross exaggeration for the *Constitutional-*

*ist* to say that "the numerous stories" about the "Smith grant" "did not only promote, but absolutely cause the election of Gov. Langdon." Smith lost the election of 1810 on issues of much more substance. The grant to Dartmouth was of little consequence.[55]

After the unpopularity of Governor Smith became evident, he was visited by a committee of Federalists asking him not to run for reelection. The group included some of the men who had, the year before, urged him to leave the bench for the governorship. He replied "that as he had taken no part in putting himself forward for the office . . . , so he should take no part in withdrawing himself from it." He became extremely bitter. "It was a standing remark of his through life," his biographer recalled, "that he had received more injury from his friends than from his enemies."[56]

At the Mont Vernon Fourth of July celebration of 1809, a toast had been offered to the governor. "May his 'twenty years' application to the study of law be fully compensated by one year in the gubernatorial chair."[57] And that was just what Smith received, one year. The election of 1810 was a repeat of the election of the year before. Foreign affairs, notably Great Britain against France, was the major issue. Smith was billed as the candidate "of PEACE and COMMERCE." The difference from 1809 was that the embargo had been repealed and better economic times prevailed. Yet the Federalist resurgence remained strong. The election was surprisingly close. John Langdon won with 16,325 votes. But Smith had 15,788.[58]

Smith had himself to blame. "Gov. Smith cannot complain if he is turned out this year," the *New Hampshire Gazette* asserted, "for his *best and real* friends advised him last Spring, not to quit a certainty for an uncertainty." Isaac Hill, reprinting the remarks of the *Gazette*, agreed: "Had gov. Smith been contented to fill the first judicial office in the State, the republicans would never have wished to disturb him, but would have honored the *man* so long as he honored the *office*," Hill told readers of the *Patriot*. "His merits and qualifications would not have been a subject of public discussion, because the people had no *immediate* influence to prolong or diminish his term of service. But as he has chosen to exchange the tranquillity of the judicial department for the more active and less permanent station of Chief Magistrate . . . he thereby challenges the strictest scrutiny of these pretensions and of his past conduct. . . . The peculiar turbulence of the times when he chose to make his debut on the political theatre, while it tends to degrade him in the estimation of the thinking part of the community, renders more certain his downfall from the eminence to which the restless spirit of party and popular folly in an evil hour had promoted him."[59]

The next year the *Patriot* said it was likely that the Federalists would nominate Smith for governor again. Why not, the paper asked? He would be a candidate to satisfy "those who wish for a monopoly of the '*twenty years*' lawyers." A month later the newspaper published "Thirteen Reasons why Jeremiah Smith should be Governor of New Hampshire." The third reason: "Because he is a lawyer and has studied law more than '*twenty years.*'"[60] We may wonder what Smith regretted more. That he had left the court for the governorship or that custom required that New Hampshire governors address the legislature.

*Chapter Six*

# In Judicial Depths

In turn-of-the-century New Hampshire, "election day" was not the day people voted, but the first day of the legislature's June term, the day when the two houses of the General Court met in joint session and counted the returns from the towns and certified the winners of elections. On Election Day 1810, Jeremiah Smith was declared to have been defeated for a second term as governor and William Plumer was chosen president of the state senate. In a very real sense the office was Plumer's reward for Smith's defeat. Some people at least credited the outcome of the gubernatorial election to five articles that Plumer had published in the *Patriot*, lampooning his former friend.[1] It was an hour of political triumph, but Plumer was not satisfied. The branch of state government he thought the most important, the judiciary, was entering a low point in its history. We can obtain a sense of how bad he thought matters were by considering Plumer's evaluation of the Common Pleas of Rockingham County, the court where he most frequently practiced. The judges of Rockingham, he charged, "are incompetent to perform their duties. They have no dignity & preserve no order—they are fickle and irresolute; & their decisions are often illegal. Their mode of proceeding occasioned great delay & unnecessarily increased expence both to the suitors & the public. That court is rapidly sinking into disgrace & contempt." The Superior Court, although by no means in so sorry a state, was in obvious decline. Under the leadership of Chief Justice Smith, the court had experienced its only period of efficiency and respectability. Now it was misleading to speak of the leadership of Chief Justice Arthur Livermore, for with Richard Evans and Jonathan Steele as his two associates, he had no one worth leading.[2]

In the minds of educated laymen, the law of New Hampshire may have possessed very little legitimacy.

It cannot be said that the public's opinion of Jeremiah Smith mellowed after he was out of office. What seems to have occurred was a sense of loss. It was not nostalgia for Smith as a man but an appreciation of what was lost, of what he had meant to the Superior Court and to the judicial progress of New Hampshire. Even severe critics sought to measure what was missing now that he no longer presided over their courtrooms.

Caius Julius, a Republican writing in the *New Hampshire Gazette* to "His Excellency Jeremiah Smith," celebrated the defeat of a governor but lamented a judge to remember. "Had the unfortunate situation to which you are reduced, resulted from the common casualty, to which all human affairs are liable, it would have been at once a subject of pity and regret," Caius Julius pointed out. "Talents like yours, without the possibility of employment; the lucubrations of thirty years lost upon us;—a world of wit, with no one to cherish its sallies, are melancholy considerations. There is a propensity in human nature to condole with the unfortunate, and to mourn the loss of virtue, the misapplication of talents, and a premature termination of brilliant prospects and splendid achievements. Not only the common principle of sympathy inspires us on these occasions, but we feel the loss which we ourselves have sustained."[3]

John Langdon's popularity is more difficult to evaluate than Smith's. He was New Hampshire's most popular governor during the era of the early republic, but why? He was notable for having little imagination and his gubernatorial addresses were void of any thought. He was seldom troubled by political events and hardly ever proposed changes in government policy, alterations in the administration of the state, or reforms in law. His address of 1810 was, therefore, unusual. The year before, Smith had devoted almost his entire speech to the judiciary, and now Langdon used his address to try to undo what lawyers thought had been Smith's most successful reform.

As soon as becoming chief justice, Smith had begun efforts to subject jury verdicts to the correction, if not the control of the court. He introduced into New Hampshire law the principle that judges should reverse verdicts of civil juries if the jurors rendering the verdicts had not followed the court's instructions. Although these reforms upset Jeffersonian jurisprudents, alarmed at any tampering with the jury's autonomy, their opposition was more limited than we in the twenty-first century might suppose. Jeffersonian legal theory in New Hampshire permitted a verdict to be overturned—but by the legislature, not by the court. A judge was not to substitute his decision for that of the jury's. The vote of both houses of the legislature to overturn a jury's verdict meant, rather, a trial *de novo*—that is, the jury verdict was nullified and the complaining party was granted a second trial, before a new and different jury. A trial *de novo* was complete relief from the judgment but not so drastic as the procedure Smith sought to introduce, the court overturning a jury's verdict and, without impaneling a second jury, decreeing a different judgment. That is, a new legal judgment was pronounced by the court, based on the facts found by the first jury, the jury that has been overturned. Yet even so restricted a reform produced outrage. It was good republicanist legal theory for the legislature to overturn jury verdicts and grant a complaining litigant what was called "restoration" to his or her law, that is, the right to a trial *de novo*.[4] But aside from that one exception, which after all was an assertion of legislative supremacy over the judiciary, New Hampshire republicanist legal theory opposed any diminishing of the jury's autonomy. During the early decades of the nineteenth century no civil institution was more emotionally defended than the independence of the jury.[5] After all, when a jury verdict was overturned by a court, the judges usually explained why, making a statement of law that might create a new legal principle or at least set a new precedent, in each instance advancing the efforts of jurists like Smith to make law independently of the elected republican legislature.

Even Langdon, who was not much interested in law or legal theory, realized where Smith's jurisprudence of responsible juries would lead. He wanted it reversed, and in his gubernatorial address of 1810, he urged the General Court to overrule the reforms. Interestingly, he sought to strengthen his argument by dressing it in the garb of a second complaint against the judiciary, the law's delay. "The Constitution of the State contemplates, that justice should be administered to its citizens promptly and without delay," Langdon told the legislators. "The present mode of transacting business in the law courts appears to me to have a tendency greatly to procrastinate and load it with intolerable expenses. I therefore think, that at a convenient season there should be a revision of the judicial system. The discretionary powers of the judges to set aside verdicts of juries appears to me never should be permitted except upon very extraordinary occasions; and so doing, should be stated at large in the records of the court, that they may be publicly known."[6]

There is no record of how Smith reacted to this speech. Langdon made two points, one of which should have angered Smith; the second, if he thought about it, could have struck him with amazement that it had been raised by Langdon and not by himself. The first point about jury verdicts being frequently set aside was intended, as Turner said, to be "a thrust at former chief justice Smith." He was the first New Hampshire judge known for setting aside jury verdicts. He did so, of course, because of what he perceived to be errors in the verdicts but also for reasons of legal theory, to strengthen the reception of common-law jurisprudence and to encourage New Hampshire lawyers to challenge verdicts that they could argue were based on erroneous law. Langdon may not have understood much of what Smith had been doing, but he knew that Republicans wanted the courts not to question jury verdicts. Two years before, in 1808, his administration had introduced a bill that might have stopped the practice had not nearly thirty Republicans voted against it.[7]

The other part of Langdon's proposed reform was far different and surely surprised Smith: the governor proposed that should a judge, because of "very extraordinary occasions," have to violate Republican principles and set aside a jury verdict, "the reasons for so doing, should be stated at large in the records of the court, that they may be publicly known." Smith had to have been flabbergasted. He had tried every argument and political manipulation he could think of to have his judicial decisions published. He had asked that state reports be printed, and the Republican legislature had said no. At least allow the court to have a reporter, he had asked, and the Republicans had again refused. They would not permit him any aspect of an official court reporting system, and now here was the Republican governor saying that judges who overturned jury verdicts should explain their reasons *on the record*. True, Langdon was not proposing official reporting; the judges were to record their legal reasoning only in "very extraordinary occasions," that is, when they overturned a jury. But lawyers could usually find reasons why there were "very extraordinary occasions" for adopting special measures, and judges could have easily converted Langdon's explanation for overturning verdicts into somewhat more detailed legal arguments, resembling formal judicial opinions explaining their legal reasoning. After all, the very procedure that Langdon was challenging—overturning jury verdicts—was then the cutting edge of the law. If a judge overturned a verdict, he was ruling that the jury had made an error of law, that the trial judge had made an error admitting evidence, or that the trial judge had misinstructed the jury. If the judge overturning the verdict had to state his reasons on the record, he could declare what he thought was the correct rule. His statement, then, especially if he explained his theories, discussed his reasoning, and presented authorities in support, would become a precedent for the rule in future litigations. The process might not start like the writing of a judicial opinion, for in theory it was limited only to the reason that a verdict had been set aside, but it easily could read like one. Had Smith still been chief justice, it is very likely he might have welcomed Langdon's criticism, say that he was acting on it, and written statements in the form of explanations that in fact were judicial opinions. He might even hope to write opinions that would prove the need for a court reporter and persuade the Republicans to reverse themselves on that issue.

The General Court did not act on Langdon's suggestion. The lower house told the governor it doubted whether the authority to set aside jury verdicts "can be defined by statute, so that the trial by jury can be holden more sacred than it now is." It is only remotely possible that some representatives realized where a judge like Smith could take Langdon's idea and thought it best that the procedure of publishing a court's reasons for overturning jury verdicts not be developed. "In approaching the judiciary," the House voted, "we ought, in our opinion, to tread with cautious and well guarded steps; lest in attempting to remedy we increase the evil."[8] The representatives did not doubt their legislative authority to correct the judiciary. But it is possible that they realized they could not predict where an experimental rule could lead, including, possibly, how easily they could accidently open doors for jurists like Smith, and how anything they might approve could be developed by the court into the very practice they were trying to prevent.

The Senate was less reserved. The senators asserted that it was their right, not the judiciary's, to define or refashion trial by jury. "This invaluable right should not be nullified or viciated [*sic*] by judicial or other encroachments," they resolved, "and as soon as a suitable time presents, we presume the Legislature will cause a revision of it."[9] Like their colleagues in the lower house, the members of the upper chamber accepted as a constitutional given that they had the power to do as they pleased with the judiciary—they just were not sure what to do. One reason may be that Plumer was president of the Senate and wrote this answer. He had not yet abandoned many of his receptionist principles. He may no longer have favored the court in control of the jury, but he would not have the jury in control of the court, as many of his fellow Republicans wanted.

Low as the prestige of New Hampshire's judiciary was in 1810, it was driven even lower by the behavior of some of its personnel. By the June court session that year, Nahum Parker was well into his third year serving both as United States senator and chief justice of Common Pleas. "The clamors against him is [*sic*] loud," Plumer wrote from the legislature. "If he does not resign his senatorship I think it probable they will remove him from that of Judge." Parker claimed that he could not resign from the court because if he did he would be giving the position to the Federalists, and "this I supposed my friends would not wish." He did not resign from the Senate, he said, for to do so would create too much work for the legislators who would have difficulty agreeing on a successor. "[T]here is one Senator and five Representatives to elect without filling my place," he told Plumer. "I am not fully determined what to do." He was soon told, however, that members of both parties had lost patience. He resigned from the Senate, and because his conduct had received little publicity, he caused less harm to the judiciary than otherwise might have been expected. But with those who knew what he had tried to get away with, the reputation of the courts suffered a bit.[10]

The judiciary's image was further damaged by Smith's one appointee to the high court, Jonathan Steele. In August, upset at something that he had read in a Republican newspaper, he wrote "an angry, insolent letter to the printer of the *New Hampshire Gazette*, forbidding him from sending that paper to him any longer." The printer knew how to handle saucy lawyers. He published Steele's letter with a reply of his own, "which excites some indignation against the judge." It was a small, unimportant incident, yet the court's reputation suffered a bit more.[11]

By October 1811 even Republicans were sending articles to the press, criticizing the Superior Court, and the *New-Hampshire Patriot* was willing to print them, at least if they also found fault with lawyers. "The administration of this department of government," JUSTUS reported of the judiciary, "is both weak and wicked. The confidence of the people is withdrawn from it." He had a complaint about the September term at Exeter, which had lasted a week. Was it possible "that the business of the Court at this place can be ordinarily performed in that time?" he wondered. "At the last term of the Superior Court in that town, there were three or four hundred cases upon the dockets for trial; but they were not noticed, the court not having arrived at them. . . . [I]s this Justice? *Short* terms and *unfinished* business suit the lawyers, but they do not suit the people."[12]

One reason the *Patriot* printed JUSTUS was probably because of what he had to say about Arthur Livermore. At that time the chief justice was thought more Federalist than Republican, and any Federalist was fair game for attack in that newspaper. "I speak now of the Judges of the Superior Court, one of whom has, for years, been the subject of the people's animadversion," JUSTUS continued. He predicted that Livermore's "constant endeavor to display an utter contempt for the people, will not be forgotten—will not go unpunished. The people are not *blind*! They have seen, and with the sensibility of freemen, that the business of our Superior Court is often directed by *fietuance* [*sic*] and *acrimony*—often directed by injustice and inhumanity. A *continuance*, a *new trial*, a *dismission of the juries*, is decreed with as little ceremony as that with which a man would put on his glove."[13]

It is a sad commentary on the status of the judiciary, but at that time the chief justice, Arthur Livermore, was more unpopular among lawyers than he was with the general public. There were members of the bar who actually discussed having him addressed from office. Livermore's inability to control his sarcasm or his tetchiness apparently became more evident as time passed. During trials he would be annoyed by quite minor occurrences, even by the tardiness of counsel, and without warning he would declare a continuance, order a new trial, or dismiss the jurors sitting on the case at bar and also the panel waiting to be called. The Republican press, including the *Patriot,* had difficulty with Livermore. It could not tar him with the brush it had used on Smith for he was not of the same caliber, the same originality, and certainly not of the same reforming zeal. There was one litigation, however, the *Hillsborough Bank Case,* where he dared to enforce a procedural rule as Smith would have, giving Republicans a chance to question his judicial restraint.

That the defendant was a bank is significant. Like many Republican theorists of the era, Isaac Hill, publisher of the *Patriot,* detested banks. They were, he contended, "instruments of public suffering." Just before the 1810 election he accused them of what was to him a serious offense. "It may be fairly said that the influence of the Banks," meaning the Hillsborough and Cheshire banks, two engines of Federalist politics, "placed Jeremiah Smith in the chair of State."[14]

It made political sense for the *Patriot* to blame the banks for the ills of New Hampshire if, as it claimed, "almost all the banks are under the control of federalists." The Republican press had a problem, however, for the Hillsborough Bank, the most notorious and scandalous failure in the state, was headed by Samuel Bell, one of the most promising younger Republicans of New Hampshire. But no matter, the *Patriot* concluded in a completely irrelevant argument, Bell was only an incidental factor. "[A]lthough its President, Mr. Bell, was a republican," the bank "was in the hands of federalists and had a majority of federalists for its directors."[15]

During August 1809, unable to redeem its bills, and sued by the holders, the Hillsborough Bank closed. Bell advertised in Boston newspapers that debts owed the bank were more than sufficient to discharge all demands, and the *Patriot* urged those holding bills to trust Bell's promises of solvency. But the lawsuit, which was based on a statute making stockholders of banks individually liable "for the redemption of bills issued from these banks," was pressed forward.[16]

When the case was finally adjudicated in April 1811, Livermore did not rule on the merits but dismissed the action because it had sought relief through an improper form of action. In other words it was a decision that applied the jurisprudence that Smith had been reintroducing into New Hampshire procedure.[17] It served Republican purposes for it allowed the *Patriot* to focus attention away from Samuel Bell and against the lawyers and what Hill considered their readiness to use technicalities to deny justice.

> The causes pending against the Hillsborough Bank were decided in favor of the ex-stockholders—not on the ground that the ex-stockholders were not bound by the terms of the charter—*that* remains to be settled when those who have already been deprived for years of their bona fide property, shall have the temerity to prosecute their actions in a different form, which after laying years in Court may, equally with the other, be decided to be brought wrong; but because a plea of *assumpsit* would not lie in this case! We believe it has been the custom, in all former cases, when an action has been brought wrong, that it should in no wise ultimately effect the merits of the final question, but that the plaintiff should have the privilege of a plea of abatement. In *this* case the action has been in a course of law upwards of two years, and costs accumulated to a great amount; and what was least of all thought of, when the time for a decision on the *merits* of the question was expected, the action was decided, we believe only by one judge, to have been brought wrong![18]

No other holding could have so well served the causes of republicanist jurisprudence and Jeffersonian demagoguery. Not only Livermore and the court but the law itself and common-law jurisprudence could all be chastised, and it was done without mentioning Bell and his fellow directors. The plaintiffs had alleged fraud, misrepresentation, and stockholder statutory liability. The action of *assumpsit* was based on the contractual elements of an enforceable promise that had not been performed, and all Livermore had ruled was that he was not empowered to grant relief as the plaintiffs had not sued on a promise unperformed but had asked for relief based on the statutory remedy. Had the plaintiffs moved a plea in abatement, they might have been allowed to amend the action from *assumpsit* to *case*. The questions that the Republican press focused on were not the merits of the plaintiffs' case but the application of a technicality and the legal theory that had applied that technicality. The *Patriot* even made an argument for returning New Hampshire to commonsense jurisprudence. "We profess to know but little of the forms and technical meaning of the law, as interpreted by our courts," Hill admitted. "We had ever conceived that common reason and justice ought to be the guides by which decisions were to be made."[19]

There is no evidence of what the former chief justice thought of the *Hillsborough Bank* decision. On one hand he could have been gratified to see the court apply the adjective law he had spent much of his time on the bench teaching to the New Hampshire bar.[20] On the other hand he could have been alarmed to see both the court and the common law castigated when no one of his ability and prestige was on the bench to deflect the criticism.

Smith was now in private practice and was stirring different interests. People with a sense of the ironic, not only in New Hampshire but in other

New England states, wondered what the atmosphere in the Superior Court would be when Jeremiah Smith appeared at the bar and Richard Evans was on the bench. We have no extended accounts, only squibs from newspapers, that tell us nothing except that there was high interest about how Smith could tolerate the humiliation of looking up and seeing Evans sitting where he had sat and having not only to address him as if Evans knew what he was about but, even more challenging, trying to make him understand the law. The first encounter seems to have been at the September term holden at Keene. "The Supreme Judicial Court of N. H. was in session at Keene, last week," the Boston *Gazette* reported. "In the *bar* was the late Governor and Chief Justice Smith; on the *bench*, Judge Evans.—Such *rank offences* cannot end in good." The local Keene newspaper felt the drama but attributed it to a turnover of political fortunes. "On observing the late Governor and Chief Justice Smith at the bar, and Judge Evans presiding on the bench," the *Sentinel* said, "*unpleasant sensations* are excited; but such revolutions must be expected to happen in a country like ours, *where public favor* depends upon the *popular voice*."[21] For some observers, it would seem, the confrontation was political, not intellectual.

In the election of 1811, the Federalists supported Smith for governor a third time. Again he was up against Langdon, who was most reluctant to be a candidate, thinking himself too old; he consented to run only when Republican party leaders could not agree on a different candidate.[22] The continued harassment of American shipping by the British navy and the inability of President Madison to deal with the international crisis brought to the Federalists much more political support than they otherwise might have had, but Smith still lost by more than three thousand votes. One might think that would have been enough gubernatorial politics for Smith, but there is evidence that he did not discourage friends from urging his candidacy for yet a fourth try in 1812.[23]

On the last day of December 1811, the *Concord Gazette* speculated about the next gubernatorial election. The two candidates, it was certain, would be Plumer for the Republicans against Smith. Pitting these two men against one another would be a fascinating contest, the *Gazette* surmised. "[F]ortunately the character of both candidates are now established in the minds of most citizens of this State," the publisher theorized. "Democrats acknowledge that one of them has been slandered without cause; and Federalists confess that the other was promoted without merit. In the result of this election we shall see how characters are estimated; how far professions and practice in the Electors agree, and which they prefer, talents with, or talents without integrity. The reputation of New-Hampshire was never more at stake than in this election."[24]

The intrigue of Plumer running against Smith was never to occur. When the Republican caucus unanimously nominated Langdon for another term he unequivocally refused, insisting he was now too old. The caucus then had little choice. Although there was some support for other Republicans, the caucus unanimously nominated Plumer.[25] It was at this point that the Federalist press, mindful of how the Republicans had bashed them for being the lawyers' party, pounced on their choice of Plumer, a lawyer for governor. NO PARTY MAN, writing in the *Oracle*, was especially gleeful: "It is truly laughable to observe the *inconsistency* of the democrats, in selecting a Lawyer for their candidate for Governor!" he contended. "Ever since the memorable Administration of the *illustrious* Jefferson, down to the wise and disinterested government of the *patriot* Langdon, every *species* of abuse has been heaped on the profession of Lawyers—Yet to such a *shift* have they been at last driven, they have announced as *their* Chief Magistrate, *William Plumer* of Epping, once a celebrated Baptist Preacher, who for years since renounced his *Godliness for gain*, and has been a *learned* Lawyer at the *Court of Common Pleas*."[26] It was a put-down of Plumer to describe him as a Common Pleas lawyer. The bottom of the bar practiced in that court. But it had some truth, as Plumer had tended not to file some of his cases in the Superior Court while Smith was chief justice.

Shortly before he was chosen, Plumer wrote to John Adams Harper, the congressman for the Laconia area of the state, that he thought the Federalists would go with Smith. "I hope the federalists will *stick* with Smith," Harper replied. "Gilman would get many more votes in the upper part of Strafford than Smith."[27] In fact, the Federalists for a time had two candidates, Smith and former governor John Taylor Gilman. Smith had lost the last two elections, and some of the older Federalists were demanding a return to their perennial winner, Gilman.[28] Plumer hoped that the Federalists remained divided, unable to settle on a candidate. "The Boston Centinel . . . announced Smith as their candidate, but [the] Portsmouth Oracle of the same week proclaimed Gilman as their candidate," he told Harper. "Last saturday the Oracle declared Smith as the real candidate, but the Centinel of the same day [said] they have 'learnt officially' that Gilman is the federal candidate. After all this oscillation, & games at *cross purposes*, it is probable they will agree; tho the *Bar* is unwilling to submit to Gilman, for they complain of his former appointments."[29]

Plumer's last point was obvious. Most lawyers were Federalists and voted for Gilman when he was the Federalist gubernatorial candidate, but they were unhappy with him. Except for Smith, Timothy Farrar, and one or two others, he had not given them the judges they wanted. Not respectful of attorneys, he was willing that there be lawyers on the courts, but he saw no reason that all the judges should come from the bar. As a group, according to Plumer, lawyers preferred Smith over Gilman, though they had to have been disappointed by his one term as governor. He had had one appointment, and the best he was able to get from the Council was Jonathan Steele, who enjoyed little respect from the bar. Even so, lawyers had to favor Smith, for, if elected, he would appoint only lawyers to the high court, and Gilman might appoint none.

The choice was not left to the lawyers. Rumors said that Smith had declined to be a candidate and, although not true, it was believed by enough of his potential supporters for much of his backing to dissipate. The Federalist press united behind Gilman. The election was extremely close. Gilman had 121 more votes than Plumer, but with more votes than that scattered among other candidates, including Smith, no one had a majority. Under the New Hampshire constitution no one was elected. The choice went to a convention of the two houses of the General Court. The Republicans controlled each house, and they elected Plumer by 22 votes.[30]

The judiciary became Plumer's most difficult challenge as governor. He had publicly pledged to raise the quality of the court's professionalization and to persuade the best lawyers to serve as judges. He also realized that the judicial system in New Hampshire at that time might politically be impossible to improve, but given his own priorities and what he wanted to accomplish in office, he was determined to try. Two of his former Federalist friends, Jeremiah Mason and Daniel Webster, had impressed him with the urgency. After he was nominated by the Republican caucus but before the election, he had attended, as a private attorney, a session of the Rockingham County Court of Common Pleas. He had been gratified by his reception. "During the term I was treated with much respect by the court & bar," he recalled. " The federal lawyers were distinguished by their attention: Mason & Webster were particularly so, tho they will both vote against me in March. They plainly gave me to understand they had more confidence in my judicial appointment than in [those of] John Taylor Gilman. They observed, our courts of law, from the highest to the lowest, were contemptible; that Livermore was ill qualified—decided cases more by passion & caprice than according to law—and that Steele was a feeble lawyer, of violent passions & strong passions." Mason may have demanded change but he was not offering Plumer the help he wanted. He would not accept appointment to the bench. He had refused Smith's plea that he become a judge, and Plumer could not expect a different answer.[31]

Jonathan Steele gave Plumer his first problem with the judiciary. Through a clerk's error Steele had collected salary in excess of what he was due. Plumer discovered the discrepancy and demanded that Steele return the difference. The judge refused. The issue was very simple. "The salaries of the judges of the Superior Court were paid quarterly by the state," Plumer explained. "A portion of those payments, however, were made to the judges by the clerk of that court, from fees received from the suitors. It was the duty of the clerk to transmit to the secretary [of state] an account of the amount paid each judge. The clerk neglected to make a report in due season; and in consequence of that neglect Steele received from the state treasury two hundred eighty eight dollars sixty six cents more than was due him on account of his salary."[32]

After Steele ignored Plumer's demands for repayment, the governor lay the matter before the General Court, and Steele resigned from the bench. A legislative committee instructed the state treasurer to settle with the judge. At the next session the treasurer reported that Steele still would not pay. A second committee set a date for payment and told the treasurer to sue Steele if he was not paid. Instead of paying, Steele incredibly published an address to the people, accusing the committee "with being influenced by *a spirit of bitterness against* him."[33] Its report, he complained, left the impression that he had been paid by "the people's hard earnings," that is, from the state treasury. Rather, his salary had come from court fees—"the contributions of poor suitors for the support of a government bound to administer justice to them—and out of whom our liberal Legislators are desirous of making a purse." Steele was playing to the public's favor by reiterating a frequent complaint of New Hampshire litigants, that the legislature set fees for filing court actions so high that it was they, and not general taxation, that supported the costs of the judiciary. Contrary to what Plumer understood, Steele insisted that his salary was paid entirely by court fees, that he got nothing from the treasury. "All the money I ever received officially, was paid to me by the Clerk, with a full understanding that it was my legal fees," Steele wrote. "I drew no money from the treasury, during my continuance in office; nor did I ever receive or accept of any as fees, with the least indication or expectation of its being paid over in trust for the State, or any of its Servants. Indeed I knew of no such practice or authority, and consequently received whatever the States' [*sic*] agent paid over to me, in fees as my own, and spent it with the same impression."[34]

Steele's theory of law was incredible, yet it was his only legal defense when telling Governor Plumer that he was not obliged to return to the state the money he had been overpaid. The clerk had been authorized by law to pay him from fees, the clerk made him an offer of money, in good faith he had accepted that offer, and now the money was his. His jurisprudence was ridiculously flawed, and Plumer did not allow him to exploit the state. The money was returned. Steele sent a letter to the *Portsmouth Oracle*, crediting Plumer with discovering the discrepancy and, for demanding that the money be repaid, concluding with bitter sarcasm that a "great obligation" was "imposed upon the people of this state by the scrutinizing eye and actively honest heart of Governor PLUMER, for first bringing to view this new claim."[35]

Plumer had been delighted to receive Steele's resignation. Few of the public events that he had been able to influence had interested him more in his younger years than recommending judicial appointments, and now as governor he had the opportunity to strengthen the judiciary as he had always sought to do since having been first admitted to the bar. Moreover, this appointment was particularly significant because of the two judges then sitting on the court, Livermore and Evans. Evans, Plumer explained, "by reason of sickness was incapable of attending the courts," so that Livermore was presiding alone over trials, both contrary to statute, though it could not be helped, and to the unhappiness of many lawyers who felt he was becoming more and more arbitrary.[36]

Like Smith three years earlier, Plumer knew exactly whom he wanted to appoint. Smith had picked Jeremiah Mason, who had turned him down, and then the executive Council rejected his other choices until he felt obliged to accept Steele, whom he did not respect either as a lawyer or a citizen. Plumer's candidate was Samuel Bell, a lawyer from the first rank of the bar, a man of strict integrity, and one of New Hampshire's most brilliant younger Republicans. Perhaps as important to Plumer, Bell was what a later governor, Charles H. Bell, described as "a dignified presence. Though accessible to all, he unbent to few." Later, when serving on the Superior Court, his rulings were deliberate and never modified. "If a persistent counsel ventured to press for a reopening of a question already passed on, 'that point is decided,' was his mild answer, and it was well understood that nothing more was to be said."[37]

Plumer surely expected that the Council would support Bell. The councilors had to realize they could never find a better associate judge to balance the impetuous and irascible chief justice. Moreover, at forty-three he could easily serve the time necessary to regain for the court some of the public respect and professional prestige that it had lost when Smith resigned and to restore to the law of New Hampshire some of its lost legitimacy. Also, Plumer was in a much stronger political position than Smith had been when he, too, had hoped to appoint Bell. Three of the five councilors when Smith was governor had been Republicans steadfastly opposing his Federalist nominees. Three members of Plumer's party were on his Council and, as three were all that was needed to confirm appointments, one would think that a decisive governor could have gotten the judge he wanted.

Bell's candidacy became the greatest disappointment and the most visible setback of Plumer's first gubernatorial term. Two of the three Republican councilors refused to accept him at all. They felt he had been too closely connected to the Hillsborough Bank failure, and no matter how competent he might be, the public did not want him on the bench. "[I]n those days when banks were personally identified with the men who organized them," Lynn Turner surmised, "farmers who lost their deposits were inclined to hold the banker rather than the bank responsible." The third Republican councilor opposing Bell supported a different candidate, who was also favored by a fourth councilor. He was Clifton Claggett,[38] a party hack who needed a job. Although a lawyer, he did not have the intellect, the learning, or the experience as a practitioner to be a high-court judge. "I thot him honest," Plumer explained, "but his talents & legal information were not above mediocrity." Yet he had to accept him. Writing of himself in the third person, Plumer told why he had agreed to Claggett's appointment. "Tho the governor considered him deficient in talents and capacity in that office, yet being unable to obtain the consent of the council to any man whom he proposed and believing the situation of the court, and the public interest required a new judge, he reluctantly consented to the nomination."[39] "It was the one act of his year in office that he subsequently had cause to regret," Turner noted, and recalling his first term as governor, Plumer said that it was the one action he wished he could take back. "I should have made a more strenuous effort to have Bell appointed Judge of the Superior Court, and should not have consented to the appointment of Claggett." Turner best summed up the results: "The superior court now consisted of Arthur Livermore, a judicial despot, Richard Evans, a chronic invalid, and Clifton Claggett, a mediocrity."[40]

A month after Claggett's appointment, Chief Justice Livermore dropped by one morning to visit Plumer and to complain about his new associate. "He observed that Judge Claggett was an honest man, but his legal talents are not above mediocrity, & he wants decision of character." Plumer agreed, and he made the same evaluation after Claggett was forced from the court, using some of the same words as those he attributed to Livermore. "His conduct, during the short time he was on the bench," Plumer wrote, "proved he was deficient in quickness of apprehension, soundness of judgment, and decision of character, and, considering the advantages he had, that he was in fact a man of moderate talents."[41]

Livermore had visited Plumer to complain as well of his other associate, Richard Evans. Plumer was not surprised. "I will not say with or without reason," he wrote a congressman. "Evans has not attended court, the state of his health forbids it." That was in March. In August Evans applied to

Plumer to pay his salary for that quarter. He had not attended a court session for eighteen months, "& there is no probability he will ever recover his health," Plumer believed. "Your sickness is a misfortune both to you and the state," he told Evans.[42]

In May of the next year, Evans visited Plumer in Epping and stayed for a couple of days. "His health was bad, & I think he has no rational prospect of recovery," the governor concluded. On the second day Evans asked what changes would likely be made in the court. Plumer said he thought both Livermore and Evans might be removed from office, meaning the legislature would address him and the Council to remove the two judges. Plumer evidently thought that Evans at least should be "addressed." "It is more than two years since he has done any duty," Plumer said of Evans. "[H]e not only receives an annual salary of $1000, but prevents the appointment of another judge, to the great injury of suitors, & of the public. If a federal administration removes him they cannot with propriety be blamed, his obstinacy in holding the office will attach all the blame to himself."[43]

Some months later Evans also visited Benjamin Pierce, sheriff of Hillsborough County and a very influential Republican. Pierce told him to resign, that it was his duty and that if he did not, the Federalists would remove him in June if they won the 1813 election. "I am poor or I would not hold the office," Evans replied, adding that "if he resigned he was afraid the governor would insist upon appointing Samuel Bell, or some other lawyer." He added that "he wished . . . [a] good man, not a lawyer, his successor." It would appear from that statement that Evans had been sincere when he had justified his appointment to the court on grounds that the judiciary always needed at least one judge who was not a lawyer. Now, he told Pierce, "he was apprehensive that if he resigned, the executive would appoint a *lawyer*, which he thot would be wrong."[44] Plumer decided that the Evans problem had to be submitted to the legislature, perhaps a tactful admission by Plumer that the General Court held the ultimate authority over the judiciary. "The judge is not only sick but indigent," Plumer explained. "Our court consists of only three judges, all of whom ought, particularly in times like the present, to be punctual in their attendance. We grant no pensions to retiring officers. But one or two things are necessary—increase the number of judges or remove Evans by address. Either of these measures are unpleasant—three judges able & punctual are sufficient, & to remove a sick man oppressed with poverty is a hardship to him but to continue him is a greater hardship to the state. The legislature must decide."[45]

At the November meeting of the General Court, a committee was appointed to report on a letter that the legislature had received from Chief

Justice Livermore. He asked the two houses to address Evans from his office as judge of the Superior Court. The committee reported that, due to Evans's state of health, the Superior Court could not meet and offered a motion that the House address the governor and Council to remove Richard Evans from the office of high court judge. It was defeated overwhelmingly—28 yeas to 142 nays. The legislators of New Hampshire may have been proverbially niggardly, but they would not address from office a sitting judge who missed every session of court for over two years but who was too sick and too poor to support himself.[46]

When, at the second session of his first legislature, he threatened to veto a judiciary bill, Plumer's colleagues at the New Hampshire bar learned how much his new Republican politics could cause him to abandon the receptionist jurisprudential principles to which he had been so committed. At the first session, in June, Thomas W. Thompson, former congressman from Concord, on behalf of a House committee, reported a bill that he and Daniel Webster had drafted. It had been revised by Jeremiah Mason, and although there is no direct proof, it may also have been worked on by Smith. His fingerprints are all over it. The bill was entitled "an act making further provision for the administration of justice," but a more accurate name would have been "an act making provision for carrying out the reforms of Jeremiah Smith for the administration of justice." The *Constitutionalist*, an Exeter newspaper, summarized the provisions:

> This act provides that the Superior Court shall hereafter have original jurisdiction concurrent with the Courts of Common Pleas of all suits wherein the title of real estate is concerned—that the Superior Court shall consist of one Chief Justice and four other Justices—that in the several counties the said Court may be holden by any one or more Justices, and shall be called the *Superior Court sitting* at Nisi Prius—that it shall be holden twice in each year by all the or a majority of the Justices at Portsmouth . . . and at Concord . . . , which shall be called the *Superior Court setting* [*sic*] *in Bench*—that the latter shall be considered in the nature of a Court of Appeals, with the power to revise, by writ of error, any judgment given in the Court of Nisi Prius. It also provides for the appointment of a Reporter of the decisions of the Superior Court of Judicature, and for the publications of those decisions from time to time.[47]

Although the proposed bill was politically astonishing, its provisions probably did not surprise lawyers. They were nothing less than the reforms that Smith would have introduced during his term as chief justice, had he not been prevented by Republican legislators. First was the ending of the Common Pleas's original jurisdiction over land titles, taking from that nonprofessional tribunal decisions over property.[48] Second was the division of the Superior Court into two types of terms, a trial term sitting at *nisi prius*—that is with juries—and a law term, *in bench* or more commonly *en banc*, convening without juries to hear motions, errors, reserved questions, and related judicial business. The *Constitutionalist* described it as "in the nature of a Court of Appeals," a word that may have made Thompson, Webster, and especially Smith cringe. Had the word "appeals" been in the bill, it would have been a red flag rallying Jeffersonians in opposition. Third was the appointment of a court reporter, which may have been included only because Smith insisted. Thompson, Webster, and Mason surely knew they had no chance to get a reporter approved and even less of a chance to have judicial decisions published officially by the state. For some reason that may never be explained, Smith was more optimistic. He expected that New Hampshire would eventually realize that it would have to report its judges' decisions or it would be getting all of its law from Massachusetts, which had just started publishing reports.[49]

The Thompson-Webster bill was a truly astonishing proposal. It was nothing else than a codification of pure receptionist legal theory. Republicans wanted nothing to do with it. The *New-Hampshire Patriot* called it a lawyer's bill, intended only "to benefit the principal members of a profession whose situation and talents have already given them an undue ascendency in society, and whose ambition is ever on the watch to grasp further at whatever the credulity of the people will surrender to their power." The proposed changes in the judicial system offered nothing to the public at large, the *Patriot* implied, except to add more delay and expense to litigation. Judgments would be stayed in most causes, for lawyers could usually find the semblance of legal error justifying an appeal to the law term either at Portsmouth or Concord, adding costs for the litigants, and lining lawyers' pockets with still more fees.[50]

The *Patriot*'s sarcasm was expected. Thompson, Webster, and Smith knew what the Republican press would argue and could have written the articles themselves, everything that was said was so predictable. Governor Plumer was more of a surprise. His opposition provided another measure of how much he could turn his back on legal principles to which he once had committed his heart and soul. At the Constitutional Convention of 1791–1792, he had devoted hours of labor trying to abolish the Court of Common Pleas, tagging it a useless tribunal, unproductive, and serving no purpose except to provide a sinecure for undeserving politicians.[51] Now he objected that the Thompson-Webster bill, by giving concurrent jurisdiction to the Superior Court, would decimate the Common Pleas, and he said that he would veto the bill on those grounds alone. "This may operate as a virtual, tho' covert, mode of annihilating the Courts of Common Pleas," he noted in a private memorandum, "for it will leave to the discretion, whim or caprice of plaintiffs, or more generally their attornies, to commence all their suits in the Superior Court, & as the Justices of the Common Pleas depend entirely on the fees of the entry of actions for their compensation, it may in fact prevent every man qualified for the Courts of Common Pleas from holding that office; & yet the Courts of Common Pleas must still exist, for this bill gives no authority to the Superior Court to lay out roads, repair gaols & court houses, appoint agents for the county, receive & examine votes for the register of deeds & county treasurer & transact all the various prudential concerns of the several counties."[52]

It does not do to overstate differences. Plumer had been a leader among the lawyers who had been working to control juries by the rule of law, but he had never been as doctrinaire as Smith. He would have limited reversal of jury verdicts to those contrary to the trial judge's instructions, but apparently he might not have overturned verdicts contrary to precedential law as Smith would have. Formerly Plumer had supported law terms that did not sit during trial terms. But once Thompson and Webster appeared to make law terms specific Federalist policy, he reversed himself. Now he objected that judges sitting *in bench*, that is at law terms, were authorized to "reverse the verdict of juries & try the fact themselves, merely because the Judges are of opinion that the jury that tried the cause at nisi prius decided the facts different from them. This is introducing a new principle into jurisprudence, & would in fact destroy the power of juries, and render that inestimable institution useless."[53] Plumer was postulating an argument of extremes, employing sheer exaggeration to concoct a case against law terms. Still, he was on safe and solid ground. What he said was pure Republican politics and mainstream Jeffersonian legal theory.

Plumer was defeated for reelection in 1813. On his last day as governor, he looked back on his term with satisfaction. "Had I possessed the same information & experience when my office commenced, as when it terminated, my conduct in a *few things* would have been different: I would have made a more strenuous effort to have appointed Samuel Bell as a judge of the superior court, & *not* consented to the appointment of Clegget." To say the same in fewer words, judicial appointments were the only actions he would have done differently.[54]

*Chapter Seven*

# Legislative Hegemony

The election of 1813 was a New Hampshire political watershed, and many people expected that year's General Court would become one of the most memorable in history. It was memorable but not for the reasons that people had anticipated. It was memorable only for legislation reshaping the judiciary. And as legislators arrived in Concord for the opening session, newspapers were reporting the first positive news in years about the judiciary. It was announced that "the Hon. Judge Evans has so far recovered his health, as to have been able to perform the duties of his office in the Courts of Grafton and Coos." It would be but a temporary respite in Evans's incapacity. For well over two years he had not attended a court session, although, the *Farmer's Cabinet* reported, "it is believed he never failed to claim his salary." With only the incompetent Clifton Claggett to assist him, Arthur Livermore had to try and clear most dockets practically alone. He complained to Governor William Plumer that he needed abler associates and told his brother "that he intended to resign as he felt himself inadequate to the task of doing the whole [judicial] business of the State."[1]

As the government of New Hampshire gathered in Concord for the opening of the legislative session that June, there was a general consensus that some action had to be taken to remedy the many and obvious defects of the judiciary system. For the first time in the state's history, there was talk about legislating the entire high-court bench from office. That possibility was a contrast with the legislative session of just the year before. Then, at both the June and November sessions, discussion had not been on legislating out the Superior Court, but of either impeaching or addressing out of office individual justices. The targets that most lawmakers had in mind were either the chief justice, Arthur Livermore, whom some of the leading lawyers of Rockingham County wanted addressed out, or Richard Evans, the absent judge, whom many legislators, especially those representing counties where court sessions were sometimes cancelled, wanted off the court.

"Complaints against the Justices of that court, particularly the C[hief] Justice, are numerous," William Plumer informed Congressman Harper three months before the legislature met. "[T]hey do not proceed from one party only, but many of both parties [are] dissatisfied." Complaints against the chief justice had been multiplying. He may have become more arbitrary as judicial pressures increased. With Evans staying at home and his other associate, Clifton Claggett, too unfit to be of help, Livermore had begun to conduct trials alone. The practice was not authorized by statute, and it does not seem to have been frequent. From what little is known the best guess is that desperate litigants, anxious to have their legal problems resolved, sought to waive their rights to be tried by two or more judges and asked Livermore to preside alone, whether such trials were legal or not. One reason that Livermore did not often have to preside alone was because he usually had Judge Claggett to sit alongside him. Claggett's presence satisfied the statutory requirement of two presiding justices but did not relieve the burden on Livermore. Having Claggett as his sitting associate may have been very much like presiding alone. From everything that contemporaries have told us about Claggett, it is safe to surmise that the chief justice had to make most of the rulings and formulate all of the decisions, and that was probably what he meant when telling his brother he would resign. He was complaining about Claggett as much as he was about Evans.[2]

For litigants there were some risks in asking Livermore to preside alone if Claggett was not available. His impatience and short temper made his trials both unpredictable and unnerving. There were, however, two sides to his contentious personality. On the negative side he could be arbitrary, but on the positive he could be quite decisive. THE VOICE OF NEW-HAMPSHIRE claimed that when Evans took sick and stopped coming to court, Livermore ordered the clerk of the Superior Court not to pay him his salary.[3]

Almost all the complaints about Livermore's conduct in court were private, voiced to friends and acquaintances by unhappy or abused attorneys but not brought against him as formal charges. As a result they are lost to history. As far as research has uncovered, only one incident was ever described in a newspaper, and it does not show him out of control, only being egocentric. THE VOICE OF NEW-HAMPSHIRE, addressing Livermore in the second person, told how the chief justice, while conducting a trial in Grafton County with judges Steele and Evans as his associates, stopped the proceedings and abruptly announced he was going home. "When the judge on your right hand expressed his astonishment at your proposal to return home, and observed that you knew that there were many great questions pending, upon which a decision was expected, you replied, 'I HAVE MEN AT MY HOUSE DIGGING A WELL, AND YOU KNOW HOW IT IS WHEN YOU HAVE HANDS TO WORK, AND ARE NOT THERE WITH THEM.'" And with that, according to VOICE, Livermore left the courtroom and was absent from the circuit for three weeks.[4]

Although we have no direct evidence, there is reason to suggest that lawyers who were angered by incidents like this or who had experienced the blunt of Livermore's sharp tongue in court were talked out of filing formal complaints with either house of the legislature. After all, if worse came to worse and Livermore was disciplined by being addressed from office, what lawyer of his caliber would be willing to make the financial sacrifice and take his place? Then, at the June 1812 meeting of the General Court, Peyton R. Freeman presented a memorial and remonstrance against the chief justice, and no one could persuade him to withdraw it. Freeman was a Hanover lawyer who had removed to Portsmouth in 1803, where he built a somewhat successful practice, for he was well trained and had a reputation for hard work. Plumer would think enough of him to appoint him Deputy Secretary of State in 1816, and a year later he became clerk of the United States District Court.[5]

It is not necessary to examine all the details. It is enough to know that, while presiding at a court session in Haverhill, Livermore became upset with Freeman and suspended him from practicing at the bar of the Superior Court. Reporting Freeman's petition to the legislature, the *New-Hampshire Patriot* published one of the very few compliments paid Livermore by the press. Saying it could not comment on the facts of Freeman's suspension, the *Patriot* did want to praise the chief justice for charges recently delivered at various sessions of the court. "[W]herein he inculcated the duty of the citizens to acquiescence in the measures of rulers chosen by, and from ourselves," the *Patriot* explained. "That charge undoubtedly has had an excellent effect on our State; and however we may have formerly disapproved of some official conduct of Judge Livermore, we cannot but approbate him in this thing."[6] The War of 1812 had just begun. The state's leading Republican newspaper, the *Patriot*, loyally supported the Madison administration but most New Hampshirites were strongly opposed to the war. In his charge the chief justice, speaking beyond the grand jurors to the general population, said they had a legal duty to aid the national government. When Livermore arrived in Concord to defend himself against Freeman's memorial, Plumer asked him whether he was changing his politics. "[H]e frankly said he had not changed his opinion upon politics." But he "supported the laws of Congress and thought they should be obeyed. And had recommended obedience to the grand juries on his last circuit. '& that some portion of the federalists were offended with him.'"[7]

Livermore had surprised the state by arriving in Concord and announcing that he intended to defend himself at the legislative hearing. Perhaps people should have expected he might do so, considering both his impetuous personality and the serious nature of Freeman's charges. Not only had the chief justice suspended him "from practicing at the bar of the Superior Court," but, Freeman asserted, Livermore did so "without any formal accusation being preferred against him," adding that the chief justice's conduct was "arbitrary and unjust, and without precedent—destructive to the memorialist in his means of living and his rights as a citizen."[8] Plumer, who was governor at the time, recorded what had happened on the first day, before Livermore arrived in town.

> At the last term of the Superior Court in Grafton County, present judges, Arthur Livermore chief justice & Jonathan Steele, the chief justice addressed Freeman stating that the court had received information that he at a public tavern immediately after the rising of the Court in the county of Rockingham, had uttered in the presence of many people, such accusations against the court, in particular against the Chief Justice respecting the court, as were not true; that they tended to destroy the reputation of the Court, & impeach public confidence in them, & that untill he explained his conduct to their satisfaction, he as an officer of that court must consider himself suspended from the practice of law in that court.

Freeman did not answer the charges, and he did not apologize. He went to his lodging and sent Livermore a note, asking for a copy of the order. The chief justice readily sent it to him. After hearing the memorial reciting these facts, which was read at one of its daily sessions, the House of Representatives referred Freeman's complaint to a committee. The committee took testimony from Freeman and then prepared a report recommending that he be advised that he had liberty to withdraw his memorial. Also, the committee "indirectly censured" the chief justice. Before the report could be considered by the full membership of the House, Livermore arrived in town and submitted a memorial of his own, justifying his conduct. The House referred this memorial to the same committee, and the committee replied that both parties should be heard by the full House.[9]

An unfamiliar, very surprising Arthur Livermore was in Concord that June day of 1812. He was an Arthur Livermore that most of New Hampshire had not seen before. The *New-Hampshire Patriot*, not given to saying anything favorable about lawyers or the judiciary, reported that his defense before the full House "was a *master-piece*." "The drift of his argument was, that the attornies were mere officers of, and removable at the pleasure of the Court," the *Patriot* summarized, "that they possessed no privileges there which were not possessed by the Clerk, the Crier, or even the humble waiter who makes and tends the fire for the Court—that as they retained no privileges as attornies by any statute of the State, so their suspension destroyed no rights which they had not in common with other citizens." Livermore then took a different tact and went off in a direction that surely astonished much of his audience. He did not question the competency of both houses, as he had on previous occasions, but acknowledged the authority of the legislature to complete and unrestricted superintendence over the judiciary. Admitting that by law he was "amenable to the House of Representatives, as the Grand Inquest of the State, for all his conduct," Livermore said that "he was liable, not only to be removed by impeachment, but by the Governor and Council, on the address of the two branches of the Legislature."[10]

Plumer was also impressed by Livermore's defense but was more interested in what the judge told him about some of the leading Federalist lawyers. Livermore claimed that he had treated Freeman no differently than he treated the best practitioners in Rockingham County and he suspected they had retaliated by persuading Freeman to file his memorial. "He observed that what was done in relation to Freeman was not done by himself only, but was the act of the court," Plumer recorded. "He observed, the court had authority not only to suspend, but to expel lawyers from the practice, and that it was a power indispensable & necessary to all courts of record. That he knew that in discharging his official duties, he had made some of the Bar his personal enemies. That he had never been obliged to order but two lawyers to sit down, & those were Jeremiah Mason & John C. Chamberlain, & that in consequence of that they were inimical to him. . . . He made allusions which conveyed the *idea* that Freeman was induced to make this complaint, to gratify the resentment of Mason, Chamberlain, & Daniel Webster, & they urged him to this course." Freeman, Plumer added, "was not only short, but cold, formal, & feeble in his reply. The result was that he had liberty by a unanimous vote of the House to *withdraw* his memorial." Federalists were surprised as well as delighted by the unanimous vote. "After the foul abuse we have heard lavished by the democrats on Judge Livermore," the *Constitutionalist* exclaimed, "we cannot consistently account for the impunity with which he escaped—but we congratulate the Judge upon the honorable nature of his acquittal."[11]

Stubbornly, Freeman drafted a second memorial, which he presented at the November session of the General Court that same year. It was described by the *Democratic Republican* as "a re-petition" of the original complaint. In addition, it charged that Livermore "at the last term of the Court at Exeter refused to hear the said Freeman as council in a case where he had a written power of attorney from one of the parties. It complains of the proceedings of the Chief Justice as violent, oppressive and extra-judicial—as destructive to the rights of the citizens, and as making the *bar* the mere automatons and machines of the *Court.*"[12]

Freeman's new memorial was submitted to a committee, which dealt with it summarily. There was no need for another hearing. The committee investigated the charges and told the full House they did not warrant a different outcome. The question was then put to the House of Representatives: "Do the facts reported by the committee . . . warrant the impeachment of the chief justice of the Superior Court of Judicature?" The House answered no, 141 to 22.[13]

At the same session of the General Court, a motion was made in the House of Representatives to address the governor and Council to remove Judge Evans from office. The vote, Plumer reported to the *Patriot*, "was ayes 28, nays 142—every federal member, I believe, voted in the negative." Once again the Republicans of New Hampshire refused to follow the example set by Thomas Jefferson and the national party. They would not use the authority of the legislature to strip a judge of his tenure in office.[14] At the next session of the General Court, the Federalists would not hesitate to do so.

When that next session of the legislature convened in June 1813, the political balance in New Hampshire had been drastically altered. Recall that the election of the year before had been one of the closest on record. It had not been settled until the General Court met and the two houses elected William Plumer governor, or as Federalist newspapers put it, "a *party, not the people*, made him governor of New-Hampshire." The balloting occurred just before the Madison administration declared war on Great Britain, and war made all the difference for the next election. Held in March 1813, it attracted more voters than any previous New Hampshire election, and its outcome depended less on state issues than had any since 1798. Gilman defeated Plumer with a plurality of 797, but he had only 242 more than needed to make a choice. The Federalists did better in the legislature, getting a dependable majority of more than twenty in the house, nine of the twelve senators; they even elected three of the five councilors.[15]

The gubernatorial election of 1813 was waged on the issue of how much and even whether New Hampshire should support the national war effort. Surprisingly, Plumer, who just a few years earlier had actively conspired with Timothy Pickering to lead New England out of the federal union, was one of only two New England governors to comply with national requisitions for the service of the detached state militia. He received four requisitions and filled them all. In his address to the General Court at the November session of 1812, Plumer not only defended his policy, he almost begged the legislators and people to join him in supporting the president, the Congress, and the military. "There is no middle course," he warned New Hampshirites. "We must support our Government, or oppose it—afford aid to our country, or countenance her enemies. If we oppose the Government, we shall inflict punishment on ourselves, protract the war, prolong the evils we fear, or compel the Government to make an ignominious and disgraceful peace."[16]

Compared to most New Hampshire governors of that era, Plumer could be eloquent, but his gubernatorial speech to the second session of the General Court in 1812 was a call that New Hampshire would not answer. "A wise government," a minority of the representatives protested, "would have enquired into the necessity, and the expediency, as well as the abstract justice, of the proposed war. We do not deem this war to have been necessary." The protest was signed by 70 of 177 members of the lower house.[17] In speech after address, lawyers, public officials, and clergymen, who once had been Plumer's friends and political supporters, denounced the war and the slaveholders who had forced New Hampshire to go to war.[18]

Opposition to the war was the issue that swung the election of 1813 to the Federalists. As Plumer had already committed New Hampshire's militia to the national military service, there was little the new state government could do to oppose the federal administration, except to refuse further cooperation with Washington. Although Gilman was inclined to support the Hartford Convention, convened by Federalists to give voice to New England's opposition to Madison's foreign policy, he found most of the party's leaders in New Hampshire hostile to dividing the union, and he concluded not to ask the General Court to send a delegation.[19]

International affairs may have determined which party controlled the government, but not what that government would do. The legislative session of 1813 was no different from any other in early New Hampshire. The General Court's time was entirely concerned with local affairs, and the most local issue of all, the one dominating all discussion in both houses during the June session, was the judiciary. There were three obvious problems: the unpopularity of Livermore and what Lynn Turner summarized as "the absence of Evans and the ignorance of Claggett."[20] Stating that something had to be done about these three judges, A Friend To Justice spearheaded a concerted attack on the judicial system itself, delineating in lay terms the shortcomings that were increasingly troublesome to lawyers. Friend probably thought that the public was not aware of one of these shortcomings but that they would understand once it was explained: motions, petitions, errors, and reserved questions had to be argued, opposed, and adjudicated at trial terms, that is, during sessions when other business, especially jury business, required the attention of the court. To accommodate lawyers needing to argue matters of law, impaneled jurors had to be put on hold and told to remain in the shire town, waiting to be called, trials had to be halted, and the process of justice was interrupted by questions that had to be argued and settled but which were nevertheless distractions from the main business of trial terms. "Sometimes there were forty or fifty questions of Law, many of them novel in their nature and difficult of decision, to be determined in a single day, and very often in half a day," A FRIEND TO JUSTICE pointed out. "The consequence was that decisions were made without hearing the proper authorities and without due deliberations. Hence it necessarily happened, the opinions delivered at one term were reversed at the next. The Judgments of the Court were inconsistent, fluctuating, perpetually changing, so that it was impossible for the citizens of the State to know what the law was."[21]

We should read between the lines. A FRIEND TO JUSTICE is not troubled that ordinary citizens did not "know what the law is." He was, rather, concerned about lawyers, saying that it was impossible for practitioners to know what was New Hampshire law. It would not have been politically productive to say so openly in 1813. The average voter did not care about lawyers' difficulties. FRIEND's complaint that complicated legal questions had to be resolved at the very session at which they were raised, usually within less than half a day, is something that is readily understood in the twenty-first century, but in 1813 it was both a challenging and a challenged argument. At that time, remember, the dominant legal theory in New Hampshire, as William Plumer, Jr., pointed out, "regarded good sense and upright intentions as of more importance than mere book-learning."[22] It was not only nonlawyers who failed to cotton to the reforms of Jeremiah Smith. FRIEND's lament that judgments were inconsistent, fluctuating, and perpetually changing, would not have troubled many lawyers of the day, including even some of the bar's leaders.[23] That FRIEND made the argument, however, is very revealing of the change coming over New Hampshire law. It shows that Smith's legal philosophy was gaining enough acceptance that it could be articulated and defended in a newspaper article and that a correspondent such as FRIEND, writing for the general newspaper reader, thought that for New Hampshire law to become legitimate, judgments had to be consistent, not fluctuating or perpetually changing.

A FRIEND TO JUSTICE tipped his political hand when telling his readers that there had been one period when the Superior Court applied law consistently. "[I]t was that period in which a man presided in our Superior Court, whose strong discriminating mind, and whose extensive legal information [i.e., education] enabled him to solve the most perplexed and intricate questions with the greatest facility and correctness," he wrote of the former chief justice. "It may with truth be said of him 'that he could untie the Gordian knot of law familiar as his garter.' But this does not prove the system a good one—it only proves what may be done by a man of extraordinary talents, profoundly skilled in the laws of his Country, even under a very bad system."[24] This tribute might have been a welcomed compliment to Jeremiah Smith had it not been written in such a political context. The purpose of A FRIEND TO JUSTICE had not been to praise Smith but to disparage the current Superior Court. He was contributing to a campaign to refashion the judiciary and that it had functioned so well when Smith had been chief justice was dismissed as an aberration, personal to him, but certainly not likely to be repeated when someone of less ability was chief justice.

It was this Federalist campaign that made the 1813 term of the New Hampshire General Court a one-issue session and determined that the one issue would be the structure of the judiciary. In the gubernatorial address of that year it was the only subject that Governor Gilman recommended for legislative action.[25] Remarkably, on the very day that Gilman spoke—the first day of the session—the House of Representatives, without opposition, appointed a judicial committee, and the next day the Senate followed suit. The House committee submitted its report almost immediately. Five days later a bill entitled "An act establishing a Supreme Judicial Court" was reported out of committee and laid on the table of the House for consideration.[26] The next day "the bill entitled 'an act establishing a Supreme Judicial Court and a Circuit Court of Common Pleas,' was taken up and discussed. Motion was made to postpone the further consideration of the bill till the next session. Negatived—ayes 77, noes 95." The bill passed both the House and Senate and was signed by Governor Gilman.[27]

The events of that week were absolutely unprecedented. New Hampshire legislators were not known to act so swiftly or so decisively. A bill reconstituting the judicial system of the state should have taken at least two sessions, if not three, to be drafted, debated, and voted on. There is no escaping the conclusion that in 1813 the Federalists had arrived in Concord for the June term of the General Court with both committee reports written and the judicial bill drafted. How else could they have been so effective or have acted so swiftly? Maybe the promoters of the new judiciary system did not lobby the Federalist representatives and senators before all were in Concord, but they knew what most of them would support and they knew they could get their votes. It was a truly remarkable triumph that must have stunned the Republicans, a unique New Hampshire legislative event not just for the nineteenth century, but for the twentieth and the twenty-first century as well. Usually New Hampshire politicians do not have to be so well prepared or so devious. And most remarkable of all, the bill was the most controversial New Hampshire legislation enacted during the first quarter of the nineteenth century. It was opposed by a united Republican party from the moment it was first proposed.

The Judicial Act of 1813 had no preamble. There was not even an opening clause saying why the Superior Court of Livermore, Evans, and Claggett should be abolished; not a single explanation stated in any of the various sections why a new court had to be created. Flush with victory at the polls and expecting to remain in power for several more years, Federalist leaders may have thought that they did not have to explain. If so, they were carelessly overconfident, passing a statute intended to revolutionize the third branch of the government, practically in secret, without any advance public discussion, without much public debate, and now that it had been made public and could be read, without any purpose stated. And it really could be read for, unlike just about every other nineteenth-century New Hampshire statute, it was readily accessible, printed in the press of both parties. In fact, it could not be missed for it was printed not only on the first page—the whole page—of the Federalist *Portsmouth Oracle* but also on the first page of the Republican *New-Hampshire Patriot.*[28]

More may have been published concerning the Judicial Act of 1813 than any other New Hampshire statute enacted during the first three decades of the nineteenth century. Yet almost nothing was written about its origins, its authorship, or the sources of its policy. Of course, people asked these questions, at least lawyers did, and undoubtedly some satisfied themselves that the answer was that the new Judicial Act was so readily drafted and complete because it was largely based on the bill that Thomas Thompson and Daniel Webster had authored just the year before. And it was, but that 1812 bill at best was only an intermediate source. The basic query for most people was how much the 1813 bill was the work of Jeremiah Smith. It was evident to lawyers that the new court that the bill created was a Smith court, cut to his specifications and tailored to prove the merits of Smith's program of judicial reform. Smith denied that he had had a hand in framing the new Judicial Act, and there is no evidence, even indirect, that he did. The most that can be proven is that Smith had friends and admirers in the legislature and at the bar, including Thompson and Webster, who both understood the reforms he had been introducing during his term as chief justice and who wanted those reforms implemented.

If we consider just the major changes introduced into New Hampshire law by the new legislation, it is readily apparent that the Judicial Act of 1813 codified Smith's jurisprudence. First, it authorized single-judge trial terms. When Smith became chief justice in 1802, the rule had been that at every session all four justices of the Superior Court be on the bench presiding, not just at criminal prosecutions but at all civil trials as well. There were exceptions for sickness, absences, or failure of appointment, but never by statute was one judge permitted to preside alone. Unable to get legislation for one-judge courts, Smith had introduced the practice on his own authority. The Republicans, especially doctrinaire legal theorists of the Jeffersonian school of jurisprudence, were vocally angry, and as soon as it had the opportunity, the General Court repealed Smith's rule, reinstating the requirement that all judges preside at every jury trial.[29]

The Judicial Act of 1813 was the first New Hampshire legislation to authorize single-judge trials, but it did so through very circumspect drafting. Two terms were established in all counties except the two counties with the smallest populations, and the dates of every term were spelled out in separate sections of the act. In section 2 each county was named and the weeks of the sessions specified. It was then provided that each term be presided over by the justices of the new court, "any two of whom shall constitute a quorum for holding the said Court." This was an important carry-over from an earlier reform. Two judges were enough. Even if a third judge was in the county, he did not have to attend. Section 3 of the act was almost identical, reciting the dates of the second term in each of the same counties. In this section, however, it was provided that "any one or more of the Justices" of the court were a quorum. The words "or more" seem ambiguous, but they had a purpose. By introducing an indefinite element, they undoubtedly were intended to dampen potential opposition by implying that single-judge courts might not be the norm. But of course the intention of the drafters of the bill and of the legislators who enacted the law was that all the second sessions in every county would be presided over by a judge sitting alone.[30]

"Intentional vagueness" is an accurate way to describe how section 6 was drafted. The first of its two parts provides that trials for crimes punishable by death or life imprisonment, and several other types of trials such as divorce or suits for alimony, be tried by two or more judges. The second part of the section continues the intentional vagueness. It provides that "all appeals from the Circuit Courts of Common Pleas, and all other actions, processes, matters and things, civil and criminal . . . may be heard, tried, and determined . . . at the court which may be holden by one or more Justices pursuant to the third section hereof." It is difficult to conclude what should be made of this clause except that the Federalist drafters were providing to the judges an opportunity to rule that just about every cause except capital and life offenses, matrimony issues, and questions of law could be settled with a single judge sitting alone.[31] If that surmise was not conclusive, the drafters added in section 16 what may have been a catchall provision: "where any two justices are, for any reason disqualified to sit in the trial of any action, the remaining Judge shall constitute a competent court to try the same."[32] Jeremiah Smith could not have asked for more.

To readers in the twenty-first century, the authorization of one-judge courts may not look like much of a reform, but it was then a huge change, a stunning departure from the judiciary system that the Republicans had insisted upon. Moreover, it was the first legislative endorsement of any element of Jeremiah Smith's jurisprudence. It may not, however, have been the most contentious part of Smith's program of reform codified by the Judicial Act of 1813. It has been claimed that the Federalist legislators used the act to introduce law terms surreptitiously. At least that is what Smith's son, Professor Jeremiah Smith, suggested in 1879. Section 5 of the Judicial Act has the appearance of alleviating some of the concerns of Republicans and other citizens apprehensive of single-judge courts. It allowed a party to a single-judge litigation, "thinking himself aggrieved by any opinion, direction, or judgment of the said Justice . . . to allege exceptions to the same," the action to be continued to the next session of the court held in the same county, the exceptions to be determined by the full court of three justices. The younger Smith says that this provision opened the door to law terms in New Hampshire.[33] The only other section relating to correction of errors provided: "That all judgments rendered in the said Supreme Judicial Court, may be reviewed in the same manner as causes have been reviewed in the Superior Court of Judicature."[34]

There is no doubt that Professor Smith was correct. Commentators at the time the act was adopted said that it authorized law terms.[35] Then, at the November session of the General Court that same year, 1813, when the act was amended, it specifically incorporated the words "law term." Section 3 provided "that all questions of law shall be decided at the law term, except by consent of the parties interested in such question."[36]

It is not easy to evaluate historically the Judicial Act of 1813. History remembers it because it was the first New Hampshire statute to legislate out of office all the judges of the high court. By creating the new Supreme Judicial Court, it abolished the old Superior Court, and by abolishing that court, it abolished the offices of the judges sitting on that court. Put in more legal terms, by abolishing the old court, it "legislated" from office the judges of the old court. For contemporaries, those thinking more of the politics of the day, at least at the time of enactment, rather than of historical uniqueness, the act was more important as legislation that codified Jeremiah Smith's judicial reforms. And for lawyers the fundamental change was the introduction of law terms—or what Turner called "Jeremiah Smith's brain child." It was the provisions in the Judicial Act of 1813 authorizing law terms that marked the difference in substance between the old judiciary statute and the Judicial Act of 1813. "This feature in the new law," THE PEOPLE pointed out, "distinguishes it more than every thing else, from the old system." Without the provision authorizing law terms, the Judicial Act of 1813 would have been no different from the act it replaced, except for allowing single-judge jury trials. But that was not how Republicans discussed it. Ignoring one-judge courts or discounting their significance, THE PEOPLE contended that the object of the act "was *not* to introduce a new system *permanently*: but, only to remove from office the old judges."[37]

THE PEOPLE was right, but he stated his conclusion incorrectly. A Republican writing in the *New Hampshire Gazette*, he, of course, was arguing that the Judicial Act of 1813 was political legislation. He discerned two purposes to the act, a political purpose—to rid the state's highest court of its Republican judges, that is, Livermore, Evans, and Claggett—and a legal purpose—to create a new court on which Jeremiah Smith would serve. To be certain that Smith would accept appointment as chief justice, the drafters had incorporated in the act some of the jurisprudential principles that he had tried and failed to make New Hampshire law. Oddly, most Republicans apparently doubted that the Federalists cared much about Smith's program of reforms. After all, had Smith's jurisprudence been their motivation, the Federalists did not have to create a new court. They could have amended the old judicial statute to authorize single-judge trials and law terms. Rather, most Republicans seemed to think that the main Federalist motivation had been to make a place for Smith, that is, to put the former chief justice back on the court. They may have been correct. Why else did the Act of 1813 raise the chief justice's salary to $1500 a year, the amount that Smith had been making when he resigned the chief justiceship to become governor? The associates were to be paid $1200 a year, the amount that Livermore was then receiving as chief justice.[38] The pay was way too much, Republicans complained. Plumer, writing as CATO, twitted Governor Gilman for boasting that the new act, with one-judge trials, "would save one third of the business and time of the Judges," yet "*added* $700 a year" to their compensation. "To increase salaries already ample, and to establish that increase in proportion not to the increase, but the *decrease* of the duties of those officers, is a system of policy, of which I believe you are the sole inventor."[39] In his extensive criticisms of the Judicial Act of 1813, Plumer never mentioned how it promulgated the essential parts of the court reforms that he had tried to write into the state constitution at the Convention of 1791–1792.[40]

Plumer's selective memory became the standard for how Republican officials discussed the Judicial Act of 1813. The Jeffersonian opposition interpreted the act by separating discussion of the statute as an entity from its elements. Anyone reading their polemics would think there were no changes in its provisions making it different from earlier court acts. The legislation when first enacted contained no clauses creating one-judge jury trials or authorizing law terms. "The act indicates no necessity whatever for the transfer of jurisdiction of the Superior Court," the House Committee on the Judiciary reported in 1816, the year the Republicans returned to power. "It only transfers this jurisdiction from these Judges to those Judges with an increase of salary, a change of the style [i.e., title] of the Court, and some little variations in the manner of holding the Courts. . . . Indeed it is difficult to conjecture any motive that could have urged to the erection of a new court, but the removal of the Judges of the old court."[41]

The Republicans on that legislative committee were not being devious when ignoring such substantial changes as single-judge terms and law terms. They did not think of them as actual reforms or even as genuine changes in the judiciary system but as statutory tricks by some lawyers to increase the business of the bar. They were spurious reforms and could be ignored. For a few Federalists the contention was not worth answering. They believed that they had other and better justifications for the Judicial Act of 1813 than merely the codification of Smith's reforms. Although, John H. Morison contended, the judiciary legislation prior to 1813 had contained imperfections, "which were remedied by the new, especially in allowing jury trials to be conducted by a single judge, and in making provision for a law term, but the main object in making the change undoubtedly was to get rid of incompetent judges."[42] That was not an immaterial consideration for the Federalists and certainly not for the lawyers of New Hampshire. After all, the year was not 1783 or 1793, when the bar was smaller and much less distinguished, but rather it was 1813, when the legal profession had increased substantially in both numbers and wealth, and the bar of one county was remarkably distinguished.[43] When they went to court they faced judges who, with the exception of Arthur Livermore, simply were not of their caliber but were, in fact, their intellectual and professional inferiors. With the resignation of the mediocre Jonathan

Steele and the appointment of Clifton Claggett, the Superior Court became the most incompetent judicial tribunal in all of New Hampshire's history as a state—the most incompetent for the years before 1813 and the most incompetent in all the decades since 1813. There were pressing reasons to legislate those judges out of office—reasons of judicial integrity and reasons of public confidence—in order to restore public confidence in the legitimacy of New Hampshire law.

*Chapter Eight*

# Dependent Court, Reluctant Chief

The legislature of 1813, the first that was Federalist controlled since 1802, "has generated and brought forth a monster," the *New-Hampshire Patriot* complained of the new Judicial Act. "The Legislature of this state," the *Gazette* agreed, "have attempted to prostate in the dust the independence of the highest Judicial power in the State."[1]

The Judicial Act of 1813 was a "judicial coup d'etat," Lynn Turner observed. It "came as a surprise, if not indeed as a shock, to most New Hampshire citizens, Federalist as well as Republicans." Most people had expected the General Court to address out of office the sickly Judge Evans and to implement some of the changes that Jeremiah Smith had agitated for but not to legislate out all the judges on the two courts and to remodel substantially both judiciaries, the Court of Common Pleas as well as the Superior Court. "If the object were to reform the court, why not change it without removing the judges?" John H. Morison wondered. "If to remove the judges, why not remove them in the way the constitution had provided, by address from the legislature to the executive department? Or if both purposes were to be answered, why not let each be done in the way which the constitution had pointed out?"[2]

Of course, the purpose was to change the system, not to remove the Republican judges, A FRIEND TO JUSTICE claimed. "If the only object of the Legislature had been to get rid of the Judges, there was no necessity of changing the system; they had only to address the Executive and the Judges would have been removed." It might be objected that to have derobed Evans and Clifton Claggett by address was politically more messy than the single, clean incision of legislating them out of office by abolishing their court, but in fact, Federalist lawyers sought to be rid of more than the judges on the Superior Court. There was also the Court of Common Pleas, a tribunal with which this study has had little concern. If anything, many judges on that court were little better than Evans and Claggett. "Some of our inferior judicatories have been rendered absolute mockeries of courts of law," AN IMPARTIAL CITIZEN complained, "and the practice in them has been a scene of catching and pulling, of nimble tricks and shifts, that would disgrace an assembly of haberdashers."[3]

MARCELLUS, writing three years later, answered Morison's questions in part by including the Court of Common Pleas in the equation. The Federalists, he pointed out, had just won a majority in all state offices except the judiciary, and they wanted all the judgeships as well. It would have been cumbersome to remove the Republican judges by addressing them from office. Once the Court of Common Pleas, which was legislated out along with the Superior Court, was counted, it could have meant up to eighteen separate addresses to the governor and Council to remove as many as eighteen judges. Each separate address would have been occasion for the opposition to arouse public opinion and to make the removal process appear undeniably political. If you wanted the judges removed, it was much cleaner and less divisive to legislate rather than address them out. Besides, "the Judges were men highly esteemed, a majority might not be obtained for removing several of them." This was a chance that the Federalists did not need to take. They wanted all the judgeships, and that was why, MARCELLUS concluded, they legislated the Republicans out.[4]

Looking back to 1813, it could easily be assumed that the judicial legislation was a partisan act of political job stealing, taking Republican offices and giving them to Federalists, a takeover of the judiciary by a party that had just won the other two branches of government, and like Jefferson in 1801, felt cheated because the third could not be changed by the ballot box.[5] It would be well, however, not to be hasty. A case can be made, not only that the Judicial Act of 1813 was good legislation, but also that it was useful, even that it was needed.

There have been other occasions when the public was dissatisfied with New Hampshire's courts, but the period from 1809 to 1813 was the last time when discontent became a major political issue.[6] "Before an alteration of our Courts was proposed in our legislature, we can most of us remember that it was spoken of by men of every party and denomination, as being very desirable," PHOCION recalled four months after the judicial bill became law. "It is indeed well known, that the defects of our former systems of judicature were such as not only to *warrant*, but to *demand* remedy." It was the sickness of Evans and the incompetence of Claggett that brought change to a head. The conditions they created—"delay of justice, and the uncertainty of decisions"—were visible, prominent, and universally understood. "One term after another of the Superior Court would pass, without doing the business necessary to be done," a legislative committee reported. "[T]he injured would wait long, and with painful uncertainty of having redress." The situation was especially bad in the most populous section of the state. "In the late Superior Court in the County of Rockingham," A FRIEND TO JUSTICE explained, "there have been but twelve verdicts in civil causes for the last twelve months. There are on the Superior Court docket two hundred and eighty-five actions." He estimated that, at the current pace of trial, it would take twenty-four years to clear the present docket. "[A] change is indispensable." Congressman Daniel Webster was in Washington when told that a judicial bill had been drafted. "Too much cannot be done or said to convince Federalists of the necessity of attending to the subject," he wrote.[7]

The Republicans were probably right in claiming that the Judicial Act of 1813 did nothing but what could have been done by amending the old court law, except for giving the governor and Council the appointment of new judges and giving the new judges the appointment of a new clerk.[8] It would have been difficult, however, to have formulated as amendments the changes that Federalist lawyers were demanding and to have entrusted implementation to the Superior Court. Those lawyers wanted nothing less than a fundamental change in the conduct and definition of judicial business by introducing the beginnings of an appellate system and continuing Smith's program of shifting from control of the courts by laymen to control by lawyers, especially control by judges who would all be law trained. There were again to be only three members of the new Supreme Judicial Court. Now, however, the state was divided into three circuits, in each of which a single judge could preside at one, at least, or possibly up to three trial sessions annually. If litigants or counsel wanted more than one judge, two were enough for a quorum. The three members of the court, therefore, might sit together only at law terms, when, it will be recalled, there were no jury trials. The judges decided questions of law, that is, issues "reserved" from cases heard at trial terms, motions that attorneys needed time to argue, and matters requiring research, contemplation, and briefs by counsel, such as writs of error, mandamus, and possibly quo warranto. If, in fact, the full court of three justices seldom met except at law terms, the law terms authorized by the Judicial Act of 1813 would soon become the beginning of appellate jurisdiction in New Hampshire.[9] It was an objective that Jeremiah Smith most likely had had in mind. Those opposing his law reforms thought so. Just as one reason (among others) that New Hampshire Jeffersonians objected to single-judge jury trials was that they threatened lay judges, who could find it too challenging to preside alone, so also they feared that law terms presaged an appellate court on which lawyer-judges would make much—perhaps most—New Hampshire law.[10]

The Federalists were somewhat cautious. They did not brag about the innovations they were bringing to the judiciary but attempted to pass off the radical provisions of the Judicial Act as merely copying the Massachusetts court system, which currently had the reputation of functioning more efficiently than New Hampshire's judiciary.[11]

And, in fact, the Judicial Act of 1813 was not as radical as some lawyers wished. It did not provide the third major reform that Smith had been struggling for: the authority to publish the decisions written by the justices, explaining judgments, and the appointment of a court reporter to prepare the opinions for publication. No other proposal was so vehemently opposed by New Hampshire Jeffersonians who understood what Smith intended. If the judges could publish their decisions and the bar cited those opinions as binding legal precedents when arguing cases, there would be no way to prevent the court from becoming the fountain of new law or changing existing law.[12] Smith was told that "provision was made for a reporter in the judiciary bill of 1813," but that it had been "struck out" before passage. It was a keen disappointment to him, but it is possible that the Federalists would not have been able to enact the judicial bill had it authorized a court reporter.[13] That is a likely reason why it was removed from the bill.

What excited interest about the Judicial Act of 1813 was not just that the personnel of the Superior Court had been swept away, although that was the most visible and striking aspect of the law. However, the way that the legislation forced the two political parties to switch positions, philosophies, and arguments was also of great contemporary as well as historical interest. The Federalists, after all, were the conservatives, the lawyers' party, and the defenders of what little autonomy New Hampshire's judiciary possessed. With this act the Federalists were not only subjecting the court system to the domination of the legislature as it had never been dominated before, they were doing precisely what they had vehemently insisted was unconstitutional only eleven years previously, when Jefferson and the national Republicans had abolished the United States Circuit Courts and had legislated out of office the midnight judges, including Jeremiah Smith. Seldom in American history had two opposing political parties so completely reversed themselves. The Republicans suddenly became champions of judicial independence and critics of legislative supremacy. The Federalists uncomfortably found themselves defending a constitutional interpretation they did not like, at least not in theory, as it led them to subordinate the courts to the legislature and to contend that tenure at good behavior meant a judge was secure in office only as long as the office was not abolished by legislation. It was unusual for anyone debating the issues to be consistent. If the Republicans' Judiciary Act of 1802, removing the midnight judges had been unconstitutional, then the Federalists' Judicial Act of 1813 was also unconstitutional; yet Republicans had to say the first law was good and the second one bad, and Federalists said vice versa. Only someone like Plumer, who had changed parties, could be consistent. The Act of 1802 had been "a violation of the constitution of the United States," he believed then, and the Act of 1813 violated New Hampshire's constitution, he said now. He took the same position both times.[14]

Familiar roles were reversed. It was not just the conservative, pro-court Federalists who legislated out an entire judiciary; just as surprisingly it was the *New Hampshire* Federalists who did so. The New Hampshire Republicans stood in sharp contrast to them. Affiliated with the national Jeffersonians, they were the supposed radical, anticourt party; yet even though they had had control of both the executive and legislature several times during the preceding decade, they had not legislated out any court, nor had they addressed out or impeached a single judge. When Langdon first became governor, Federalists had been certain that he would adopt Jefferson's Republican national policy and remove Federalist judges. He did nothing, not even complaining that all the high-court judges were Federalist. Several lawyers, including Plumer, were so surprised that they wrote him their gratitude.[15] The only difference between the Federalist court when Langdon was first governor and the Republican court legislated from office in 1813 was the quality of the judges. Jeremiah Smith presided over the Federalist court while, by contrast, the Republican court of 1813, with the exception of Arthur Livermore, was pitiful. A not unbiased committee of Federalist legislators, appointed at the General Court's October term that year, drew a picture of the Republican court that was both intentionally partisan and not quite accurate. "The languid and imperfect state of the late Judicial system," the committee summarized, "the feeble and slow administration of justice; complaints of suitors who prosecute claims for redress of grievances; and the general discontent of the people at large; all unite to prove, that it was the duty of the Legislature to make the judicial department an object of their particular attention. One term after another of the Superior Court would pass, without doing the business necessary to be done; the injured would wait long, and with painful uncertainty of having redress."[16]

An extensive, bitter debate over the legality of legislating from office the entire Superior Court took place, lasting until 1816 when the Republican party again took control of the executive and of both houses of the legislature. Many New Hampshire newspaper readers may have felt that they were being treated to a protracted lesson in constitutional law, but in fact, the argument was generally a repeat of the debate eleven years before over the constitutionality of Jefferson's ouster of the midnight judges. Again the bone of contention was the mutability of judicial tenure at good behavior. The act of 1813, one side insisted, violated the constitution by preventing the three Superior Court judges from enjoying good-behavior tenure. That was reading the constitution too narrowly, the Committee on Memorials of the House of Representatives answered. Good-behavior tenure meant tenure "*during good behavior in office, or as long as the office exists.*" A FRIEND TO JUSTICE agreed with the committee. That was the precedent that had been established by repeal of the statute creating the midnight-judges jurisdiction. When Congress enacted that legislation, it had created a rule determinative of New Hampshire's good-behavior tenure as well as of federal constitutionalism, that "a judge shall hold his office during *good behaviour* so long as the office continues to exist; but that when the office ceases to exist, the Judge must cease to hold."[17]

DEFENDER OF THE CONSTITUTION denied that tenure at good behavior meant tenure while a judge behaved well and while the office continued to exist. It would be more constitutional, he contended, to define good behavior in contractarian terms. When good-behavior judges were commissioned, "the Constitution attached to their offices, and guaranteed to them the independency and permanency in their offices, defined in our charter of rights." For judges the constitutional guarantee was a contract that "says to them, that the tenure of their offices shall be during good *behaviour.*" If they behaved properly, honestly, and with competence, they should remain judges no matter what happened to the office. Writing thirteen years later, Plumer agreed, for otherwise a judge's tenure would "depend not on his *good behavior*, but on the mere *will and pleasure of the legislature*," that is, a judiciary neither independent nor permanent.[18]

New issues introduced in this debate that had not been raised during the earlier federal-law controversy over the midnight-judge repeal were sprung from the New Hampshire constitutional provision for addressing judges out of office. Most importantly, the existence in New Hampshire's constitution of an authority to address judges from office—a power not authorized in the federal constitution—forced the Federalists to abandon another element of their judicial philosophy. The universal constitutional givens of an independent judiciary that was a separate branch of government, equal with the executive and legislative, were challenged for the first time. Confronted by the argument that legislating out the Superior Court violated the principle of judicial independence, the Federalists answered that the New Hampshire judiciary had never been truly independent. All one had to acknowledge was that judges could be addressed out of their judgeships by the two houses, the governor, and the executive Council, for any reason or for no reason at all. "This does not look like the independency of the Judiciary which some seem disposed to magnify above all control," the *Constitutionalist* argued. "You know perfectly that a Judge may be removed from his office whenever the legislature and executive departments may think proper," A FRIEND TO JUSTICE pointed out, "and it is very clear that it creates as great a degree of dependence to take the Judge from his office, as the office from the Judge."[19]

Since the two other branches could remove a judge without a finding of transgression or even assigning a cause, the *Newhampshire Sentinel* asked, "[a]re not the Judges therefore, completely tenants at will of the Legislature?" If so, how could the authority to legislate a judge out of office be unconstitutional? The Committee on Memorials made the same point when asserting the General Court's right to exercise that authority. "It is here admitted that both Houses of the Legislature, and the Governor and Council, may remove a Judge when they think necessary," the committee argued. "If they can remove this year, they can next, and so on every year; so that the office of Judge, in this view of the Constitution, is held by the precarious tenure of the will or opinion of both Houses of the Legislature, and the Governor and Council." It was a conclusion too obvious to be denied, A FRIEND TO TRUTH insisted: tenure at good behavior, no matter how defined, did not exist in New Hampshire. "The tenure by which a judge holds his office in this state is, *in fact* a tenure at the *will* of the Legislative & Executive departments. . . . Although the spirit of the constitution requires, that there shall be no removal except for *good* reasons, yet these two departments being the *judges* of what reasons are good, may remove the judge *without reason*."[20]

A Republican answer was sounder in logic, though perhaps not in law. The clause in the New Hampshire constitution vesting the legislature and the executive with the discretionary power of addressing judges from office, Republicans asserted, was not, by analogy, constitutional authority for legislating out. Rather, it was the opposite. The power to address out, together with impeachment, was the constitutional method for removing judges. The fact that the addressing-out power was in the constitution and legislating out was not even hinted at in the constitution meant that addressing out was constitutional but legislating out should not be. Although the executive and the legislature "may remove the Judges, it cannot be done by abolishing their offices—that it must always be done in a particular way, that is, the Legislature must address the executive" and state its pleasure that a judge be removed. "Can this pleasure be made known to the Executive in one way only?" A Friend To Justice wondered. "Why can't they make the pleasure known in the form of a legislative act as well as in the form of an address?" "The answer is obvious," William Plumer pointed out. "[T]he one mode is established by the constitution, and the other is not." The constitutional power of addressing out was not a mere legislative power, as it required consent by the governor and Council. Legislating out was an exercise of legislative power, over which the governor had a veto—but not the Council, whose members could not veto legislation. Therefore, by analogy, the power of legislating out was unconstitutional because it excluded the Council.[21]

As with just about every argument in this debate, the constitution could be read from the opposite perspective. "Where is it said in the constitution, that the General Court shall not abolish a judiciary after it has once been established? . . . [O]r that the Superior Court as heretofore established, shall always be the Supreme or highest court of Judicature in the State?"[22] "The office must exist before it can be held," the Committee on Memorials explained, "and the power that creates it has a right expressly, or by implication, to annex such condition to it as shall seem proper."[23] Obviously, one condition could be that the office should no longer exist. In other words, whatever court or whatever court office the legislature created, the legislature could always destroy. This reality followed directly from the fact that Plumer and Smith had failed to have the Superior Court entrenched in the constitution of 1792.[24] Had they succeeded, the legislature could have altered a court's jurisdiction and increased the number of judges, but it could not have taken the office from a judge because each office would have been constitutional and unalterable.[25]

The ultimate constitutional conclusion was much more serious than anything Plumer and Smith had feared when they tried but failed to entrench the court in the constitution of 1792: in New Hampshire the highest court was not independent. It was, rather, a dependent institution, subject to the superintendence of the legislature. The committee of the General Court explained the sources of judicial dependency. "On examining the Constitution, we find no power is given the Judiciary to rise above the other departments of Government," the committee contended. "In the 37th article of the Bill of Rights, it is said, 'The three essential powers of Government, to wit, the Legislature, Executive, and Judicial, ought to be as separate from, and independent of, each other, as the nature of a free Government will admit.' This very expression, '*as the nature of a free Government will admit*,' pre-supposes a dependence."[26] Not only was the judiciary dependent, but the legislature was supreme.

Exercising the legislature's role as the final interpreter of the constitution, the joint committee pronounced judgment: the Judicial Act of 1813, legislating out of existence the courts of New Hampshire and with them all of the judges, "is constitutional."[27] But was the committee competent to decree that rule? Shortly after the law had been enacted, DEFENDER OF THE CONSTITUTION had concluded that it was not. A Republican writing in a Republican newspaper, he argued that "the Legislature is not the proper tribunal to decide upon the constitutionality of the act."[28] But if not the legislature, who was competent? "We say, the Judges of the Superior Court," the *New-Hampshire Patriot* answered, "but, say others, the Superior Court no longer exists."[29] The *Patriot* provided the best summary of what momentarily was the Republican theory: "That the late Superior Court, was *created* (not by the Legislature but) *by the constitution*, and therefore 'has the sole power of interpreting the laws,' and 'alone must decide the constitutionality and unconstitutionality of any act of the legislature.'"[30] This argument might have been persuasive had the court been constitutionally entrenched. It was not entrenched, however—a fact giving the Federalists solid grounds for claiming that the Superior Court was not competent to decide. "[T]hey can have no more authority to determine the question, than any other individuals in the community," A FRIEND TO JUSTICE argued. "By *sitting* therefore they determine that they *are* Judges and of course that the act is unconstitutional; and after having *prejudged* the question they proceed to consider it and to pronounce their opinion. They first *decide* and then *examine* the question."[31]

Constitutionality could not have been resolved in the political excitement of 1813. The issue was just too contentious. But repetition, even without theory, creates precedents. How can we question the constitutionality of the Judicial Act of 1813 when we know that New Hampshire courts would be legislatively abolished and reorganized five more times between 1813 and 1901, and on each occasion the power to legislate judges out of office was accepted as constitutional by both the judiciary and the public?[32] No matter how controversial, the successful exercise of authority, consistently accepted by those adversely affected by that authority, is persuasive precedent for the authority. When the highest court in the jurisdiction ruled the authority not subject to review,[33] constitutionality became conclusive.

The process may be constitutional, Plumer warned, but the costs were high. Legislating out "has a direct and powerful tendency to destroy the independence of the judiciary," he contended, for although he knew judicial independence did not exist in New Hampshire law, he, like most lawyers, continued to argue as if it did, hoping, we must imagine, to establish it by analogy to general American principles. It was an argument that newspaper readers of New Hampshire had drummed at them by constant repetition. "Without an independent Judiciary, the people have no security for property, liberty, or life itself," DEFENDER OF THE CONSTITUTION warned, for example. "[F]or, if the judiciary of a State can be thus prostrated, and Judges deprived of their seats by the strong arm of power," AN AMERICAN explained, "every thing dear and valuable we possess, depends on the *insolence* of party."[34]

The extensive newspaper debate over the constitutionality of the Judicial Act of 1813 became a great civics lesson, teaching New Hampshirites the importance of having an independent judiciary—or at least what independence could mean. Every platitude and slogan important to lawyers and constitutionalists about separate government powers and how independent judges alone had the ability and mandate to protect property, liberty, and life were repeated so often that every reader of newspapers surely understood why the better lawyers argued that their judiciary had to be free of the legislature or they, the citizens, would themselves not be free.[35] It is not farfetched to suppose that more than any others in the United States, the people of New Hampshire learned to cherish an independent judiciary—even though it was at most a theoretical constitutional ideal that they did not possess. And should they feel the loss, they were told by the Republican press who was to blame: "Who violated the Constitution of the State of New Hampshire and thereby threatened the destruction of all law and order? The *Lawyers*. Who now adheres to the courts which were created by the violation of that sacred instrument? The *Lawyers*."[36]

The lawyers might be blamed by the Republicans, but for the moment they had won. With the Judicial Act of 1813, they had legislated from office the crippled and discredited court of Arthur Livermore, Richard Evans, and Clifton Claggett. And now Governor Gilman and his Council faced a troublesome task. With every voter in the state watching and ready to criticize, they had to appoint three different judges to the new court. Their decisions were both difficult and easy. They were difficult because opposition to the new system was so widespread; it was apprehended that few potential candidates would consider appointment. Certainly no Republican lawyer could accept, and there were Federalists who were just as opposed. Moreover, anyone selected would be subject to unusual scrutiny. One of the chief arguments for passing the Judicial Act, after all, had been that the old court of Livermore, Evans, and Claggett had been so incompetent that it had to be replaced. That meant that Gilman had to find judges of a quality high enough that the public would readily see a substantial difference, and then maybe some of the criticism might subside. The selection was easy for one of the judges. There was only one man a Federalist administration could consider for chief justice. Gilman knew it. He and the Federalist majority on the Council had no choice but to appoint Jeremiah Smith. "On all sides," Smith's biographer concluded, "it was considered impossible for the new court to get under weigh, unless Mr. Smith would consent to be the chief justice."[37]

Smith knew he would be appointed chief justice, and he had to have been preparing for the day; yet when the appointment was made he gave the governor no answer. As time went on and he was not heard from, New Hampshirites were puzzled, especially those convinced that he was the author of the Judicial Bill of 1813 or that he had aided Thompson, Webster, and Mason to draft the 1812 version of the act. Smith said that he had nothing to do with either bill. That quite a few people were unwilling to believe him may explain why he tried to persuade Timothy Farrar that he had not been a party to legislating the old court out and opening a place on the new court for himself. During Smith's first year on the Superior Court, Farrar had been an associate justice and was still a close friend. If we can accept what he said to anyone, Farrar would be the man. Not only was Farrar still active in public affairs, his son was an associate of Daniel Webster and he would have known had Smith collaborated with Webster. It is unlikely that Smith would have felt he could mislead Farrar, so it is revealing that he told Farrar that not only had he done no work on the new Judicial Act, he had not wanted it enacted. "A very bold step has been taken, in which I had no agency, and as to which I was not even consulted," Smith claimed. " It is a step, too, which I should not have advised, though two things have been gained by it of great consequence, the trial of jury causes before a single judge of the supreme court, and the chance of obtaining better men than the old system was calculated to give for the common pleas bench. But the step has been taken, and if it does not succeed well, it will do an infinite deal of mischief."[38]

"To him," John Morison summarized, "it was a source of extreme perplexity and vexation. He heartily disapproved of what had been done, and yet by consenting to be placed at the head of the new judiciary, he must expect to encounter all the difficulties, and to bear all the odium connected with it." After three months had passed and he had not accepted, Republicans began to hope that he would refuse. "We have it on good authority," the *Gazette* reported, "that Judge Smith declared, while at Cambridge, that he '*very much doubted*' whether he should take a seat on the bench under the new Judiciary system." If that proved true, the new court might never meet.[39]

Smith had persuasive reasons not to accept appointment. It would, for one thing, mean a sizable cut in income. In his reestablished law practice he was making more than two times what the new chief justiceship would pay. Also, he knew that with passage of the new Judicial Act, good-behavior tenure had lost most of its security. "Good behavior" now meant, the *Patriot* warned, "only 'during the pleasure of the legislature'—during the prevalence of a faction in that legislature—nay, what is worse during the pleasure of two or three influential members of the bar." And worst of all, for him to endorse the Federalist legislation removing the judges of the Superior Court from office would make him the hypocrite for everything he had been saying about the judiciary, including publicly denying the constitutionality of legislating judges from office. He had signed a memorial to Congress, written by other of the midnight judges, claiming that the constitutional tenure protecting judges serving at good behavior from being deprived of either their offices or their compensation was "among the first and best established principles in the American constitutions," and just four years previously he had warned in his gubernatorial address against subjecting the judiciary "to the revolutions of political parties."[40]

There were, however, some fairly persuasive reasons why Smith should have accepted the chief justiceship. Except for the damage that acceptance could cause his reputation, those reasons may have appeared to him to be stronger than the arguments not to accept. Lynn Turner wrote the best summary. "It was," he contended, "because Smith was the spiritual father of the new judicial system and felt a sincere obligation to accomplish reforms for which he had striven since the day when he was a neophyte in the profession that he accepted an appointment which could only bring financial loss, merciless criticism, and an indelible blot upon his reputation for consistency."[41]

Those friends urging Smith to accept the appointment seem to have been members of the bar. Knowing the professional strength he would bring back to the court, they could discount the personal sacrifice they were asking him to make. The most notable was Jeremiah Mason, who would never have made the sacrifice himself. Telling Smith that he had to again become chief justice, he wrote from Washington where he was in the Senate and Daniel Webster was in the House of Representatives. "I am confident the success of the system will depend on you. Should you decline, I cannot see how it will get into operation," Mason argued. "[Y]ou must in my opinion accept and hold it for a time, or prepare to see disappointment and confusion ensue. . . . I will only add that Mr. Webster and others here, entirely agree with me in the wishes I have expressed on this subject." In a follow-up letter Mason added, "I see by the public papers, you have been appointed chief justice; I hope I shall soon see that you have accepted. Nothing else will put down the clamor raised against the system. Should you decline I think I see danger of confusion." Mason assured Smith that he had written these words "with the utmost sincerity." He received all the newspapers from the state and had "been informed of the feelings of the democratic party," so he knew the political venom that poured over Smith, but still he wanted his friend to accept the appointment.[42]

By the time he had received Mason's first letter, Smith had accepted appointment to a second term as chief justice. "I would hardly believe that anything could have given me so much perplexity as this," he told Mason in reply. He knew he faced much trouble and doubted he would receive the support that he needed because even legislators who had voted for the Judicial Act of 1813 now knew that it had been a mistake, or so he reported. He may have been serious about how the bill had been enacted, but it is doubtful. "I verily believe our path is beset with difficulties," Smith lamented. "[O]ur members in the legislature were chock full of courage when they were at Concord, stuffing themselves with brandy, and each other with big swelling words of their own importance. But when they got home and came to be sober, the scene was sadly changed; they were most piteously frightened. . . . I sincerely believe if they (the General Court) could get back the act, they would see the devil have it before they ever passed another such."[43]

It was legislating the Superior Court judges from office to which Smith objected and the reason that he said the legislators who had voted for it would take back the Judicial Act if they could. It was legislating from office the court with two Republican judges that ensured that Smith's second term as chief justice would be the target of constant political criticism and that, more likely than not, would doom the new Supreme Judicial Court to a very short life. Smith realized all of this. We do not know whether he suspected that the Federalist resurgence might only last the time of the war and that once peace came, New Hampshire's Republican majority could reemerge. The best guess is that he did not appreciate how precariously the Federalists held on to power. He seems to have expected that when the war ended the Federalists would remain strong enough that neither party would be in complete control of the state government, and the Federalists' Supreme Judicial Court would not be legislated out for a few years to come.

Yet, even had Smith been more politically acute and understood that his court would not survive half a decade, if that long, it might not have made a difference in his decision to accept the chief justiceship. He agreed to become again a judge not for his future employment but because of the potential of the Judicial Act of 1813. The court that the act created, introducing to New Hampshire jurisprudence single-judge trials and law terms, was the reason that he felt obliged to return to the bench. If he had his wish and served only for a year, he could still expect to demonstrate to the public that a single judge presiding at trial term was not only more efficient than multiple judges but would strengthen rather than endanger the right to trial by jury and would deliver a more consistent system of justice by ending the delays so frequently caused by the old requirement that at least two judges, and more often three, had to be present for trials to be held. If he could establish the merits of that reform, Smith would have taken a giant step toward completing the judicial program that he had been introducing into New Hampshire law during his first term on the bench. If they faced the prospect of having to preside alone over jury trials, laymen were much more likely not to seek appointment as judges. If so, and if only lawyers accepted nomination to the high court, Smith would realize one of his major objectives for changing the judiciary; the remaining challenge to creating the court system that he wanted for New Hampshire would be to find qualified lawyers willing to serve as judges.

Smith had an idea how to attract those better lawyers to the court, and that gave him another reason for accepting the chief justiceship. Economics was his motivation. Judicial salaries had to be raised—and raised substantially. He had been made more aware than ever of the sums of money that would be needed through his recent success at the bar. He had done very well since losing the governorship and being out of public office. Reopening his law practice had been a pleasant surprise. Everyone acquainted with him knew how unhappy he had been to return to his law office. He had not only told friends, he had told the general public that he did not like being a practitioner, for he found the work to be drudgery. Instead, when he hung out his shingle after losing the gubernatorial election of 1810, he discovered that practice, even the aspect he had disliked the most—having to attend court—had "not been irksome to me" and was much more lucrative than he had expected. He soon was at the head of the bar, even though practicing in the same county with Mason, Webster, and George Sullivan. But now, once the new court system was created, he explained to Farrar, "many people" told him he was indispensable for its success, that he therefore had to become chief justice of the Supreme Judicial Court, or it might not be accepted by the public, and the reforms for which he had been working would be written off as failures, perhaps not to be tried again. "If this experiment should not succeed, it will destroy all hopes of any improvement in our judicial system in our day," he warned. "Except so far as regards myself, there is doubtless weight in these observations. At the same time it is equally true that I cannot hold the office of chief justice with the salary annexed to it. I have made such arrangements on the score of expense, as forbids it."[44]

If we are willing to accept Smith's own account, he decided to become chief justice for a second term in part for reasons that had threatened to drive him out of his first term—to fight for raises in judicial compensation. But this time it would not be for the purposes that most people in the state, including many of his friends, believed. He was no longer primarily seeking to increase his own compensation. If New Hampshire ever was to persuade the better lawyers in the state to become judges, all judicial salaries had to be raised substantially. He knew that he would have better opportunities to force the issue if he was on the bench. After he had served a reasonable time, he planned to complain about his own low pay, hoping to obtain raises for all judges, even those on the Court of Common Pleas. He intended "to procure better salaries for others," hopefully high enough to "command the services of those best qualified," he informed Farrar. "It is not necessary for the state, as little for me, that I should be a judge, but it is my sincere desire that the office should be raised; because I am persuaded that the character of our judiciary will rise with it. I am willing to be thought avaricious, (which I am not,) and to be evilly spoken of, if it will conduce to this end. I know this is not the road to popularity, and I do not like it the worse on that account."[45]

Smith began his agitation for higher salaries almost immediately. He had been appointed chief justice over a week before writing Farrar and Mason that he intended to accept, but for a month after that he still had not told the governor. The *Patriot* thought it knew why. Smith, it claimed, was holding out for more money, an unbelievable sum according to the *Patriot*.

> This delay which has been protracted to a great length, begins to excite serious alarm among the knowing ones in the federal ranks. Some pretend to say that the Judge is employed in nicely calculating the relative advantages of his business at the bar, and those of the employment offered him by Governor Gilman and his Council—that in this sort of account current between possession and expectancy, the Judge declares that . . . he finds the sum of fifteen hundred dollars, with the honor of being Chief Justice which, *under existing circumstances*, he believes not worth regarding, is far from being sufficient to balance the fees and emoluments of his practice at the bar—and that if they wish to get him on the bench again, they must give him *two thousand dollars*, instead of *fifteen hundred*.[46]

The *Patriot*'s figures were wrong. The chief justice of the Superior Court, that is Livermore, had been paid $1200 a year. Anticipating Smith's acceptance, the legislature had already raised the salary to $1500, the amount that Smith had received during the final years of his first term as chief justice, and that was the sum he accepted when he took the office for a second time. It would be several months before he began writing Sullivan, Mason, and Webster, saying he was thinking of resigning because of the pay. That was how he got the issue of compensation once again into legislative debate. He enlisted some of the state's leading lawyers, who lobbied their friends in the General Court to raise the amounts.[47] The legislators did not respond as Smith had hoped they would, and one reason is that Republican members questioned the lawyers' sincerity, at least the motivations of the lawyers of Rockingham County. They certainly wanted the judicial salaries raised, Republicans suspected, but not just to ensure that Smith remained on the Supreme Judicial Court, reforming the judicial process. No, some Republicans said, lawyers were urging that the pay be increased to keep him from returning to law practice. The lawyers of New Hampshire, AN INJURED PEOPLE charged, had conspired "to evict" Smith from the bar and into the chief justiceship, "for his practice would be sufficie to make up a deficiency in the practice of a score of ordinary attornies." The lawyer most wanting Smith on the bench and not at the bar was said to be Sullivan, "who, living in the same town with Mr. Smith, and being far inferior in points of talent and capacity, soon found when Mr. Smith returned to practice, that his own business, which before had been lucrative, was diminished one half." But once Smith was elevated to the court, PHOCION added, "his extensive business falls into other hands, principally into those of Mr. Sullivan, who gains by this event at least five hundred dollars a year. . . . But Judge Smith's practice was not confined to Exeter, nor even to the County of Rockingham—it extended through the whole state—lawyers met him, to their sorrow, at every Court. The monster must be destroyed, or he would devour all before him. There was therefore a sort of general conspiracy at the bar to get rid of Smith." At least one Republican was bold enough to claim that the Judicial Act of 1813 had been passed not to rid the judiciary of an incompetent Superior Court but to rid the bar of a practitioner who was too competent. New Hampshire lawyers, A FRIEND TO TRUTH asserted, "have combined to *ridicule* and *run down all the Courts*, with the design finally to displace every republican Judge, and restore Judge Smith to the bench, who, Mammoth like, has been devouring all the fruits of the most lucrative part of the practice."[48]

All this supposition was written with a good deal of tongue in cheek and even more exaggeration; yet there is one smattering of truth lurking beneath the hype: the great success that Smith enjoyed at the bar after leaving the governorship. What indirect evidence we have indicates that in those years of practice Smith may have been the highest-paid lawyer in the state. Remember, his biographer Morison says that he was making three times at the bar what he would make as chief justice. That would have been $4500, which seems too high an estimate. But even twice the judicial salary would have been $3000. Compare that to Daniel Webster's claim that while working in Portsmouth his practice was worth nearly $2000 a year. It is evident, then, that Smith's income was certainly as high, quite likely somewhat higher than that of his most competitive rivals at the bar.[49] The Federalists could have claimed that although they exercised unprecedented power in legislating from office the three judges of the Superior Court, the people had received their money's worth with the chief justice who replaced them.

*Chapter Nine*

# Contesting Courts

Doubts concerning the wisdom, political propriety, and constitutionality of the Judicial Act of 1813 were not the only reason that Jeremiah Smith hesitated in accepting the appointment to a second term as chief justice. It was important to him to learn who his associate justices would be. He would be satisfied in one regard. One of his chief reforms was implemented. Despite the fact that Governor John Gilman would select the new justices, everyone knew that all three would be lawyers. For only the second time there would be no laymen on New Hampshire's highest court.

It is difficult to believe that Smith could have been pleased with one of his associates, Arthur Livermore. He had been chief justice of the legislated-out Superior Court, so his appointment as an associate was a demotion. At that time he was being investigated by the legislature and, of course, was still despised by a sizable portion of the bar, including leading Federalist lawyers, primarily for what Plumer described as his "passionate" and "imprudent" conduct on the bench.[1] Smith was one of the few members of the bar who got along with Livermore. One reason was that Livermore, to the best of his ability, supported much of Smith's jurisprudential program. It deserves to be especially remarked, that when he was legislated off the court for the last time in 1816, The Voice Of New-Hampshire accused Livermore of "having done all the harm in your power" when he was chief justice, "by depriving the trial by jury of its consequences in our juridical tribunals." This complaint is a bit of evidence that during the four years that Smith was off the court and Livermore was the chief justice, he had continued to implement one of Smith's most major reforms, controlling the jury, and with enough effect that he irritated Jeffersonian critics such as Voice Of New-Hampshire. He was not, however, a supporter of all that Smith sought to accomplish. When Governor Plumer had told him in 1812 that he thinking of vetoing the judiciary bill written by Thompson and Webster, Livermore did not object but, from Plumer's account, apparently encouraged him. "He said the information [i.e., education] & habits of the people were not sufficient to support such a system, & doubted if five men could be found in the State qualified to administer it as judges. We have been more in the habit of expecting justice, than quibbles & sharp points." Livermore was telling Plumer both that single-judge court terms could not succeed in New Hampshire because there were too few potential judges capable of conducting jury trials alone and also that Smith's campaign to impose stricter standards of procedure would fail in New Hampshire because people wanted the equitable "justice" of commonsense jurisprudence; they did not want the "law" of sharp-pointed quibbling over niceties of common-law process.[2]

The second associate justice was almost a complete contrast to Livermore, not only as a lawyer who defined law as Smith defined it, but as a man whom Smith respected, both professionally and personally. He was Caleb Ellis, a native of Massachusetts and graduate of Harvard College, who had opened his law office in Claremont, where, according to Plumer, he "attended to his professional business with propriety and success. At the bar he was distinguished as a reasoner, & for his faithfulness to his clients; but claimed no merits as an orator."[3] Perhaps because he was not a polished speaker, he had no "desire for appearing in public," and was elected to office only because the Federalists brought him forward as a candidate. He served one term as a state representative and one in Congress; he was twice a member of the executive council, the first time was when Smith was governor. In 1811 he was a state senator, and in 1812 he was a presidential elector, opposing Madison and the war.

In 1809 Governor Smith had wanted to appoint him to the Superior Court, but Ellis absolutely refused to serve; yet only four years later he accepted. Smith claimed that Ellis changed his mind because he considered the Judicial Act of 1813 such "a great improvement in the jurisprudence of the State." If Smith understood Ellis correctly and reported his words accurately, Ellis's change of mind deserves special attention. What he said is striking evidence of the expectations of some of the better lawyers in the state for the benefits that the law would derive from the Judicial Act of 1813. What he is saying is that he, who refused to accept a judicial appointment to the Superior Court of Judicature from Governor Jeremiah Smith, readily accepted the same appointment to serve with Chief Justice Jeremiah Smith on the Supreme Judicial Court because he expected that the changes in judicial practice mandated by the act would actually make a substantial difference.[4] It is not certain just what Ellis expected, but if we take into account the efforts that he, as a judge, would make to assist Smith, it is a safe guess that he anticipated that the introduction of single-judge trial terms would expedite New Hampshire justice and advance the pace at which common-law pleadings were introduced.

Ellis would become Smith's most cherished associate, and it cannot be wondered why. Governor Charles H. Bell reported that the "only criticism made upon his intellectual methods was that he was perhaps sometimes too refined and subtle in his distinctions to be easily understood by a jury," which meant that he approached the law as Smith did, as precedents, principles, and process, not as general questions submitted to jurors who then, in reply to the court, told the judge the legal rules, definitions, and policy deciding the outcome of the case at bar. Of the lawyers who served on New Hampshire's highest court before 1816, it can be argued that, aside from Smith and Samuel Livermore, Ellis was the most admired. "He was," the *Farmer's Cabinet* summarized, "learned, candid, patient, firm, and of the most unsuspected integrity and uprightness." Just about the only observer to speak less of him was Plumer. "Caleb Ellis," he noted when hearing of his appointment, "is a man of talents, of a fair moral character, but rather of an arbitrary despotic temper & disposition, is a decent lawyer, but not well acquainted with men & manners, & is more inclined to be governed by metaphysical subtleties than plain common sense."[5] That appraisal is another indication of how much Plumer's rhetoric, if not his jurisprudence, was changing. Five years earlier he would not have accorded to common sense a higher status than metaphysical subtleties.

The education of the people of New Hampshire on the meaning of an independent judiciary did not end with the passage of the Judicial Act of 1813. At the time when Smith, Livermore, and Ellis were preparing for the opening sessions of the new court, ordinary citizens became unusually active politically. Spurred on by Republican anger over the Judicial Act, they were urged to write protests to newspapers against the new judiciary and, in town meetings, to vote petitions to the legislature demanding repeal of the Act. That a majority of the electorate in town after town, including, it seems likely, most lawyers in the state, believed the new court unconstitutional raised some very serious questions that were never answered. What if Smith and his colleagues tried a defendant for murder and the verdict was guilty, A FARMER asked? "Should such a court take the life of any person, although the guilt be *clearly* proved. Let me make the solemn inquiry, would it not be *murder*?" DEFENDER OF THE CONSTITUTION warned that lawyers "who believe the act unconstitutional, having sworn to support the constitution, will violate their oath by practicing in the new court." "Will you presume," the *New Hampshire Gazette* enquired of the three judges, to act "upon the property, character, and lives of your fellow citizens? Will such conduct in fact be any thing short of public robbery of our estates, and lawless violence towards liberty and life?" On the day the court was scheduled to open its first term in Portsmouth, the *Gazette*, quoting from the state constitution, urged the judges to ask themselves "whether they derive the tenure of their offices from the constitution, whether they are 'as *impartial* as the lot of humanity will admit,' whether they are as 'independent of the legislature as the nature of a free government will admit' or whether they are not wholly dependent upon the will & caprice of a legislative majority—whether if the act which gave them a Judicial existence, is constitutional they have any more authority to take away the property of their fellow citizens than any other three individuals, who would assume the name of Judges and pretend to hold a court?"[6]

The Judicial Act of 1813, the *Farmer's Cabinet* suggested, "seems to have awakened the sensibilities of every class of people throughout the state." There were even addresses to sheriffs urging them "to refuse obedience to the commands of the newly-created Courts." Before the year was ended, the two houses of the General Court were awash with memorials demanding the repeal of the Judicial Act. The custom of the lower house was to read petitions aloud. At the November 1813 session there were so many memorials opposing the new judiciary that the member from Peterborough became angry, declaring "they were not worthy the attention of the Legislature—that the memorialists were the very scum and dregs of society—that they were ignorant as the Hottentots or Chinese Tartars!" By the following session, June 1814, there were simply too many to be read. When a member presented a petition from Goffstown, praying repeal of the Judicial Act, the House "voted it should not be read." The presenter protested that there were more petitions yet to be received "from various parts of the state." The House then voted "that no more remonstrances against that act should be presented this session." The Republicans, of course, protested, but the gag order stood.[7]

The House of Representatives alone received so many petitions that it appointed a "Committee to Consider Memorials for Repeal of the Judiciary Act of 1813." Controlled by Federalists, the committee members displayed the political arrogance toward public opinion then characteristic of the New Hampshire Federal party and which would help bring about its downfall. Dismissive of the petitions as a whole, members of the committee even questioned the sincerity of the memorialists' constitutional contentions, treating their arguments as political rhetoric rather than as sincere statements of principles or of legal theory. Summing up the petitioners' central theme, the committee reported that the "minds" of individual citizens were "represented as agitated in the highest degree, with fear of losing their liberty and property, and all that is dear because the Legislature undertook to revise and alter the Judicial establishment of the State."[8]

The Federalist committee members would have served their cause far better had they shown some respect for the petitioners: certainly they should have given thought to answering the one major legal argument running through all the memorials. The Judicial Act of 1813, the argument contended, was unconstitutional because "it removes from office Judges appointed to hold their offices during good behavior; and thereby making them dependent on the Legislature." In the process of drafting these petitions, the ordinary voters of the town meetings, who had no education in law or government, not only learned and relearned constitutional principles, but their constitutional perspective was extended to embrace values they probably had not understood before or at least had never previously articulated. The Portsmouth memorial may have been an exception. Signed by John Langdon and other leading Republicans, it was probably drafted by lawyers, or certainly college graduates, yet even so, its substance was not much different from the memorials sent from further inland by small farming communities. "For a great portion of the blessings we enjoy we have been indebted to our Courts of Justice," it contended. "Our lives, liberties, property and character have hitherto been protected, and secure against lawless or arbitrary power." Obviously, these Republicans were drawing more from common-law or Hamiltonian values than from Jeffersonian jurisprudence.[9]

The memorial of the small town of Chester went further than Portsmouth's in the direction of receptionist or common-law legal theory. Not only espousing the principle that the judiciary should serve as a check on the legislature through judicial review, as Portsmouth's did, the Chester petition anticipated the doctrine, still emerging in New Hampshire, that the constitution was the supreme legal authority even over the collective will of the people, which was then the ultimate authority in republicanist legal theory. "The Constitution makes the Judiciary a check upon the Legislature," the Chester town meeting contended, "by investing it with the power to declare legislative acts invalid, when repugnant to the Constitution, the supreme, irrepealable, and controlling statute, enacted by the people. This is a check indisputably necessary to the security of the rights of the people: without it, the Constitution would be a mere dead letter, subordinate to the will of a Legislative majority who would be above all control, a despotism itself." Almost as if to round out the theoretical circle and outdo the Chester Memorial in reversed arguments, the Federalist majority of the Committee on Memorials reported that the General Court had to have power to legislate judges from office or it would not be able to check the pretensions of the judiciary to declare statutes and other legislative actions unconstitutional.[10]

The memorials against the Judicial Act of 1813 may have been partisan, and some of the petitions may have been drafted by Republican politicians to make political points, not to argue legal merits, but even so, they damaged the effectiveness of the new Supreme Judicial Court. They were popularly voted in town meetings and mustered the weight of public opinion against Smith and his two colleagues. Every person voting for their passage, and every town leader signing them, was saying that the new court was unconstitutional. Even zealous Federalists seem to have been wondering whether the Judicial Act of 1813 had gone too far. "In organizing this new system the Governor & Council have felt much anxiety & fear," Plumer suspected. "The further they progress the more they feel it is the creature of party, & the more they apprehend it will put them down." Writing as CATO for the *Patriot*, he warned the judges that they stood on shaky constitutional grounds. "Your system is the creature of party," he scolded. "Republicans can repose no confidence in such judges. Their independence is at an end. They no longer hold their offices by *the tenure of good behavior*; but by the pleasure of a *dominant faction*." The legitimacy of the court could hardly have been weaker even though, as Turner observed, "[n]o one could deny that the new judiciary was infinitely superior in ability to the old—even the raging *Patriot* printed the argument that good judges could not compensate for unconstitutional appointments."[11] In truth, no one could deny that it was the most competent court in the history of New Hampshire. But to much of the population that fact was irrelevant.

The court may have been New Hampshire's best, but it was not helped by the fact that Arthur Livermore was one of the members. It was universally perceived that his status had been diminished by surrendering the chief justiceship to Smith and becoming again an associate justice. Worst, some of the finest lawyers in the state, including Jeremiah Mason and Daniel Webster, were upset that he had been reappointed; they continued to want him off the bench. With his usual cynicism Plumer thought he knew why Livermore had been reappointed. "He is not popular with many of the leading federalists," he explained, "but they had apprehensions that if he was not appointed, he with Evans & Clagget[t], would hold terms of the superior court under the old law & declare the new one unconstitutional."[12]

We cannot be certain, but there may be something to what Plumer said.

The Federalists could not know whether Evans and Claggett would actually go to the shire towns and oppose the new Supreme Judicial Court at the scheduled trial terms. But they surely thought that, if the two judges planned to challenge the new court, they needed the assistance of Livermore if they hoped to make their opposition effective. It is even conceivable that some Federalists had urged the governor to appoint Livermore to the new Supreme Judicial Court at least in part to divide the old Superior Court and prevent him from meeting with his former colleagues, Evans and Claggett. If so, Governor Gilman and his Council were surely disappointed. Livermore did not exactly join his former colleagues on the old bench. In fact, he was careful to avoid sitting with them. But he still did what Plumer implied that the governor and Council had hoped to prevent. He publicly agreed with their legal argument that the act legislating them from office was unconstitutional.

Judges Evans and Claggett did not need Livermore's active participation in order to mount a campaign against the new court. Despite what most lawyers thought of their legal talents, they claimed that they knew the law and, as they had neither been impeached nor addressed from office, they were still, along with Livermore, New Hampshire's only high-court justices. Passage of the Judicial Act of 1813 had had no effect on the validity of their commissions. "I consider the law in question unconstitutional, and an outrage upon the good sense and essential rights of the people," Evans wrote to a Federalist newspaper. His court, the Superior Court of Judicature, he explained, was "RECOGNIZED" in the state constitution, and that fact meant that the constitution "gives to the Superior Court an authority not within the control of any other department of the government."[13] Claggett agreed. Quoting several clauses in the New Hampshire bill of rights and the constitution, he asked, "[C]an this Court, thus *established by the Constitution*, be abolished?" The Superior Court, he asserted, had "a *constitutional*" jurisdiction. To be precise, both Evans and Claggett were contending that because their old Superior Court had the same name as a high court mentioned in the constitution, it was constitutionally entrenched. They argued, that is, as if Plumer and Smith, at the constitutional convention of 1791–1792, had not failed but had succeeded in constitutionally entrenching the state's high court. "I now respectfully ask," Claggett concluded, "by what authority can the Legislature abolish the Court?" When it passed the Judicial Act of 1813, the General Court attempted to exercise "unlimited power," not constitutional power.[14]

When Federalists charged that Evans and Claggett claimed they still were judges not for reasons of constitutional principle but in hopes of keeping their salaries, the *Patriot* replied that Evans and Claggett "saw the unconstitutionality of the late act, and they were bound by their oaths to perform a duty as well to the people as to themselves." It was a contentious suggestion, but it was not unique. Other Republicans urged the judges to defy the "unconstitutional" Judicial Act of 1813 and to conduct court proceedings as if the tribunal of Smith, Livermore, and Ellis did not exist. It was, in fact, their duty, DEFENDER OF THE CONSTITUTION argued, "without regarding the said act," for them "to proceed in the ordinary and usual mode of administering justice."[15]

The Judicial Act of 1813 did not change the time and places of holding most court sessions. The new Supreme Judicial Court was scheduled to meet in Strafford County, for instance, on the same day and hour when the old Superior Court would have met. The first term of the new court was to be holden at Dover, the shire town of Strafford County, on the morning of 7 September. Smith apparently hoped to use the session to demonstrate to the public how sufficiently and swiftly the new system of single-judge trials would operate, for he assigned only one judge to attend. Ellis had had no experience as yet conducting trials and could not be expected to try cases with the dispatch that Smith wanted. Livermore, by contrast, had been on the bench longer than any other high-court judge then living and had tried many more cases than anyone else, including Smith. So he was the judge sent to Dover to prove the value of the new judicial system. Quite likely, before the first week had ended, Smith wished he had gone himself.

Judge Livermore arrived in Dover on the morning he was scheduled to open the new Supreme Judicial Court. There he found his associates from the old Superior Court of Judicature, Evans and Claggett, waiting for him. They told him that they three were the only legally appointed high-court justices in New Hampshire, that he was the state's only chief justice, and that they intended to hold trials in the courthouse as required by the earlier judiciary act, the only valid judicial legislation and the statute under which they had been commissioned. Again, Livermore's reaction surprised most citizens who knew him. Although Evans and Claggett were informing Livermore that they were planning to take the courthouse from him that morning, he did not react in his usual manner. He may have argued with them, but he did not become angry. Rather, he explained, "I treated them with the respect due to gentlemen and with the kindness due the unfortunate."[16]

Some Republican newspapers reported that Livermore went to the courthouse with Evans and Claggett and "took his seat on the bench with the two old Justices," staying at least long enough to tell those assembled outside the bar that the Judicial Act of 1813 was "unconstitutional." Livermore denied going to the courthouse or speaking there that morning.

Both during that very week, and many years later, he insisted that he had never sat with Evans and Claggett. "When the court hour approached, Judges Claggett and Evans took up their line of march towards the court-house enveloped in a dense concourse of people," while he instead went to Dover's meetinghouse, where he had all along intended to hold his court. Smith's biographer understood that when Livermore found the two judges determined to convene their session in the county courthouse, "he compromised the matter by agreeing that they should have the court-house in the forenoon, and he in the afternoon." Livermore also denied that. "I made no compromise, no agreement of any kind whatever, with these honorable judges," he insisted. The fact that, even before arriving in town, he had apparently made arrangements to use the meetinghouse, or what today would be called Dover's Congregational church, indicates that some agreement had been reached, but it may be that Livermore simply told Evans and Claggett that they could have the courthouse, that he would not confront them, and that he was going to use the meetinghouse.

After watching the two judges and the "dense concourse of people" depart for the courthouse, Livermore, "unattended by any person except Sheriff Barker," went to the meetinghouse. Once there, he apparently waited and what occurred set the pattern for the future. The clerk of court seems to have been at the courthouse when Evans and Claggett arrived. On learning the situation, he gathered his documents and went to the meetinghouse. So, too, did all the lawyers in town and the grand jurors. Evans and Claggett were left with a small audience of supporters but no means of carrying on judicial business. They appointed a clerk; Evans delivered a long address, condemning the Judicial Act of 1813 as unconstitutional and inoperative; and then they adjourned until the next morning. Some accounts say that they spent the remainder of the week trying to convene a court. A more reliable witness, Livermore, said that they left Dover that afternoon and that he was able to preside at the courthouse that afternoon and for the remaining days of the two-week term.[17]

Livermore had acted with unaccustomed restraint, handling Evans and Claggett with a surprising tact that surely puzzled his critics and must have pleased his friends, especially Chief Justice Smith. If we consider only the publicity he received, it could well have been his most successful half day as a judge, but as was so usual with him, the remainder of the day was spoiled for Livermore by his own impulsiveness. That afternoon he reconvened his adjourned session at the courthouse where the main order of business was charging the grand jury. He could have done so without difficulty as he had addressed grand juries ever since Smith had appointed him chief justice three years before. His charges had been neither controversial nor notable, attracting slight attention from the press. On this occasion, however, some impulsion led him to give his opinion on the Judicial Act of 1813. The charge became extremely contentious. Just what he said was disputed, but the version the public first read was from Republican newspapers, and unfortunately for Livermore, although his argument may have been surprising to some, the belligerence and impassioned tone that was reported was exactly what many people expected from him. "He assailed the act with the utmost virulence and denounced it as a work of a dominant faction in the legislature," the *New Hampshire Gazette* reported. "He declared that the leaders of that faction had perjured themselves—that the act was altogether unconstitutional—that it was a base, insidious, dastardly attack on the independence of the Judiciary—that its creators did not dare attack the judges in an open manly manner—that the act did not remove the judges—that the judges were not removable except by impeachment or by address upon good reasons—that they still hold their offices under the constitution, and, to remove them by mere [legislative] act, would be as unjust and unconstitutional as by a similar act to take away their estates, confiscate their property, and proscribe their persons." It must be reemphasized that this account is from the Republican press. According to that same source, Livermore concluded by observing that, if the legislature really had intended to introduce judicial reforms, those reforms could have been written into the old statutes as amendments but were not because "the only object of the framers of the act was *to remove the judges.*"[18]

This charge to the Strafford grand jury was another extraordinary occurrence in Arthur Livermore's judicial career. Once again Livermore was at the center of events and almost immediately was under legislative investigation. The "*harangue*," the *Portsmouth Oracle*, a Federalist newspaper, complained, "has no *precedent* in the whole *history of our jurisprudence* and seemed extraordinary and unwarrantable for the occasion on which they [*sic*] were delivered and under circumstances of such peculiar delicacy." FAIR PLAY was puzzled. "What object can such an official public declaration be intended to effect?" he asked the *Oracle*. "What else is it but to destroy the credit and authority of the existing Courts altogether? And what purpose can it subserve unless it be that of a resort to open violence by the people against the execution of the law?" The *Farmer's Cabinet* also questioned whether doubts about the legality and purpose of the Judicial Act belonged in a grand-jury charge. "[W]hat business had he *there*, in his official capacity, *to say any thing* about it, without it legally before him? If he thought the new law 'unconstitutional, arbitrary,' and 'in his conscience wrong,' how *in his conscience* accept his new office, and become the *willing instrument of error?*"[19]

As a judge, Livermore had been investigated by the two houses of the legislature several times before and now again had to explain himself to both the legislators and to the general public.[20] This time was particularly difficult, not only because he had to justify why he had spoken at all, but as he struggled with his explanation, it became quite evident that he was not sure just what he had meant.[21]

"Having been turned out of office with others by a legislative act, and having accepted a new appointment in the Judiciary," he told the lawmakers, "I thought it my duty to all present and future Judicial officers, and to the public, to protest our removal in the way and manner in which it has been effected, lest by my silence I might seem to approve of what in my conscience I think wrong. To deprive Judges of their authority and salaries by a legislative act, or by any direct or indirect means other than impeachment or address upon a full and fair hearing of them by themselves or friends, is, in my opinion arbitrary and unconstitutional." Apparently, what Livermore had intended was to raise questions about the legislature's policy of unrestricted supervision of the judiciary. But in his explanation he was careful that his criticisms of the General Court did not go that far. The only unconstitutional action effected by the Judicial Act of 1813, he now said, had been legislating himself, Evans, and Claggett out of office. "I have ever thought that I said the law in question in every other respect constitutional."[22]

There were New Hampshire people who claimed not to understand what Livermore meant when he asserted that it had been "unconstitutional" to legislate the old court out of office. Why then did he consider Evans, Claggett, and himself legally removed from office, Junius wondered? "If the act be unconstitutional, it can have no binding force, inasmuch as the Constitution is the law of the land, and renders inoperative and void in a legal sense, every act of either department of the government, militating with its provisions." Livermore's argument "that he was removed by a legislative act," Junius concluded, "appears too much like an excuse for having accepted an *un*-constitutional appointment."[23]

Junius did not understand Livermore because they were applying different meanings of "unconstitutional." Junius's was a newer definition, the American understanding that the word "unconstitutional" also meant illegal and void. Livermore's definition was older, similar to the meaning of "unconstitutional" in today's Canadian law or what in Britain during the eighteenth century was referred to as an "act of power" rather than an "act of right." An act of power was contrary to custom, to precedent, and to the established, traditional ways of doing things and often unconstitutional, but if enacted by the two houses of Parliament, it was just as legal as an act of right that conformed to custom, to precedent, and to the established, traditional ways of doing things. Livermore drew this distinction in a letter "To the Editor of any Newspaper in the State of New-Hampshire." "In mentioning the consequences that I thought would flow from an admission of the principle that Judicial officers are removable by Legislative act," he explained, "I speak of what a dominant faction may do," that is, the majority of legislators. "In saying that the new Judicial Act violates the Constitution, which the framers of that act had solemnly sworn to support, I mean no more than that the Act is unconstitutional."[24] It was unconstitutional to legislate from office Evans, Claggett, and himself, but they were legally removed because the statute legislating them from office was enacted by the General Court and signed by the governor. It may be thought that JUNIUS's definition was the correct one, for, after all, it is the definition of the future. But considering the General Court's exercise of legislative supremacy over the judiciary, its assertion that it, not the judges, was the final arbiter of the constitution, and the fact that in less than five years New Hampshire's highest court would rule that the law-of-the-land clause in the state bill of rights meant whatever the legislature said it did, Livermore's definition was better New Hampshire law than that of JUNIUS.[25]

It may be wondered whether Livermore himself knew what he meant. "[W]e believe no one knows what he did say or mean," the *Farmer's Cabinet* said of the grand-jury charge, "and, indeed, the Judge himself appears not to know; for he now says, 'I had not idea,' nor 'did I *intend* to say,' 'I mean no more,' 'I might seem,' 'I thought,' and 'I ever thought I said,' &c. &c. It appears whatever he *did* say, does not amount to much."[26] Once more Livermore was damaged by his own words. He was not even credited for having had the gumption to tell the public what he believed: that it had been unconstitutional for the Judicial Act of 1813 to legislate from office the judges of the Superior Court. Jeremiah Smith, by contrast, never stated publicly whether he believed the Judicial Act was constitutional.

Such a careless address may seem unimportant today, but at the time Daniel Webster thought it yet another serious harm done to the Federalist judiciary and to Chief Justice Smith's program of judicial reforms. He had attended that first session of the Supreme Judicial Court at Dover and had heard Livermore. "We had a very strange speech here," he wrote a fellow member of the bar who practiced in Grafton County. "It did a great deal of hurt, and we shall long have reason to regret that the power of making it existed." He was regretting that Livermore had been reappointed to the bench and as a result had "power" to address the grand jury. "It is not however what will ensue at Exeter," he assured his colleague. "We expect the Ch. J. will open the court there."[27]

Webster was right. Smith would have to preside at the second session of the Supreme Judicial Court, although because it was held at Exeter, the town where he lived, he probably had been planning to preside no matter how Livermore's session at Dover had gone. Evans and Claggett, apparently deferring to Livermore, their former chief, seem to have left Dover after conducting their token morning session, although most newspaper accounts reported that they remained for the first week, taking over the courthouse every morning and relinquishing it to Livermore in the afternoons. Now that they realized that Livermore would not join them, however, they had resolved to convene the old Superior Court whenever and wherever it had been scheduled to meet and to remain in the courtroom for the full two-week session. They were not acting alone but had much encouragement from other Republicans. Stephen Peabody, who had been admitted to practice two years before and whom Evans and Claggett had appointed their clerk of court, made an effort to round up support. He instructed Plumer, for example, "to take charge of the *venires* of Epping," where Plumer lived, to make sure "they may go to the old Court," rather than to Nathaniel Adams, the previously appointed clerk of court, who, at Dover, had elected to serve the new Supreme Judicial Court, rather than follow Evans and Claggett. It was expected that Federalist lawyers would converge on Exeter for the court's opening, and Peabody wanted Plumer there to oppose them. "You are requested to attend early on the first day," he wrote. It may be that both sides tried to obtain active supporters. Claggett's son wrote Levi Woodbury to come down from Francestown with as many "Republican lawyers" as possible. "So far our victory is complete at Dover and there is a good chance of nullifying the new court at Exeter since the sheriff is with us."[28]

Support from the sheriff was very important. Should confrontation, even violence, occur between their supporters, the two rival sets of judges would find themselves in a difficult situation. Each court depended on the Rockingham County sheriff to maintain order, and if there were conflicts between them, the sheriff could not be neutral. If the two courts issued him conflicting orders, he could obey only one. The situation left him no choice but to regard the "other" court as illegal. "What will you do?" JUSTICE asked the sheriffs of New Hampshire, and he answered the question himself by giving all the sheriffs the most inane advice of the entire affair. "Gentlemen," he wrote, "there is no other way, than for you to examine the constitution and determine for yourselves." A FRIEND TO JUSTICE disagreed. He did not think the sheriffs had to decide for themselves. They should listen to the advice they were getting from all over the state, telling them that they would "be guilty of *perjury*, if they should aid in carrying out the Judicial Act into operation; because the act, as these advisors say, is unconstitutional." If Smith's court was unconstitutional, he had no authority to order the sheriffs to do anything, VOICE OF THE PEOPLE pointed out. "We ask you Gentlemen, at least to *suspend serving or executing* any precept from an *unlawful* or *void* authority," until they had instructions from Evans and Claggett.[29]

Although their legal position was not as threatened as that of the sheriffs' could be, there were questions confronting the lawyers appearing in the Exeter courthouse that might be difficult to resolve. None of them were so certain about the law as to know "what court to prosecute their suits in." A wrong guess could be embarrassing for their professional standing and costly to their clients.[30]

Smith was joined at Exeter by his new colleague Caleb Ellis. Livermore did not attend. The two judges had been told by the sheriff that he would not obey them. He would, he said, follow the orders of Evans and Claggett. Soon after Smith and Ellis had entered the courthouse and had taken their seats on the bench, Evans and Claggett came in and, carrying out their resolve to occupy the courtroom, seated themselves beside Smith and Ellis, one on the right, the other on the left. Thus began what was almost a comedy of court proceedings, two tribunals, two sets of judges, both occupying the same bench, attempting to function at the same time, in conflict one with the other. The judiciary of New Hampshire had descended to depths unprecedented in American law. Smith, paying Evans and Claggett no heed, directed the crier to open the Supreme Judicial Court, which the crier did. Evans then directed Sheriff Josiah Butler to open the Superior Court of Judicature, which he did. Smith then ordered the grand jury sworn. Clerk-of-Court Adams administered the oath as Smith directed. Smith then prepared to address the grand jury, but before he could begin, Evans ordered his clerk, Peabody, to repeat the oath, saying that the oath Adams had administered was unauthorized and illegal. Peabody started to repeat the oath when Smith forced the first confrontation between the two sets of judges, probably feeling that he had been compelled to by Evans's claim that the first oath was illegal. He announced that a second swearing should not be tolerated. In what was the decisive moment of that session, all the jurors—Republicans and not just Federalists—refused to stand and raise their arms. Evans again ordered them to be sworn but no juror obeyed. It was then evident that the court of Smith and Ellis would prevail. Smith announced that it would be best to adjourn for a short break, and the two-court session was temporarily concluded.[31]

There is conflicting evidence about when Smith charged the grand jury. Most sources say that he delivered the charge that morning, that the adjournment he called had been to allow him time to consult with Mason, Sullivan, and Webster, who were seated within the bar and who advised him not to adjourn for the morning but to reconvene and address the grand jury as scheduled. They and other lawyers who were present then advised the jurors to ignore Peabody if he tried again to swear them, and that apparently caused Evans to be quiet momentarily. Smith not only was able to deliver his charge, but before breaking for the noon dinner, he called up some entries that had been left over from the docket of the old Superior Court.[32]

Whether Smith spoke to the grand jurors that morning or waited until the afternoon, as a few of our sources report, two facts are clear. One is that the grand jurors refused even to stand for Evans and were advised not to put up their hands by all the attending lawyers, most notably by Mason, Sullivan, and Webster. The second is that after Smith delivered his charge, he and Ellis remained seated on the bench while Evans addressed the jury, telling them that the only constitutional court was his and Claggett's. There is no reason to believe that his constitutional theory as to why he and Claggett were the legal judges was any more sound than his explanation of the legal status enjoyed by Smith and Ellis. "We acknowledge that these men are judges by *appointment*," he said of Smith and Ellis, "but not Judges of the Superior Court of Judicature, nor of the Supreme Judicial Court. . . . To *us* they may have an inferior jurisdiction; with *this* Court they have nothing to do." When Evans finished, Claggett arose and, uninterrupted by Smith, said that he agreed with everything Evans had said.[33]

As far as can be determined from available evidence, Evans and Claggett received no support from members of the bar or from any court officials except for the sheriff of Rockingham, Josiah Butler, and his deputy. Before adjourning for the noon recess, Smith asked the sheriff to furnish a bailiff to attend the jurors and to provide a place to keep prisoners waiting to be tried for crimes. Indicating that he adopted Evans's unprecedented constitutional theory of two legitimate sets of judges, with Smith's Supreme Judicial Court an inferior tribunal to the Superior Court, Butler replied that he "could not obey the orders of the said Supreme Judicial Court, when sitting at the same time and place with the Superior Court, or when their orders counteracted the commands of the Superior Court; but would furnish officers to attend said Supreme Judicial Court at any other time or place, and obey the precepts thereof, not inconsistent with the precepts of the Superior Court—that, possibly, the Supreme Judicial Court, *so called* might have some *inferior* jurisdiction, but that the Superior Court was the *constitutional* court, *exercising the highest jurisdiction*."[34] There was really nothing Smith could do. Sheriffs were, like most officials in New

Hampshire, appointed by the governor and Council, and a chief justice did not have authority to appoint a substitute sheriff.

The spectators who had crowded into the Exeter courthouse could have expected that Evans and Claggett had suffered enough humiliation and that they would relinquish possession of the courtroom as they had in Dover. Instead, the two not only returned that afternoon, they even obtained the upper hand, at least momentarily. When the two courts had recessed for the morning, the Superior Court judges had set their time to reconvene before the Supreme Judicial Court was scheduled to come back. Evans and Claggett, therefore, were seated first. When Smith arrived, he found them on the bench in the center seats, Evans already well into a speech of an hour and a half, again explaining why the new court was unconstitutional. At this point Smith demonstrated one of the most judicious traits of his character—his readiness to accept public insults rather than insisting on rights that need not be enforced. Seeing the bench occupied "and having already been assured by the Sheriff, that he would not obey their orders," but would serve only Evans and Claggett, Smith and Ellis avoided a confrontation and went to the Council Chamber in the same building "and there held their court."[35] Of course, Smith wanted to avoid trouble with the rival judges, if possible, but he also had a practical reason for retreating. He really did not have a choice after the sheriff had told him he would provide the "inferior" court support only if it met at "any other time or place" than where the Superior Court was sitting. He and Ellis needed at least one bailiff and also a guard if there were any criminals who were apt to decamp or to cause a rumpus. The Supreme Judicial Court had to convene somewhere besides the Exeter courtroom. So Smith and Ellis left those chambers and convened in the Council Chamber. With them went not only the lawyers and most of the audience but also the sheriff's deputy, who had been instructed to obey Smith's requests.

The Council Chamber must have been sizable, for much of the public and almost every member of the bar sought audience at the Supreme Judicial Court. Only one lawyer did business in the Superior Court. The Federalist *Portsmouth Oracle* dismissed him as "some little attorney, or would-be attorney," and in truth his attendance added no prestige to the court's status, for he was Claggett's son, William. He filed some actions having no legal substance; their main purpose was to give the court the appearance of business, and of course, his motions and filings were never litigated. The *Oracle* said that Evans and Claggett "did not dare grant judgment and issue process," but a better explanation is that there was no way for them to even begin to try an action. All the jurors were at the other court, and there was no opposing counsel present to represent the defendant's side.[36]

Smith and Ellis, by contrast, had everyone of any consequence in attendance except for Sheriff Butler. And most important of all, they had the Superior Court's docket. They spent the afternoon calling actions from entries filed at former sessions, and there were many of these since the court of Livermore, Evans, and Claggett had failed to convene several terms of the Rockingham County court, especially during the period of Evans's protracted sickness. Ironically, Evans was plaintiff in one of these suits, in which he was seeking "judgments to a very considerable amount." The Federalists said the case showed that he acknowledged "the authority of the same Court which he declares is no Court and whose proceedings he endeavours so indelicately and illegally to embarrass."[37] But in fact the action was an old entry, held over from prior terms, and Smith, finding it on the docket, possibly saw a chance to embarrass Evans by calling it up. More likely he thought it one more action that had to be disposed of.

Evans and Claggett did not have any business to conduct, but attended by the sheriff, they kept opening their court every morning and afternoon that the Supreme Judicial Court remained in session at Exeter. Although the fact is not certain, it appears that Smith and the members of the bar were content to allow them the courtroom while they held trials in the Council Chamber. When Smith and Ellis left Exeter for Amherst, where during the first week of October, they opened the fall term of their court for Hillsborough County, Evans and Claggett went there too. The sheriff of Hillsborough, Benjamin Pierce, was a Republican, and realizing that the rival tribunal would again preempt the courthouse, Smith arranged to use the schoolhouse, most likely a one-room building. Arriving at the courthouse, Smith found that he was correct: Evans and Claggett had taken over the courtroom, and "to prevent collision" he went to the school. The sheriff opened the Superior Court and did not attend the Supreme Judicial Court, but like Rockingham's sheriff at Exeter, he did for Smith and Ellis whatever he could as long as he did not have to cooperate in person and was able to serve Evans and Claggett. He "sent his deputies to open the court, and execute the orders thereof."[38]

Even more than at Dover and Exeter, the events at Amherst were reported along partisan lines by New Hampshire newspapers. The Republican printers gave a remarkably different account from that given by the Federalists. "[T]he [Superior] Court attended by the sheriff and some deputies entered the court-house, accompanied by a vast concourse of citizens," the *New Hampshire Gazette* reported. "The bar was occupied, or rather thronged with Lawyers." The local Amherst paper told a very different story. Evans and Claggett, aided by the sheriff and well attended by people, did open court, but then "[t]he crier of the new Court came into the court-house and notified all persons having business with the Supreme Judicial Court to attend in the school-house; when the people principally withdrew, and the bar and the [court] house were nearly deserted. . . . A few individuals remained, curious to view and witness the novel scene of a *court* without juries, business or power."[39]

The Evans-Claggett court had no jurors because their former clerk was still with Smith. There was only one clerk for the court statewide—not a different clerk for each county, as there would be in later years—and the jury venires were returned to Nathaniel Adams, the previously appointed clerk, apparently even by Sheriff Pierce in Hillsborough County for, as at Exeter, all jurors attended Smith's court. It must be supposed that the county courtroom was an empty place, with no jurors, no lawyers, and no business, but the Republican newspapers sought to make it appear that the court was busy. Evans and Claggett, the *Gazette* reported, not only had Sheriff Pierce to open their session, but the Amherst minister officiated as chaplain, assisted by a clergyman from Milford. The two judges then found a way to fill the day. "[T]he Hon. Judge Clag[g]ett delivered his opinion upon the late Judiciary act in a very handsome manner; an opinion that evinced both the lawyer and the scholar," the *Gazette* bragged. "In the afternoon we were gratified with the opinion of his hon. Judge Evans in a style both solemn and impressive."[40] It was only by reading between the lines and considering what was not said that readers of the *Gazette* could realize that the court had no judicial business.

Unless people read the Republican newspapers carefully, they could have received the impression that the Evans-Claggett court did substantial business. On one day of the session, it was reported, the court heard some actions. "A motion to supersede an execution issued from the Supreme Judicial Court (so called) was made, heard, and disposed of."[41] That motion, however, seems to have been the only action the court heard while at Amherst, and it was filed by William Claggett, "son of the Judge." Because he had refused to appear before Smith and Ellis at the Rockingham County term at Exeter, he told the court, "an action against his client, had been defaulted in the Supreme Judicial Court." He was saying that at the Exeter term Smith and Ellis had proceeded as everyone had expected them to, that is, as if the Superior Court no longer existed in law. When the younger Claggett did not file an appearance and did not answer when his case was called, Smith defaulted his client and issued judgment against him. At Amherst, in his father's court, Claggett moved "for a certiorari or supersedeas to issue to stop the proceedings."[42] He was asking Evans and his father to assert the supremacy of the Superior Court and overrule Smith. They refused, or more likely, they did not dare to act. Rather, they continued the motion nisi, ruling that they needed more evidence. The *Gazette* implied to its readers that substantial legal issues were being adjudicated. "Had the evidence been at hand," it claimed, "the motion would have been granted immediately, and a true test applied, to convince the public, which Court was the highest Tribunal." The *Gazette* professed to believe that Evans and Claggett were ready, willing, and bold enough to go that far. "This test *will be applied* and that soon, not only in one case, but probably in most, if not all the cases, that have been decided by the new Court." That statement, we must assume, was intended to put on notice litigants filing actions with Smith's Supreme Judicial Court. If they won judgments and executed them, and later the Supreme Judicial Court was ruled by the legislature to have been unconstitutional, they evidently would have to repay any money they received.[43] The warning seems to have had no effect. There is no evidence that anyone but Claggett's son hesitated to file actions in the new court. What the *Gazette* called "the test" was never applied.

Evans and Claggett could have easily applied "the test" had they dared and had there been lawyers—Republican lawyers with Republican clients—willing to appeal to them. The Supreme Judicial Court had been handing down numerous judgments that could have been challenged. That, in fact, was the theme of Federalist newspapers. Smith was obviously using the term at Amherst to demonstrate how well the new judicial system operated. He was a smashing success. By the end of the second week of the term, he had "nearly cleared the docket of its numerous entrances, which we understand the court intends to complete before it rises," the Federalist press boasted. "The ability and precision with which the new court conducted the business, has met the admiration of all the attendants in and out the bar. And we trust will convince every one, not *otherwise* influenced, of the expediency of the Judiciary system."[44]

The chief element of the new system that Smith and Ellis were seeking to prove a success was the single-judge jury trial. At the Amherst term the chief justice thought of a rather dramatic way to convince the public. When it came time to adjourn and to leave for Keene to open the term for Cheshire County, he sent Ellis there to preside alone while he remained in Amherst clearing the docket of the backlog of cases that the old court of Livermore, Evans, and Claggett had allowed to accumulate. He then went to Keene to join Ellis. Smith had the satisfaction of feeling that the public surely saw that, of the two rival, competing courts, his was the legitimate tribunal. First of all, the lawyers, even Republicans, followed his court wherever it met. All of New Hampshire's judicial actions for three trial sessions had been started in the Supreme Judicial Court. None had been heard in the Superior Court of Evans and Claggett. Perhaps even more satisfying, he and Ellis had established the legitimacy of the reform procedure introduced by the Judicial Act of 1813. With jury trials being conducted by a single judge, presiding alone, the dockets were actually being cleared.

Evans and Claggett did not go to Keene. They surely understood that there was more for them to lose than to gain by following the Supreme Judicial Court from term to term, yet they tried to maintain the pretense. They directed the sheriff of Cheshire County to open the Superior Court "in form" and then to adjourn it until May, when the next term was scheduled. They had an excuse for going home. They were not "in possession of the records." The clerk had again taken them to the rival court. So at Amherst, as the *Constitutionalist* reported, they adjourned "*to meet no more*." They had no records, and they had no jurors, and with the bar attending the other court, they had no lawyers, and therefore they had no cases to try.[45]

## Chapter Ten

# Judicial Interregnum

"The Judiciary department of the state government upon the stability and independence of which depend the security and happiness of the people is now in a condition at once unprecedented and melancholy," Portsmouth's *Gazette* bemoaned during the week that Chief Justice Jeremiah Smith allowed his negligible rivals, Richard Evans and Clifton Claggett, to take possession of the courtroom in Exeter and to sit in chairs that in the minds of almost every New Hampshire lawyer by right belonged to him and Caleb Ellis. "Two courts pretending to a supreme appellate jurisdiction holding their term at one and the same time and place and counteracting the proceedings of each other exhibit a spectacle which chills every social feeling."[1]

There is no need for a poll. Nor do we have to guess. We know that most lawyers thought Smith and Ellis belonged in that Exeter courthouse, not Evans and Claggett. Members of the bar voted by their attendance. The entire bar and most of the public left the courtroom and followed Smith and Ellis to the council room when Evans and Claggett preempted the bench. The same vote was cast in Amherst. The bar chose the Supreme Judicial Court and repudiated the Superior Court. The outcome of the rivalry was never close. Yet not every lawyer put the blame on Evans and Claggett. Arthur Livermore's brother, with his usual bad temper, said the blame belonged to the Republican governor and to the longtime New Hampshire practice of putting on the bench untrained, uneducated, and inadequate men. "All this difficulty has arisen from the folly and wickedness of John Langdon and the other violent Democrats in making such men as Evans and Clagget[t] Judges," he wrote a Portsmouth lawyer. "Nothing but party insolence and madness could have induced any man to think of such men for Judges of the Supr Court except he intended to bring the administration of law and justice into contempt and ridicule."[2] That was one perspective—the idea that Langdon was responsible for the absurdity of two rival courts, the low point in New Hampshire judicial history. As contended in chapter one, nineteenth-century New Hampshire would have the most distinguished small-state judiciary in America, but not in 1813, not with the likes of Evans and Claggett challenging and embarrassing one of the most memorable legal scholars of the early republic, Jeremiah Smith. Langdon was the cause, but though he can be blamed for appointing Evans to the high court, perhaps he should not be censured. He never appreciated why Evans did not measure up or why men educated in the law, like Smith and Plumer, believed that only lawyers, to the exclusion of laymen, should be appointed to the bench. Most New Hampshire Republicans did not understand.

Richard Evans certainly did not think he was at fault for putting Smith out of the courtrooms. He had, in fact, been doing his constitutional duty, and he even had the nerve to petition the government to be paid for insulting Smith and disrupting the judicial process. "Your memorialist, believing it a solemn duty imposed on him by his oath to maintain the constitution," Evans prayed the two houses, "still attended the terms of the superior court in Strafford, Rockingham and Hillsborough [counties], and there endeavored . . . to maintain its independence." Estwick Evans, although a lawyer, was even more audacious, for he made his argument in a pamphlet, hoping to arouse public opinion. His brother and Claggett had not only acted properly, they had been forced to confront Smith, who was the usurper, Estwick Evans argued. Smith was the judicial pretender. Evans and Claggett, he concluded, "rendered no small service in continuing judges, ready at all times, to administer the constitution and laws of the land, and to shield the people from oppression. They might have resigned and sought some other business; but would not such a step have been truly injurious and dishonourable."[3]

If we can believe Judge Evans, it was a special session of the legislature called by Governor Gilman to address from office the Republican sheriffs of Rockingham and Hillsborough counties that caused Evans to end the judicial charade. He claimed that he had planned to match Smith session for session until the General Court convened. The decision of the legislators to join the governor and to address from office the two sheriffs who had obeyed him and Claggett, rather than Smith and Ellis, was the reason why he stopped following Smith from shire town to shire town. Although that contention may appear to be more of an excuse than a real explanation, Evans's experience at Dover, where the sheriff supported Livermore rather than him and Claggett, could have convinced him that there was no point continuing if there were no Republican sheriffs to support him with at least the appearance of holding court. Appearances were not what led Gilman to convene the special session, though his motive can easily be misconstrued. Lynn Turner supposed that the governor had no choice once sheriffs Butler and Pierce "made it virtually impossible for the new supreme court to function in Rockingham and Hillsborough counties," not exactly a correct assessment of what the sheriffs' refusal to act for them meant to Smith and Ellis. A superficial survey of newspapers, even Federalist newspapers only, shows that Turner is wrong. In both counties Smith's court did function; he and Ellis had been able to conduct full terms, especially at Amherst, where they cleared away most of a very overcrowded, badly backed-up docket. Thanks to the deputy sheriffs who had been assigned to aid them, Smith and Ellis had had all the assistance they needed. True, they had not had the personal support of the two sheriffs themselves, but the sheriffs' direct participation had not been necessary. Their deputies did everything the sheriffs usually did—escorting the jurors, restraining the prisoners, maintaining order, and doing whatever the judges directed. Possibly Gilman reacted prematurely. He issued his proclamation calling the legislators to convene the day before Smith opened the court at Exeter. The Rockingham sheriff had already announced that he would serve only Evans and Claggett if they showed up, not Smith, and the Federalist press was warning that there could be trouble if both rival courts continued to attract followings. Evans and Claggett, or their supporters—"*a few factious and desperate individuals*"—the *Portsmouth Oracle* warned, were "endeavouring to obstruct the administration of the laws, and to excite among the people, a spirit of anarchy and rebellion."[4] Gilman may have anticipated troubles that never occurred.

Opening the special session, the governor, as usual, offered no leadership, hoping he might "be excused from being more particular, more especially, as there are many Members of the Legislature, who saw and heard, and can give full information respecting these unexampled proceedings."[5] Even Republicans thought he should have been more forceful, though they may have suspected that his ambivalence was intended to allow the Federalists in the General Court to set the agenda.[6] The legislators did, deciding to proceed against the sheriffs and to take no action against Evans and Claggett.

The two sheriffs, Butler of Rockingham and Pierce of Hillsborough, were addressed from office. With Federalist majorities in both houses of the legislature, Republicans could do little more than protest the process. "If they were guilty of the conduct with which they were charged, they ought to have been impeached and tried by the Senate," THE PEOPLE argued in the *Patriot*.[7] As a matter of due process and procedural fairness, THE PEOPLE was right. But addressing out was not only perfectly constitutional, it was simpler and much quicker than impeachment. The Federalists understood, undoubtedly correctly, that the power to address from office was not encumbered by rules of due process or of procedural fairness. The constitution mandated no substantive procedural rules that had to be honored. The sheriffs could have been put on trial had the legislators so decided, but they would have had no right to defend themselves. In fact, there was no hearing at all. Addressing out was summary, and the accused did not even have to be present. The process—or lack of process—seemed to HONESTUS, also writing in the *Patriot*, clearly unconstitutional. For surely, denying the sheriffs the right to answer the address or even to provide evidence, "privileges which are guaranteed to every person by the Constitution," he wrote, "is nothing more or less than a palpable violation of that sacred instrument, and downright tyranny and despotism."[8] Sixty Republicans in the lower house agreed.[9]

Federalist lawmakers were less certain how to deal with Evans and Claggett. After all, the judicial law they had enacted in June of that year had legislated the two judges out of office. There were doubts whether the legislature and executive could address from office judges who no longer had an office.[10] Besides, what was the point? Some Republicans implied that Governor Gilman had been preparing the public for impeachment when he accused them of criminality,[11] but that was not true. Few Federalists wanted to prosecute the judges. In fact, the committee that drafted the formal charges against the two men was surprisingly restrained. Although both Evans and Claggett "have assumed the shew of being Judges," it reported, their pretensions to judicial authority had been mostly verbal. Attempting nothing judicially constructive, they had only sought to interrupt "the proceedings of the regular courts," to excite "public attention," and to declaim "against the justice and propriety of the law abolishing the Courts of which they had been members." The committee apparently concluded that the two men were relatively insignificant, saying, "They have tried no cause; they have issued no process; and in whatever causes *one* of them had been concerned professionally, or the *other* of them was deeply interested personally, all such causes have remained for trial and judgment in the Court which has jurisdiction of other causes and other suits. Notwithstanding the assurance with which they have pronounced themselves to be invested with Judicial authority, and to constitute the Supreme Court of the State, it does not appear that they have been willing that any interest of their own should depend on the judgment of such a tribunal."[12]

The committee was remarkably uncritical. Instead of faulting Evans and Claggett, the report belittled them, dismissing the affair of the two courts with humor. Even though Evans and Claggett had challenged Livermore at Dover and had occupied the courtrooms at both Exeter and Amherst, displacing Smith and Ellis, they had committed no acts requiring the legislature to add new sections to the criminal code. Their offenses—disorderly behavior, disturbing the public peace, and interrupting courts of law—were already misdemeanors. Their attempts to incite support had been so meaningless that there was no need for legislation making it a crime for citizens to harass adversaries by suing them in spurious courts lacking authority in law. "Not so many as fifty persons in all the places in which this spectacle has been exhibited, have appeared to be present for the purpose of countering the proceedings," the committee pointed out. Most importantly, no one asked them to hear causes or render judgments, not even one person "among those who have regularly accompanied them in their circuits, and who were loudest in support of their defunct power and jurisdiction." In fact, "no citizen of the State has imagined any more than themselves, that they had authority to hear his complaint, redress his grievance, or try his cause."[13]

Voting 99 to 74, the House of Representatives accepted the report, ending for all political purposes the rival-courts incident.[14] Evans and Claggett were the losers. In June, when the General Court had legislated them from office, New Hampshire public opinion had been shocked, and despite their reputations as incompetent and absentee judges, they received much sympathy. But the good will quickly dissipated as they paraded from Dover to Exeter to Amherst, protesting shrilly their ouster and forcibly excluding Chief Justice Smith from two courtrooms. Their conduct, Amherst's politically unaffiliated newspaper remarked, "appears to us, at the least, 'reprehensible,'" and a large section of New Hampshire's population agreed. The two would-be judges did enjoy one accomplishment to salve their reputations. Both men rewrote their harangues against the Judicial Act of 1813 that they had delivered from the benches in Dover, Exeter, and Amherst, publishing them in a pamphlet which reads very much like official judicial opinions, which, though not scholarly or conclusive, are unexpectedly respectable. "Those arguments are more able than I thot those men could make," a surprised William Plumer observed. "[T]hey do them honor, & will, I think, produce a favorable effect upon public opinion." He was undoubtedly wrong, for it is unlikely that more than a handful of people read them. But they were the judges' only publications on law, and although not legally persuasive, they were a thorough discussion of the politics of the 1813 act.[15] It must be supposed that someone helped them write the "opinions," but if so, we will never know who. Certainly it was not Plumer. He would have left a record.

It is amazing how swiftly public opinion could change in such a small state during the second decade of the nineteenth century. In just the month and a half of the two court terms for Rockingham and Hillsborough counties, Evans and Claggett came to be held in almost universal contempt, and the good reputation of Chief Justice Smith, so badly damaged by his governorship, was nearly restored.[16] Of course, it helped that his associate on the bench had been Ellis, especially as their restraint and forbearance made a strong, even lasting impression. "It was the aim of the chief justice and Judge Ellis," Smith, writing in the third person, explained of the Exeter session, "to conduct with the utmost mildness, and to bear with any acts of rudeness, and even insult, offered to their persons, as far as they deemed consistent with the honor of the court and the administration of justice. They were willing to impute many things to ignorance and mistake."[17] He would have been less confident of being able to tolerate "rudeness" and "insult" had Arthur Livermore been sitting beside him.

Smith had gone to Exeter to prove to the New Hampshire public the value of judicial changes far more important than his or Ellis's benignity. He went there, and then to Amherst and Keene, to demonstrate the utility of the reforms of the Judicial Act of 1813, especially the effectiveness of single-judge trial terms and the purpose, value, and practicality of law terms.

In each county the opening term of the Supreme Judicial Court was especially crucial to make an impression if the chief justice hoped to convince New Hampshire voters that single-judge trials would be fair, legally efficient, and economical. That is why he had sent Livermore to Dover to preside alone and why he sent Ellis to Keene while he remained at Amherst, clearing the Hillsborough County docket. At least the evidence published in newspapers indicates he did quite well. "We understand that between forty and fifty causes (more than double the number at any one session in this county for a number of years) were tried by jury, and the docket nearly cleared," the *Oracle* reported for Hillsborough after Smith had left to join Ellis at Keene. He got just as good results for Cheshire County, which was fairly easy as Evans had regularly been missing recent circuits in Keene and a backlog of cases had piled up. The committee appointed by Federalists in the House of Representatives to consider petitions demanding repeal of the Judicial Act of 1813 cited the four successful trial terms conducted by Livermore, Smith, and Ellis presiding alone, to prove that the act should not be repealed. "[M]ore causes have been tried in the counties where the Courts were holden, since last June," it reported, "than have been tried before in the same counties for eighteen months." That fact alone, Federalists claimed, showed that single-judge courts were efficient and would save much money.[18]

William Plumer disagreed. One of the chief contentions against the old court system, he pointed out, had been the long delays in justice. "It will be recollected," he said of the legislative debates on the judicial bill, "that 'everlasting delay of Justice' has been the fruitful topic of the advocates of the new, against the old system." He was referring to the fact that the Federalists had defended introducing single-judge trial courts because so many scheduled sessions had recently been cancelled when one judge, generally Evans, failed to appear. A less-often cited cause of delays was Claggett's incompetence. "But the most serious charge was, that in the Superior Court, at Exeter, a year since, there were 'but twelve verdicts in civil causes.' . . . That there were then 285 actions on the docket." That was the docket that Smith and Ellis had largely cleared when sitting in the Council Chamber, while Evans and Claggett were whiling away time in the courtroom.[19]

The Federalists tried to make much political gain by bragging about how Smith and Ellis had reduced the docket, leaving the backlog of cases in Rockingham County the lowest it had been in years. At the time that the judicial bill was debated in the General Court, it was estimated that to have continued trying cases at the pace of the old Superior Court, "it would have taken about 24 years to get rid of the actions which were then on the [Rockingham] docket." Smith and Ellis, it was now said, had demonstrated that all that was needed to clean up the arrears were competent, professional judges allowed to preside alone. Writing as ARISTIDES in the *Patriot*, Plumer did not discuss how many cases Smith and Ellis had adjudicated, but he sought to leave his readers with the impression that there was no difference between the old and new judiciaries, that there were still too many delays, "[b]ecause about 319 causes were continued to give the lawyers more fees."[20]

Plumer may have written these remarks deliberately ambiguously, to create the impression that "the 319 causes" that had been continued were similar to the actions that had piled up on the docket under the judiciary of Livermore, Evans, and Claggett. He hoped that readers would conclude that there was no substantial difference between the old and new judicial systems. What he did not say was that the "319 causes" were not continued by the same rules according to which cases had been continued by the former Superior Court—they were not unfinished business put over to the next term. They were, rather, reserved questions, motions, errors, and other legal issues of a like nature continued to the law term, that is, held over to be disposed of at the new terms of court when the judges would convene without juries and hopefully have time to read briefs and other papers filed by counsel and perhaps even be able to study relevant law and find precedents for guidance and as authority to cite. For commentators of the Jeffersonian legal perspective, causes continued to law terms were just as much justice delayed as were causes continued as unfinished business to the next regular term because there had not been time to dispose of them. Holding actions over to law term was still delay, but delay with a difference. It was a purposeful delay, permitting lawyers time to brief questions of law and the judges opportunity for study and reflection. It was also a delay that permitted the bench and bar to downgrade the role of the jury, for if the court did not have authority to reserve questions for the law term, most of those questions would have been decided by jurors at the trial term. And of course, law terms did often provide lawyers with additional income, because holding actions over for a new term of the court meant at least one additional appearance to be filed and an additional filing fee for a lawyer to charge his client. That was what Plumer referred to when he said that the "319 causes were continued to give lawyers more fees."[21]

The dispute over the merits of the two judiciary systems turned as much on law terms as on the clearing of dockets. Writing in support of both the Supreme Judicial Court and law terms, A Friend To Justice asserted that, at the pace the old Superior Court had been working, it would have taken more than two decades to have cleared the Rockingham County docket, reducing the controversy to a matter of procedure. "Where," he asked, "is the inconsistency in saying that the operation of the late system was such, that questions of law were too hastily, and questions of fact too tardily decided—that with respect to the former, there were sometimes forty or fifty of them to be decided in a single day; that with the latter it was almost impossible to obtain a trial of them at all?"[22] Seen in terms of process, then, the backlog left by the old system was not due alone to incompetent judges; it was also caused by inefficiency. The court would have disposed of more business had the legislature allowed Smith, during his first term, to have law terms. The shortcomings of the old court could be blamed on too much legislative control over the judiciary, as much as on incompetent judges.

The two sides were divided by more than the politics of judicial appointments. They disagreed about process and for whom they wanted law to work. Long before Judge Livermore opened the first session of the new Supreme Judicial Court at Dover, the Federalist press, led by Portsmouth's *Oracle*, was saying that the new tribunal would operate with greater efficiency than the old. The improvement was guaranteed by the Judicial Act of 1813, ridding from the docket petty actions of less than one hundred dollars, and authorizing a single judge "to hold a Court for the purpose of taking verdicts of Juries," which meant that "the Court will be able to try at each term all the causes that are ready for trial; and therefore justice will be administered *promptly*."[23]

According to Smith, he had accepted appointment to the Supreme Judicial Court in part to prove that promise of judicial promptitude, and, he insisted, he had done so most reluctantly. He would later insist that Governor Gilman understood and agreed that he would resign once the new judiciary system was "fairly established." During the summer of 1814, after less than a year in office, Smith concluded that he had accomplished enough, and he could leave the bench with his reputation untarnished. It was, moreover, an auspicious moment to depart, as the legislature at its current term had refused to raise his salary, and he could use the resignation to call public attention to the niggardliness of New Hampshire's lawmakers. He was dissuaded, however, by friends, all of whom, despite knowing that he would surely be legislated out of office once the war ended and the Republicans returned to power, opposed his resignation. One of the strongest objections came from Judge Ellis, in whom he had particular confidence. Ellis had personal reasons, of course, for telling Smith that he had to remain on the bench, also contending that Smith owed it to the public. Undoubtedly, too, Smith felt he owed much to Ellis for agreeing to serve as his associate.[24]

Morison, Smith's biographer, claims that "the whole bar" joined in telling Smith not to resign. Three—Sullivan, Mason, and Webster—were more persuasive than most other lawyers because they understood the jurisprudential changes he was attempting to introduce, they supported them completely, and therefore they were better qualified than just about all other members of the bar to voice apprehension about the consequences of resignation. Mason, speaking for Webster as well as himself, sent Smith a long, influential letter stressing the negative effects of resignation. True, the legislature's refusal to raise salaries had been "very provoking," he admitted, but Smith owed the public a duty that overrode his financial disappointment.

> Your resignation would immediately throw the judiciary into utter confusion. . . . [T]he council is so composed that no successor could be appointed. The ghosts of Judges Evans and Claggett would again rise, and re-act the mad pranks of the last year. It is impossible to say what would be the event. The scene would be filled with nothing but disgrace, in which we should all share. If you will permit yourself fairly to consider the consequences, I think you cannot come to the determination of resigning. I never made loud claims to any extraordinary share of patriotism. But since you request me to consider what I would do in your situation, I do not

> hesitate to say that, if in your situation, and possessing your talents for discharging the duties of the situation, I would not under any circumstances, resign the present year. I think you cannot do it without endangering your own character. Should you, contrary to my wishes and expectations, determine on a resignation, I sincerely fear that you, together with all good men in the state, would soon have ample cause of repentance.[25]

Smith's biographer insists that the chief justice made the right decision in staying on the court. Smith, he concluded, had reestablished his former prestige, and "notwithstanding the circumstances under which he had been appointed, he enjoyed the same confidence as before on the part both of the public and the bar." It is doubtful that Smith thought his old public respect had returned. He knew, as did his close friends and admirers, that, as the House Committee on the Judiciary would report in 1816, the Judicial Act of 1813 had made the court "a common object of party contention" and was no longer "the *sanctum sanctorum* of the people's rights," as it had been when he had become chief justice the first time. "The respect of the people for their courts is less; and their confidence in their Judges diminished," the House Committee on the Judiciary would report in 1816, when the Republicans were again in the majority. "The courts are no longer considered as permanent, nor the Judges as independent, but a change of men who administer the justice of the State is expected to follow a change of the men who administer the other branches of the government." The constitution had been intended to make "the Judges as independent as possible," and now, after the Superior Court had been legislated out by the Judicial Act of 1813, the House Committee opined that they were not independent at all.[26]

When the second session of the General Court that promulgated the Judicial Act of 1813 finally adjourned in November, a committee consisting of three members of the House of Representatives was appointed to sit in recess, conduct an investigation, and report its findings to the two houses at the 1814 legislative term. The committee's specific rule was "to inquire into the official conduct of Arthur Livermore, Esquire . . . since his acceptance of his commission as Associate Justice, under the act establishing a Supreme Judicial Court."[27] And so, as he began his new term as chief justice, Jeremiah Smith again found a cloud hanging over the high court. And no one in New Hampshire was surprised that the cloud was Arthur Livermore.

At the next new legislature, the first one elected following the adoption of the Judicial Act of 1813, the Federalists, though the majority party, were on the political defensive. Members of both parties agreed that by constitutional law the legislature was the superior branch of the government. The question was whether, with the Judicial Act, the General Court had taken its supremacy too far. It is indicative of how New Hampshire lawmakers thought in that constitutional era that when the issue was raised, it was not supremacy over the judiciary that troubled the legislators. What was questioned, rather, was legislative supremacy over the executive branch. The Judicial Act of 1813 could be interpreted as a statement by the legislature to the governor and Council that it, the General Court, did not want the current judges to remain in office but wanted them removed and other judges appointed in their place. If so, was the legislature usurping the executive's authority to make judicial and executive appointments? It would be "a new and unprecedented exercise of power on the part of the Legislature—unknown to the Constitution; and dangerous to the independence of the Executive," PHOCION explained. "The Constitution says, the different branches of the government shall be independent and distinct. Yet one of these branches says to the other branch, 'We are not pleased with certain of your appointments—we therefore request you to remove these men and appoint others more agreeable to us.'" If the governor complies, PHOCION wondered, "where is the Independence of the Executive?"[28]

Boxed in politically and constitutionally, the Federalists had no choice but to adopt a principle that made some of them uncomfortable both politically and constitutionally. They had to defend legislative supremacy over both the executive and the judiciary—supremacy, in fact, over all except the people themselves. Remember, the Federalists cautioned, when the constitution had been drafted, the people had made "all Executive and Judicial power answerable to the Legislature," and the legislature "answerable to themselves." Therefore, the Joint Committee on the Judicial Bill contended, it followed that "if the Legislature were next in power to the People, and other powers answerable to them, whatever they do for the intended good of the whole, is to be adjudged right or wrong only by their immediate constituents." It was a sweeping, almost constitutionally reckless doctrine that would not have stood muster in a constitution that strictly applied the principle of balanced government. Having few other choices, the committee accepted the consequences and boldly denied that there were three equal branches. The constitutional authority to make "such laws as the public good may require," it reported to the two houses, on one hand "must be nugatory, if a minor power in Government [the judiciary] has a right to arrest the progress of the Legislature, and say that every act they pass is not required for the public good, and consequently bad and void. Such an evil as this the People could not correct by a new election: nothing but an entire subversion of Government would restore them to their rights. On the other hand, should the Legislature abuse the power entrusted to their care, they are immediately answerable to the People: the remedy is quick and easy: the evil can be corrected by a new election."[29] That was the theory, just about as extreme a claim to legislative supremacy as ever made by American lawmakers in the nineteenth century. Had it not been an expedient argument of the passing moment but taken as established law, it would have constituted the New Hampshire General Court as supremely powerful as the parliament of Great Britain or as the Pennsylvania assembly had been before the adoption of that state's constitution of 1790.

The Federalists on the Committee were writing with an eye on the election of 1814. William Plumer was to be the Republicans' candidate for governor, and that party intended to distract voter opposition to the war by concentrating attention on the Judicial Act. Plumer also hoped that New Hampshire would vote Republican because people were growing disgusted with Federalist opposition to every aspect of Madison's administration. "And last, but not least," he assured Jeremiah Mason, "the judiciary law of last June operates much against them."[30] Plumer was right. The Judicial Act of 1813 and the legislation from office of the Superior Court judges dominated the gubernatorial election of 1814. He was wrong, however, to suppose that these would be mainly Republican issues. The Federalists did not have to rely on antiwar sentiment alone. Thanks to the rapid revival of Chief Justice Smith's personal and judicial prestige, the new court was soon an issue that the Federalists were as ready to put forward and defend as the Republicans were to attack.[31]

Federalists were so confident that Smith had proven the superiority of the new court with its single-judge trials and law terms that they expected to rally enthusiasm simply by arguing that, if the Republicans regained control of the state government, the Judicial Act of 1813 would be repealed and the state would revert to the old judiciary of protracted delays and cancelled court sessions. "Instead of the present excellent Courts," a CITIZEN warned, "we should have . . . those who were Judges, again on the bench. Smith and Ellis must be removed, and Evans and Claggett, take their place." The nonpolitical *Farmer's Cabinet* believed that the objective the Republicans most sought was repeal of the Judicial Act of 1813. "We have found the Judiciary laid prostrate in the dust," the *Farmer's Cabinet* quoted the party platform, "and a set of minions created to minister to the extravagant practices of a dangerous and desperate junto. We turn with indignation from them and consign them to everlasting infamy." For Republicans, both the Act of 1813 and Jeremiah Smith were election issues calculated to bring them victory.[32]

The Republicans found an abundance of riches in the many issues they had with which to attack the Federalist administration. One that they exploited to the limit was the special session of the legislature called to address from office the sheriffs of Rockingham and Hillsborough, an unusual expense that CALCULATOR called "Governor Gilman's Indirect Tax" on the people of New Hampshire.[33] The question on which both the Republican and Federalist press expended the most energy was whether Smith's court had cleared the dockets of their backloads. That was a promise the Federalists had made to the public—that the Supreme Judicial Court would relieve the congestion of cases that had piled up, year after year, when Evans and Claggett were deciding cases on the Superior Court. It was not just the additions of single-judge trials and having questions reserved for law terms that would move matters along but the more competent judging of Jeremiah Smith. Federalists had long boasted of his efficiency, especially when justifying his high pay. He had, the *Constitutionalist* had claimed just three years before, saved the state "ten times the liberal salary it then allowed him, by the inimitable faculty and rapidity with which he transacted the business of the Court."[34]

A study of the controversy over clearing the docket does not prove as enlightening as good history requires, because the local newspapers, our chief source of data, were more intent on scoring political points for the party they supported rather than reporting facts correctly. Also, they were not equipped to collect the figures needed to reach definitive conclusions. They had to rely on raw, cumulative numbers and even on courthouse gossip. When the Supreme Judicial Court adjourned its last session before the election, Republican newspapers attempted to squeeze the best they could from inconclusive statistics. "There were 218 actions on the docket, of which ONE HUNDRED AND FORTY TWO WERE CONTINUED. Many of these actions were continued to the law term in November next."[35] Smith and his colleagues had disposed of seventy-eight, which was impressive work for little more than two weeks. But the important statistic, which the Republican printers may have intentionally not reported, was the number of continued cases that were reserved for the law term, where Smith, Ellis, and Livermore could dispose of them much more quickly than if they had to be resolved at a trial term. The Republicans printers did not break down the numbers into specific categories, such as "continued to next trial session" or "continued to law terms," preferring to imply that all cases continued for whatever type of term were held over only to increase lawyers' incomes. When the previous November term had ended, leaving the 142 "continued" actions on the docket, CALCULATOR sought to give the impression that they had all been continued so that the attorneys filing them could double their fees. One hundred forty-two "actions continued," he wrote, "by which (estimating only $5 as a fee to one lawyer on each side) the lawyers drew from the pockets of their clients 1420 [dollars]."[36]

At the start of their tenure on the court, Smith and his two colleagues set out a very specific agenda: to demonstrate that, with the new judicial system of single-judge trials and law terms, they could clear the dockets better than any court had done for the previous twenty years. After their first term the *Farmer's Cabinet* praised them for doing exactly that. Unequipped to gather counterstatistics, Republican printers could do little except disparage Smith's accomplishments, claiming that some litigation was not cleared but only postponed by suitors "not willing to trust their causes to the caprice of a single Judge" and that lawyers "are willing to indulge them in a continuance, because thereby their fees are enhanced."[37]

The figures of backlogged courts and cleared dockets may have been inconclusive, yet they could have tipped the scales in the election of 1814. When the contest ended, the Federal Party's newspaper, the *Constitutionalist*, was able to boast that "[a]fter all the *hue & cry* about the Courts" and published claims "that Evans and Clagget[t] were better Judges than Smith and Ellis,"[38] the Federalists still prevailed. It was remarkably close. Of a total of 38,542 votes cast, Gilman got a majority of only 881 over Plumer,[39] not a good showing considering that in previous elections Gilman "received five sixths, in others eight tenths and in one ten elevenths of the votes."[40] The Federalists also won both houses and control of the Council, and so Smith's court was safe. It would not be abolished for at least another year.[41]

Safe from being legislated out, but not safe from legislative criticism. At the next two sessions of the legislature, the Supreme Judicial Court took a verbal pounding. "The *ghost of the Judiciary* appears at each session," the *Patriot* reported, referring to the two sessions following passage of the Judicial Act of 1813, the October session of 1813 and the June session of 1814. There was so much criticism that the Federalists appointed a joint committee at the October term to defend publicly the new judiciary. It asserted that Smith had already proven one-judge trials more efficient and certainly just as reliable as multi-judge trials. One proof offered was that the dockets still were being cleared. "[M]ore causes have been tried in the counties where the Courts were holden since last June," the committee boasted, "than have been before in the same counties for eighteen months."[42] Still the opposition continued and it was unusually vocal. As in the session of the year before, the lawmakers felt themselves smothered with petitions attacking the Judicial Act of 1813, one-judge trials, and law terms. One memorial, from Goffstown, was twenty-five feet long. Between fifteen and twenty petitions, signed with 3,000 to 6,000 names, were received.[43]

Three weeks before the election of 1815, New Hampshire learned that the Treaty of Ghent, ending the War of 1812, had been signed.[44] The news would produce Republican victory at the polls, the *New Hampshire Gazette* predicted, but the *Patriot* knew differently, reminding voters that they cared more about local than international or national issues and that the most important local issue was the Judicial Act. "On Tuesday next we hope every man will go to the polls with the conduct of faction which has ruled the State the two last years, full in view," the *Patriot* urged. "We hope he will remember that our excellent Judiciary system has been broken down, and the judges of our Courts rendered the mere creatures of a dominant faction. We hope they will not consider the question to be decided a mere party question—but whether we shall exclusively be governed by *Lawyers*, or whether the agricultural and manufacturing interest shall prevail."[45] Neither issue, however, proved sufficient to give the Republicans victory in the election of 1815. The Federalists won once more. Gilman defeated Plumer for governor by a majority of 558, but the Republicans won a majority of the members of the Council, a clear indication that the Federalist plurality was slipping away. Although the margin of victory was reduced from 1814, it was still enough to keep Smith as chief justice for a third year.[46]

The General Court paid much less heed to the judiciary at the 1815 session than it had in the previous two years, perhaps anticipating that soon the Republicans expected to be back in power and the Judicial Act of 1813 would be repealed. Claggett again petitioned, "claiming his salary as a Justice of the late Superior Court." He was paid nothing. The chief justice also got nothing when he asked that his salary be raised. Despite the fact that "he could continue in office only at great personal sacrifice," Smith's biographer explained, "his duty was too plain to be mistaken, and he remained in office."[47] He did receive $355 for his "faithful and able services" in collecting, revising, and rearranging the laws of New Hampshire and supervising their printing, a task he had contracted to do in 1814. His two fellow commissioners received $100 each, less than a third of his stipend, indicating that Smith did most of the work.[48]

Members of both political parties were anxiously anticipating the election of 1816 when, in December of the previous year, John Taylor Gilman announced he would not serve again as governor. Fourteen terms was enough. The Federalists were hard pressed to find an acceptable substitute. No one of serious political reputation was willing to be their gubernatorial candidate. The party had little choice but run the not very popular James Sheafe, who had been a loyalist during the Revolution and had even been imprisoned for a time by the colony. "It would appear," the biographer of Levi Woodbury wrote with some exaggeration, "that the Federalists were determined to lose the election."[49]

Despite the demise of the Federalists, the election of 1816 was the most memorable political campaign in New Hampshire history. William Plumer contested for the governorship on a platform of three major issues: (1) disestablishment of the Congregational Church; (2) revocation of the charter of Dartmouth College, converting the private school into a public institution, renamed Dartmouth University; and (3) legislate from office the three justices of the Supreme Judicial Court, Jeremiah Smith, Caleb Ellis, and Arthur Livermore.

Most recent writers have assumed that the contest turned on Dartmouth College. "[T]he New Hampshire election of 1816," it was claimed in 1983, "was waged on the issue" of Dartmouth.[50] Newspaper printers at the time did not think so. They gave more attention to the status of the college than to the status of Congregationalism but even more emphasis to the status of the judiciary. The *Farmer's Cabinet* told the electorate not to be concerned with Dartmouth. "They have higher interests to contemplate," it editorialized. "Among the local concerns of the state, that of the Judiciary calls loudest for their consideration."[51] The *Concord Gazette* agreed. "Awake to your duty!" it urged the voters. "It is not a contest about names. It is not merely whether JAMES SHEAFE or William Plumer will be your Governor. It is rather whether JEREMIAH SMITH and CALEB ELLIS shall continue to administer justice to the people of New-Hampshire, or whether they are to be again dependent on the *opinions* of Richard Evans and Clifton Claggett. Not merely this. It is whether the whole Judiciary system in all its branches, the excellencies of which you have tested in its speedy administration of justice, and reducing by more than one half the number of actions on the docket from term to term . . . is to be prostrated in the dust, and the old one, with all its encumbrances restored."[52]

The election campaign bore especially hard on Jeremiah Smith. He was disparaged as a person and ridiculed for permitting himself to be called "chief justice." "True we now have a form of judiciary—but no constitutional judges," WASHINGTON wrote. "For those who now hold the scales must be considered as *usurpers*, without authority." JUNIUS would not flatter Smith with the title of chief justice. "True it is, you exercise the authority of Chief Justice," he explained. "But because Oliver Cromwell usurped the Regal authority, was he, therefore, the rightful king of England?"[53] Even Smith's professional opinions were dug up and vilified. He had ruled against customs officials, holding that, without a warrant from a justice of the peace, they had no authority to seize smuggled goods during their passage from Canada to their destination in New Hampshire. Since the goods came from Canada, a British colony, he was accused of undermining the country's war effort, and because his judgment overturned a jury verdict, he was said to have "*invaded*" the right of trial by jury, "the bulwark of liberty against the corruption and wickedness of Judges," a rather simplistic argument today, but quite telling then for it expressed a principle that the Republicans held very highly.[54] In another case, which his critics exaggerated, he was said to have exempted "the property of congregational ministers from taxation." A LEONIDIAS, with a cleverness undoubtedly lost on most readers, called it Smith's "MANSFIELDIAN decision."[55]

The main line of Federalist attack was against Evans and Claggett. If the Federal party lost the election, the *Oracle* warned voters, "you will have your present Judiciary overthrown, and suffer the misfortune, (and a great misfortune too), of having the former weak, tardy and every way wretched Judiciary system reestablished." Even worse, PLAIN TRUTH predicted, Evans and Claggett would claim their salaries back to the time they were legislated from office, something no New Hampshire taxpayer would want. It was an old argument. If the Judicial Act of 1813 were repealed and Evans and Claggett restored to the bench, A CITIZEN had written two years earlier, "every person whose property or body had been taken by process of the present Courts, might bring suits and maintain them against those who had attached their body or property."[56] A minor but interesting sidelight to the old-court, new-court debate was that the *Farmer's Cabinet* again abandoned its strict neutrality in politics. It not only came out very strongly in favor of Smith's court, it was dead set against the return of Evans and Claggett.[57]

Despite its tradition of political neutrality, the *Cabinet* was remarkably emphatic, insisting that Smith had accomplished all he had set out to do. "Is it the interest of the people that *justice should be administered promptly?*" the newspaper asked on the tenth of February. "The present system proves such promptitude," it answered. On March 2, just before the election, it put the question differently. "Is it for the public benefit, that justice should be administered *with as little expence as possible*?" it asked. "A diminution of expence necessarily follows a greater degree of promptitude and dispatch. It is believed to be capable of the clearest proof, that the improvement of the constitution of the courts, has caused a saving to the people more than sufficient to defray the expenses of all the courts now in existence in the State."[58]

During the election of 1816, the docket was even more extensively debated than it had been in the previous two contests. JUNIUS scolded Smith for continuing cases, "nearly four thousand actions." Most were actions held over for law term but that meant, CALCULATOR added, that the chief justice was authorizing lawyers to collect fees in amounts previously unimagined. "No wonder," he concluded, "that the system is pleasing to lawyers and judges."[59] The Federalist *Oracle* was apparently much more accurate when it claimed that Smith had begun his second term as chief justice "with upwards of a thousand actions on the docket, [while in contrast] at this time [3 February] there are pending only one hundred and ninety one actions in the same Court." The figures, the *Oracle* claimed a week later, were "a proof plain and intelligible to all, both of the *promptitude* and *cheapness* with which justice is now obtained. Parties are not compelled as formerly to attend Court, paying counsel and witnesses, term after term, unable to obtain a trial of their causes."[60]

The numbers undoubtedly counted for very little. Neither side is likely to have won over any voters not already convinced for or against Smith's reforms. At most, the statistics shored up the resolve of those already persuaded and, hopefully, got them to go to the polls. Surely many Republicans knew the figures they were quoted could not be depended upon as reliable facts but were useful chiefly for maintaining political conviction. Today there is no reason to take seriously the arguments of either side, although there is reason to believe that Smith and his associates did, indeed, succeed in clearing the docket much as they had set out to do in 1813. The most convincing evidence comes from the *Farmer's Cabinet.* It published numbers for the eight jury terms of Hillsborough County before the Judicial Act of 1813 took effect and then for five jury terms and three law terms for the same county after the new court system was in operation. For the period from the November term 1809, until the April term 1813, when the Superior Court of Livermore, Evans, and Claggett was trying jury cases, the *Cabinet* reported that 1,979 actions were continued. For the jury and law terms between October 1813, and December 1815, when trials were conducted by the Supreme Judicial Court of Smith, Ellis, and Livermore, it found that 698 actions were continued. That made 1,281 more actions continued for the same number of terms before the coming of the new court than since. The Republicans could doubt the accuracy of the *Cabinet*'s count, but they could not protest that the comparison was unfair because eight trial terms were measured against five jury terms and three law terms. That difference illuminated one of the reforms that Smith had set out to demonstrate: that law terms in conjunction with trial terms were more efficient than trial terms alone. Law terms did result in fewer cases being continued and meant that the docket carried over to the next session of the court would be less crowded.[61]

With the election of 1816 the question of the size of the judicial dockets lost its political importance. The Republicans, having mounted a remarkably well-coordinated campaign centering on local issues were triumphant. Besides, the peace treaty with Great Britain was by no means as disastrous as the Federalists had predicted, and the war's conclusion was punctuated by the great victory at New Orleans. The Republicans were swept back into power, winning both houses of the General Court and the executive Council and electing William Plumer governor "by about 2000 majority." By New Hampshire standards the victory was overwhelming.[62]

Jeremiah Smith's future was ordained. He would not be chief justice for many weeks longer. "The public opinion is decided on the subject of the Judiciary," Isaac Hill, publisher of the *Patriot*, warned the governor-elect's son. "[S]hould that opinion be disappointed, the cause will suffer great injury." By "the cause" he meant the Republican Party. "The affairs of our College and the *Judiciary* will probably be the most interesting subjects ever presented for the consideration of our State Legislature," the *New Hampshire Gazette* observed. History may think that the course of events was inevitable. After all, for the leaders of the Republican Party, such as Hill and Plumer, it was payback time, but in one respect the Federalists knew that the Republicans of 1816 would not be undoing the "reforms" of 1813. The legislature of 1813, the *Portsmouth Oracle* pointed out, had been "charged with making the law, merely to get rid of incompetent judges and placing better men on the seat of justice." The legislature of 1816, by contrast, "will be justly charg[e]able with making the change, not for the sake of removing incompetent judges, but to place their own creatures in power totally regardless of the prompt and due administration of justice."[63]

*Chapter Eleven*

# Addressing Out the Judges

The thesis can be confidently asserted and plausibly defended that the election of 1816 was the most memorable in New Hampshire history for two reasons: First, starting with its victory that year, the Democratic Party would be absolutely dominate in the state for two decades—until John Parker Hale staged a temporary revolt on a free-soil platform—and then again for ten more years until the rise of the abolitionist movement and the new Republican Party. Second, it was an election of unusually interesting issues: the Republicans, who now were also being called Democrats, promised three major reforms. The least controversial was to disestablish the Congregational Church. The second was the pledge to transform Dartmouth College from a private to a public institution. And the one that most voters at the time thought the consequential issue was to legislate from office the Supreme Judicial Court of Jeremiah Smith and restore the Superior Court, which had been voted out in 1813.

With the war no longer a factor the Democrats were certain of victory. Still, the election was not the runaway expected. With over 38,400 votes cast, Plumer won by 2,300.[1] Yet the future was forever changed. The Federalists never again ran a serious campaign for governor in New Hampshire.[2]

The legislative session that June of 1816 was the busiest that New Hampshire had ever experienced. Plumer started the activity with an address which the Federalist press disparaged and his biographer said was "another evidence of Plumer's capacity for 'wheeling about,'—or a surrender to political expediency." "The leading measures, which he recommends," the *Portsmouth Oracle* sneered, "relate to repealing charter's [i.e., Dartmouth's], turning out judges, and the abolition of law generally."[3] It was a session that would enact ninety-six new laws, elect a United States senator, vote to build New Hampshire's first state house in Concord, and nullify the charter of Dartmouth College, but for Plumer the most satisfying accomplishment was "the overthrow of the Federalist Judiciary Acts of 1813."[4]

To rally people for the repeal of the Act of 1813, Plumer in his gubernatorial address relied on a constitutional principle that most of his listeners knew was incorrect. "By our constitution," he told the two houses, "all the judges of our courts of law are to hold their offices during good behavior, until they arrive at the age of seventy; and cannot legally be deprived of their seats by the other branches of the government, except on impeachment . . . , or by the Governor and Council on the address of both Houses of the Legislature. . . . Notwithstanding these fundamental and salutary principles, the legislature in 1813 in effect removed all the justices of superior court of judicature." He not only denigrated the Judicial Act of 1813 for creating "a supreme court," he especially faulted the Act for entrusting "a single member of it with the power of deciding important questions deeply affecting the property, liberty and character of our citizens." To make his case against single-judge trials, he turned to a surprising source: the principles of his political party. "The powers thus delegated," he said, "appear better suited to the nature of a monarchical than a republican government," an assertion rooted in pure Jeffersonian politics. "To repeal these laws," he concluded, "will not be innovating, but restoring a system of administering justice, that has, in substance, been coeval with the early settlement of the country." Plumer also departed from the jurisprudence of his earlier years as a lawyer by urging the legislators to undo Smith's efforts to control the law by taking legal questions from the laymen on juries and placing them exclusively under the authority of the courts. "As the *trial by jury is an inestimable privilege,*" he contended, again calling for implication of Republican political policy, "and jurors by their oath are bound, not simply to decide the fact, but the *law* arising in the case, it merits enquiry whether judges have not too often set aside the verdicts of juries." Plumer thus adopted extreme Jeffersonian principles that he had never supported so publicly before. Previously he had worked with Smith to promulgate the rule that jurors were the judges only of fact, not of law. But he did concede to Smith one aspect of his reforms, concluding this part of his address by agreeing that there were erroneous jury verdicts that might be overruled. "A law explicitly defining the only causes for which judges should set aside verdicts would be an improvement in our system of jurisprudence," he admitted.[5]

The address was both political hypocrisy and expediency at their worst, and at the same time it was Plumer at his best. Seldom would New Hampshire have an executive so in charge of the government, so certain of the program he wanted enacted, and so capable of getting it passed. Yet, as Lynn Turner concluded, "[t]he Governor thus pleaded for the restoration of a judicial system which he had spent a lifetime in criticizing and asked for the overthrow of reforms that he himself had advocated."[6]

Plumer did not emphasize the jury again. The legislature had enough to do without dealing with an issue about which most members had strong but differing emotions and about which, we have every reason to believe, the governor really did not care. The central purpose of the address was to repeal the Judicial Act of 1813, and in their replies to the governor, the state senate and the joint committee on the courts agreed with him that the Act had been unconstitutional. Although both the executive and the legislature were emphatic on that point, the authority to legislate judges out of office was a power that they could not bring themselves to renounce. Say what the Republicans might in 1816, the authority of the General Court to legislate from office the judges of any court remained constitutional in New Hampshire law. Plumer must have expected that it would. What may have bothered him was the committee's vote for "a restoration of things as nearly as may be to the state where they stood" previous to passage of the Act of 1813. He was more comfortable with the "answer" that the senators voted to his address, telling him that their priority was "to restore the judiciary to its former constitutional state." That wording was more to Plumer's liking, for that was precisely what he wanted to do, restore "the former constitutional state," that is, restore the Superior Court that had been legislated out by the Judicial Act of 1813. He had good reasons to understand, however, that a majority of the lower house, and maybe even the Council, wanted to do more. They wanted to restore the members of the court itself, that is, the court of Livermore, Evans, and Claggett.[7]

So much time of the legislative session was taken up by the debates on the Dartmouth College question that Plumer had to keep the new judiciary bill as simple as possible. It primarily provided that the acts of 1813, legislating out of office the Superior Court of Judicature and the Commons Pleas, were repealed and "all acts, and parts of acts" that had been repealed by the acts of 1813 "be and the same are hereby revived and declared to be in full force, except such acts only, and parts of acts, as are inconsistent with the provisions of this act."[8]

Plumer became upset by the numerous delaying tactics that the Federalists employed and also because Daniel Webster, "active & overbearing," came to Concord, hoping to persuade some Republicans to vote against repeal. Plumer was not concerned, just annoyed at Webster. He knew that whatever Webster did would be wasted effort. "[T]he bill will pass before we rise," he assured his son. "[I]f it does not it will cover the Republicans with disgrace." Jeremiah Mason also showed up. For some reason he thought he had a chance to persuade Plumer to reappoint Smith. As much as he admired Mason, the governor must have been amused.[9] When he signed the bill repealing the Judicial Act of 1813, he did more than reinstate the Superior Court of Judicature. He legislated out of office Jeremiah Smith and Arthur Livermore. Neither man would ever again be a judge.[10]

Repeal of the Act of 1813 might have ended the judicial controversy in most other states but not in New Hampshire, where judicial independence and judicial status were not the prime considerations among lawmakers. Costs and payrolls had higher priority with a majority of legislators. As a result there remained what Lynn Turner described as "a somewhat messy but necessary mopping-up operation." It resulted from an unresolvable disagreement among lawyers about the consequences of legislating from office judges of good-behavior tenure. Some legal observers maintained that legislating a court out of existence was always constitutional, that there was no difference in law between the Federalist act of 1813 and the Republican repeal of 1816. Both ended the tenure of the judges who had been members of the courts being abolished and also ended any constitutional claims they had upon the state. Other legal theorists stressed that the judges legislated from office by the abolition of their courts had held tenure at good behavior, and although the judges had no bench to sit on as their offices had been eliminated, they still enjoyed tenure at good behavior and therefore might have a claim for compensation until they died or reached age seventy. At first Governor Plumer hoped to maintain the rule that only the Act of 1813 was unconstitutional and that Smith and Livermore knew it. In fact, Livermore, at that first court session in Dover, had said so. As a result, both men had accepted a judicial office under a law they knew violated the constitution that they had sworn to uphold, all of which made them unfit to be judges. They were, at best, usurpers and, once legislated from office, they had no claims against the government.[11]

By the time he had arrived in Concord as governor, Plumer had changed his mind, fearing his theory that Smith and Livermore had been judicial usurpers was too strained. But he also knew that some Republican legislators supported a different legal theory so extreme that, if it won a following, it could turn the current legislative session into a political brawl the likes of which New Hampshire had never experienced. The contention was that the repeal of 1816 did more than deprive Smith and Livermore of their judgeships. Passage of the repeal act was a legal judgment that they had been in violation of the constitution or, more bluntly, they had been committing illegal actions by pretending to be judges. They had never been entitled to the compensation they had been paid, and therefore they should be required to repay their salaries "upon the well established principle of law and equity, that no man shall profit by his own wrong."[12]

With the fight over Dartmouth College unresolved, Plumer did not want distractions. The safest legal theory for dealing with Smith and Livermore was that they had been "judges *de facto*," at least, "if not *de jure*," and it followed that "they were 'entitled to the same rights, immunities and privileges in their office as other judges;' and, therefore, that, if they were removed, it must be under the constitutional provision, on address of the Legislature, by the Governor and Council."[13] To avoid any legislation that might recognize Smith and Livermore in constitutional law as judges still sitting, the governor set in motion one of the most anomalous episodes in American judicial history. He requested the legislature to address from office the judges whose offices the legislature had just eliminated—in other words, to remove from judgeships that had been abolished judges who had been addressed from office and therefore who no longer were judges.

Most likely Plumer did not have to persuade many Republican members of either house. It was generally accepted Republican theory, at least during that legislative session, that legislating a court from office was unconstitutional. After all, the legal justification for the repeal act of 1816 was that the Judicial Act of 1813 had been unconstitutional and that the Act of 1816 only repealed an unconstitutional statute, it did not legislate out a constitutional court. Yet, as the House Committee on the Judiciary pointed out, "No doubt is entertained that any court can be abolished, whenever the public good may require it." It was not the court's abolition but the purpose of removing the sitting judges from office that "is apprehended to be a direct violation both of the letter and spirit of the constitution." The proper method, provided by the state's constitution, was "removal of the judges by the governor with consent of council upon address," the committee concluded. "[T]hat being done the constitution seems to present no obstacle to the abolition."[14]

Having legislated from office Chief Justice Smith and Justice Livermore, the two houses of the General Court later that very same day voted to address the executive "to remove" them "from their respective offices of Justices of the Supreme Judicial Court," and two days later the governor and Council "removed" them.[15] It was a unique moment in American judicial history. On that one day the legislature of a state both legislated the judges of that jurisdiction's highest court from office, and it also addressed those very same judges from the same offices.

Plumer had even more business for the Council and General Court. He wanted them, in one day, to address from office more New Hampshire judges than probably were addressed off the courts of all the other states during the nineteenth and twentieth centuries. He was worried because supporters of Judge Richard Evans, legislated from office by the Judicial Act of 1813, were agitating that he receive back pay for the three years that the Superior Court had not been functioning. Once the repealing bill had been enacted into law, they argued, Evans and his colleague, Clifton Claggett, "should have been immediately restored to their stations, and their salaries, with interest, promptly paid." Here was another contention that could have disrupted the harmony of the Republican Party, for it could have become more divisive than the Dartmouth College controversy. There was surprising support for the principle that Evans and Claggett were judges again once the Act of 1813 was repealed. Worse, Evans was in desperate need of money, and his Republican friends knew it. Some in the House of Representatives were apparently threatening to raise the question. There was little possibility they would succeed, for nineteenth-century New Hampshire legislators were dead set against paying salaries to officials who had not been working, and they would have been especially upset if they had to compensate a judge who had missed trial terms over a period of more than two years due to sickness.[16]

The contention was both plausible and uncomplicated. It was based on the legal theory that the Judicial Act of 1813 and the subsequent functioning of the Supreme Judicial Court had no constitutional bearing on the rights, the tenure, or the compensation of Evans and Claggett. "The establishment of a thousand courts, either of exclusive or co-ordinate jurisdiction, would not deprive the judges of the courts then existing of their offices and salaries," Estwick Evans pointed out. By simply insisting on their continued tenure and holding themselves to the public as ready to conduct trials, Justices Evans and Claggett had maintained judicial independence and had earned their pay. "The constitution has been grossly violated by depriving the judges of their employment; but far greater will be the injury should you deprive them of their salaries; for here the great source of an independent administration of the law will be dried up. . . . So far, however, the judges were independent; they were still entitled to their salaries, and of course were still bound, both by duty and interest to shield the people, by a faithful administration of the constitution and laws of the state. . . . The people of New-Hampshire in 1813, did not, however, require the judges of the old courts to perform this duty; they were willing their official functions should remain inoperative, until the constitution should be restored." But, the argument concluded, if the Judicial Act of 1813 is held to deprive Evans and Claggett of their salaries, the decision would "destroy every barrier to the independence of your judiciary."[17]

The salary issue was not a surprise. In 1813, after the Federalist Judicial Act had been passed, the *New Hampshire Gazette* had predicted that, when the Republicans returned to power, "the constitutional Judges would be reinstated, and have their salaries." Before the election of 1816, the *Concord Gazette* had warned that if Plumer became governor and the Act of 1813 was repealed, "the salaries of the old Judges must be paid out of the State treasury," which meant, the *Portsmouth Oracle* feared, that the taxpayers would "be saddle[d] with TWELVE TO FIFTEEN THOUSAND DOLLARS, to pay the tribe of ex-Judges, that were never able to earn half their salaries, while they were *in office*."[18]

There were, to be sure, just about as many constitutional observers who insisted that judges legislated from office were not entitled to pay as those who said they were.[19] Although the question was never judicially resolved in any jurisdiction, there is good authority for concluding that many of the lawyers who believed that judges serving at good behavior and legislated from office had a constitutional right to receive their compensation at the sum set by statute for the remainder of the term they had been serving also thought they did not have any legal process with which to enforce that right.

There were exceptions, that is, lawyers who insisted that some remedy had to be available. The jurist who potentially could have had the most influence establishing such a rule was Justice Samuel Chase of the United States Supreme Court. He told Chief Justice John Marshall that, if the question came before their court, he would have recognized the right of the circuit judges—the midnight judges, including Jeremiah Smith—legislated from office by Jefferson's Judiciary Act of 1802, to recover their offices by what he termed an "action of assize of Office" and to continue receiving their pay by the even more vague "action to recover the Salary." Some of the circuit judges legislated from office who wished to sue for their salaries must have believed that they had a cause of action. Chief Justice Smith never resigned his office as a midnight circuit judge, and the best guess why is that he believed that somehow he continued to have a right, if not to the office, at least to the salary.[20]

Plumer was only taking the safe side of the doubts when he asked the General Court to address from office all the remaining judges besides Smith and Livermore who had just been legislated out, that is, to address from office the judges of the Court of Common Pleas, which had been created in 1813 when the Supreme Judicial Court was created and the judges of which had then been appointed to that court by the Federalist governor, John Taylor Gilman. There would have been no reason for addressing them except for the salary problem. Plumer was worried enough that the judges legislated out, especially the estate of Richard Evans, which gave every indication of suing for compensation "earned" between 1813 and 1816, would make good a claim for back pay. That is why he decided to go as far as possible and address from office every living ex-judge previously legislated out. What he was telling the General Court was that the legislature had to do more than address from office Smith, Livermore, and the Federalist Common Pleas judges appointed to the tribunal created in 1813. The Republican judges whom the Federalists had removed in 1813 also had to be addressed. After all, by repealing the act that put them out, he had given them a legally persuasive argument that, even if they had been legislated out by the Federalists, they had been restored to their judicial offices when he signed the repeal act of 1816.

Again the Republicans in the two houses of the General Court obliged their governor. Citing the two pieces of legislation—the act of 1813 that had abolished the Superior Court and the Courts of Common Pleas, and the act just passed to abolish the Supreme Judicial Court and the newer Court of Common Pleas that had been created in 1813—the legislators explained that "doubts have been entertained as to the effects of the before mentioned acts on the offices of the Justices of the Superior Court of Judicature and of the Courts of Common Pleas who were in office at the time of passing the . . . act." Therefore, they resolved that the governor and Council "remove all the Justices of the Superior Court of Judicature and all the surviving Justices of the said Courts of Common Pleas in each and every County . . . from their said respective offices."[21]

Even for New Hampshire it was a strange, unprecedented episode. Every judge on all the courts, except probate, was removed, even those whose courts were nonexistent. And Plumer may have been right that he had to go so far, although there is no way to prove that he did. If nothing else, to be addressed from office dashed the pretensions of Clifton Claggett, who claimed that with the repeal of the Judicial Act of 1813, his old Superior Court of Judicature had been reestablished and he was again a judge. Plumer could have argued with him or ignored him, but why bother? It was easier just to address him from office.

There was a bit of comedy along with the farce. Claggett, who had been elected to the House of Representatives, had voted to address himself out of office without realizing what he was doing. In December he called on Plumer to say that he no longer would support him. "He said I had approved of an address for removing all the judges [in] which he must be included," Plumer reported. "I asked him, if he did not vote for that address, he said he did, I enquired why he blamed me for approving of an address which he himself supported? He replied because he did not know that it included himself, & I did." Plumer, who had slight regard for Claggett's intellect before, now had even less. "I observed the address was plain & simple, & a man capable of being a judge of a court of law must understand it."[22]

The turn of events must have been even more embarrassing for Arthur Livermore. He became the only judge in American history to be addressed from office twice in two days. On the twenty-seventh of June, the legislature addressed the governor and Council to remove Livermore as a judge of the Supreme Judicial Court. The next day the two houses addressed that he be dismissed as a judge of the Superior Court of Judicature abolished in 1813. Once again, judicial legislation made Livermore the one who lost the most. This time it did not cost him a smaller salary than his colleague had been paid or mark him of less prestige than a fellow judge. But it did make him the butt of an event that one historian called "comic."[23]

*Chapter Twelve*

# A Receptionist Court

By legislating from office Jeremiah Smith and Arthur Livermore, and then addressing the two off the court along with every other ex-judge then living, the Republicans had taken the first two steps in their program to reinstitute the Superior Court and place it under the control of the political majority. The next element in the process promised to be more difficult. Governor Plumer had to persuade three competent lawyers, acceptable to at least three councilors, to become high-court judges. There was not a single judge left in the state except those of probate, and Plumer knew exactly what he wanted and what he did not want. Except for Jeremiah Smith, Arthur Livermore, Daniel Webster, and a few others, he sought the best lawyers he could find, because, he believed, a majority of New Hampshirites would "form their opinion of the court & its usefulness, more from the character of the men who composed it, than from the principles of our laws." There was no surer way, he seemed to be saying, to restore legitimacy to New Hampshire law than by placing the finest caliber judges on the highest court. He also wanted to find appointees "from both parties." The Federalists, he explained, "had rights we were bound to protect—they had good men, some of whom we ought to appoint." He "could not," he explained, "consent to have all the judges selected from one political party—such a measure partook too much of political intolerance to be supported."[1]

Those were the governor's two objectives: to appoint Federalists as well as Republicans and to appoint the most competent lawyers he could persuade to serve. Despite his adherence to political Jeffersonianism and his adoption of some of the more extreme Jeffersonian rhetoric disparaging English traditions, Plumer was not a committed convert to legal

Jeffersonianism. He always remained the receptionist of English common law that he had been when first admitted to the bar and especially when he was a leader of judicial reform at the Constitutional Convention of 1791–1792.[2] As much as Jeremiah Smith and Daniel Webster, he wanted the New Hampshire judiciary to receive and follow the methodology of English common law, and he gave no indication of compromising. More particularly, he sought a court before which lawyers of the education and caliber of Smith and Webster could practice, confident that their motions for demurrers, exceptions, errors, and reserved questions, would be understood and knowledgeably acted upon.

Plumer's first problem was that the court to which he had to appoint judges had been brought into being by repeal of the Judicial Act of 1813. The governor had to decide what repeal meant. Was it only that the Supreme Judicial Court no longer existed; or, also, that the former Superior Court of Judicature had been reconstituted? The law of 1816 implied that it created a new Superior Court, rather than bringing the old one back, but it did not say so explicitly. And if the old court had been brought back into being, what of its members who had been serving at good behavior? Were they reactivated with the court? There had been three: Richard Evans, Clifton Claggett, and the chief justice, Arthur Livermore. Evans expected to go back on the court but died not long after the repeal act passed the legislature. Livermore, accepting the fact that he had been both legislated and addressed from office, made no claim. Besides, as he had been paid as a member of the Supreme Judicial Court since 1813, he could never have persuaded New Hampshire lawmakers that he was owed back pay for doing nothing on the Superior Court. Claggett was different. He wanted both the office and the compensation. After being addressed out, he personally demanded that Plumer reappoint him, insisting that he had a legal, political, and moral right to reappointment.

Claggett's demands put both political and personal pressure on Plumer. True, no one then made a study so there are no precise numbers, but it is safe to guess that at least a sizable minority of Republicans in both houses said that Claggett either was already reinstated as judge or had a legal right to be reappointed, and there is good evidence that a majority of the Council told the governor they would vote for Claggett. Leading the fight for Claggett was his son William, a militant, outspoken, very active politician, who openly threatened Plumer with concerted opposition if his father was left off the bench. Worse for the governor, his only daughter, Sarah or Sally, who was very close to him, had just married the younger Claggett.[3] She may have tried to avoid being actively involved, but was unable to do so, writing at least one letter to her oldest brother, telling him she knew their father would reappoint the judge if it were not for "secret enemies." Her letter was very carefully worded. Her father-in-law, she wrote, had suffered so much that he was "owed" the judgeship. But she did not say that it was her father who was owing; rather, it was the party. Claggett had served the Republican Party, and it was the Republicans who must return him to the bench. "[H]e has suffered as much, and perhaps more, than any man in the state, for the cause of the republicans," she observed. "[H]is reputation has been impeached, his property very materially injured, and his peace of mind disturbed, these are considerations, which ought to have had weight with the republicans."[4]

Sally's brother, who shared most of their father's jurisprudential principles, was at first uncompromisingly opposed to Claggett's reappointment, calling him "totally unfit."[5] But the brother not only lived in the same town as Sally and her husband, he boarded in their house[6] and could not avoid his brother-in-law's hostility. William made it clear to him that he would no longer be welcome if the judge were not reappointed. His father, William said, was "willing to bear with *fortitude* & *resignation* his *severe* fortune" and wanted his son to adopt the same attitude. But, the son told his brother-in-law, he would not "follow the counsel of my father." "You may pacify my Father," he warned, "[n]ot so with me." Within a month the younger Plumer could no longer hold out. He wrote his father to reappoint the elder Claggett to the Superior Court, adding, "There will be no peace in *this quarter*, if he is not appointed."[7]

The elder Plumer did not want to hear anything about either of the Claggetts. Two days after addressing out all the judiciary except the probate judges, he met with the five members of the Executive Council. They agreed with him that judicial appointments absolutely must be the first order of business. "[A]s we now had to appoint all our judges of all our courts of law," Plumer told them, "our object should be to select men of talents[,] information [i.e., education] & character suited to those important offices, to effect this that we should not confine ourselves to one of the great political parties but select from both, & if possible for us all to unite in the appointments." He knew but was not deterred by the fact that the appointment of Federalists would encounter much political opposition. He willingly anticipated "a censure from both political friends & foes, both are illiberal, both are unyielding, but the interest of party must, so far as I am to act, yield to the interest of the state I govern. . . . My motives will, I am confident, not be duly appreciated by either party."[8]

Futile as the prospects might be, Plumer forged ahead looking for Federalists to appoint. In fact, even before the election, he had asked the man who was, after Jeremiah Smith, the Federalists' best lawyer, to accept appointment, and Jeremiah Mason had refused. Later, after the repeal act of 1816 became law, the two men met in Concord, and Mason gave the governor two reasons why he would not accept. The first, of course, was the compensation. That was his excuse earlier when rejecting the chief justiceship, and there was no chance that he could afford to accept the low salary Plumer offered. His second reason is more difficult to evaluate historically, as Mason wrote little about the court system, except for telling Smith that he had to stay in office if the Judicial Act of 1813 was to be proven successful. It is, certainly, very significant that he raised with Plumer the subject of the reestablishment of the Superior Court and maybe almost as significant that Plumer recorded what he said. Mason was especially opposed to the return of multi-judge trials. "Experience has I think demonstrated, that if the judges are required to be present, at each jury trial, they can never do the business of that Court, in a manner satisfactory to themselves or beneficial to the public," he explained. "If the judges are competent for their places, I think there can be no danger, in confiding to a single judge the power of ruling the evidence, and directing the course of ordinary trials of issues of fact by jury, subject to certain exceptions."[9]

Without Mason, Plumer knew, it would be much more difficult to get a bipartisan bench. There was so much opposition among Republicans, that his son William Plumer, Jr. was now advising him to abandon the idea. Newspapers of both parties were strongly critical,[10] and so, most importantly, were the members of the Council, so much so that Plumer began to waver.[11] Most troubling was the reaction of some of his appointees, especially Judge Timothy Farrar, whom Plumer thought a friend. When Farrar received his commission as judge of the Court of Common Pleas, he expressed contempt not by returning it but posting it in a "grog shop." Plumer was deeply hurt, but then he never appreciated the alarm and anger he had created by his proposed legislation to revoke the charter of Dartmouth College. Farrar was bitter that the school's independence was attacked, and his son, a Portsmouth lawyer, would soon be working with Daniel Webster to educate the public about the interests and the constitutional principles that were at stake. "The virulence of party will not allow good actions to proceed from good motives," Plumer lamented. "My candor & liberality gains no credit with either party."[12]

Persuaded by the governor, the Council appointed to the Superior Court George Baxter Upham, "a good lawyer, & a man of fair irreproachable character." After some hesitation Upham returned his commission at the urging of Webster and other Federalists lawyers, or so Plumer believed.[13] Certainly in New Hampshire, the Era of Good Feelings had not begun, and Plumer, Jr. again urged his father to abandon his bipartisan program. "I find no body that likes your plan of putting Federalists on the Bench," he wrote from Portsmouth. "Judge Claggett expects (or at least his son does) that he should take the place of Upham."[14]

Remarkably, Plumer had the opposite experience appointing Republicans. He not only found ready candidates for the high court, but surprisingly, despite the low salary, they were not only good, they were leading lawyers. After Mason rejected the chief justiceship, the governor selected William Merchant Richardson, who, although born in Pelham, New Hampshire, had spent his life in his mother's home state, Massachusetts, where he was educated and, after admission to the bar, elected to Congress. He had little interest in participating in politics and even less in living in the District of Columbia, where he found "many things to disgust" him. "The administration of justice, or injustice, in this city, is detestable," he wrote of Washington. "Men of all colour are taken and sent to goal for small offenses with less ceremony than we [New Englanders] use in impounding a hog. The poor negroes stand no chance."[15]

As a member of Congress, Richardson had supported President Madison and had voted for the war against Great Britain, but, unhappy in Washington, he decided to make a change and move back to the state of his birth when the president offered to appoint him as federal district attorney for New Hampshire. He accepted, left Massachusetts, and moved to Portsmouth. Governor Charles H. Bell thought it "really very singular that such an office was assigned to one whose acquaintance in New Hampshire must necessarily have been quite limited," but Richardson had many friends in New Hampshire, especially lawyers, and it seems that in reputation he was thought less partisan than, in fact, he was. As a legal theorist he, like Madison, was almost as much a receptionist jurisprudent as he was an adherent to Jeffersonian political theory. In 1801 he had delivered a Fourth of July oration in tones of classical republicanism, expressing unmistakable Federalist thoughts about the French Revolution.[16] Joel Parker, who would succeed him as chief justice, described Richardson as the perfect successor of Jeremiah Smith, the very caliber of judge that Smith had long struggled to have appointed to the bench. "His stores of legal learning did not consist merely in a treasury of precedents and decisions," Parker thought, "but he studied the great principles of the science; made himself an adept in special pleading, which requires not only acuteness and discrimination, but patient and laborious investigation and reflection; and to this he added diligence in the examination and preparation of the evidence and talents of an advocate which commanded a very respectable share of forensic practice."[17]

If we read between the lines of a lawyer-judge praising a fellow lawyer-judge, it is evident that Parker was saying more than that Richardson was a professional and intellectual clone of Jeremiah Smith. By describing him as "a well read and accurate lawyer," less interested in "the niceties and technicalities of the system" than in resting "a case upon its substantial merits," Parker was saying that he was a good advocate but not one able to fit into the first ranks of the fierce competitors at the Rockingham County bar.[18]

To be Richardson's associate justice, Plumer selected Samuel Bell. He had nominated him before, in 1812, during his first gubernatorial term, telling the Council that Bell "possessed handsome talents, was a sound lawyer, and that his manners, habits, & decision of character qualified him to discharge the duties of the office." But because Bell was so much involved in the failure of the Hillsborough Bank and was blamed by much of the public for widespread financial hardships when it suspended payment on its notes, the councilors would not accept him, some fearing that "if Bell were appointed that the creditors of the bank would have him arrested and imprisoned for debt." Instead, the three Republicans on the Council had insisted on Clifton Claggett and finally, though he knew Claggett had scant lawyerly talents and only mediocre legal education, Plumer had been forced to agree. It was the most distressing experience of his first term, which he was determined not to repeat.[19]

In 1816 Plumer again had to deal with a divided Council, three Republicans and two Federalists. Just after he was elected governor, he had been visited by Bell; Plumer told him that he "must be a judge." Bell declined, saying "the state of his health would not permit it." Three months later Bell changed his mind. "Considerations arising out of my feeble state of health and long absence from practice and legal studies induced me to think that I ought not to accept appointment," he reminded the governor. "Upon further consideration I have concluded that under existing circumstances it was my duty to accept the office for the present."[20] Plumer had already nominated him, the month before, at the first meeting of the Council.

At that first meeting the governor had nominated Mason, Richardson, and Bell. The Council unanimously accepted Richardson, but the Republican majority absolutely opposed Mason. All of them urged Arthur Livermore instead, forcing Plumer to speak at length, explaining why he would never appoint Livermore. The Federalists, from two inland counties, Cheshire and Grafton, were dead set against Bell, claiming that his bank disaster made him odious to the public. The three other councilors supported him, however, so Plumer obtained two out of three of the appointments he needed. He then proposed as the third Superior Court judge, George B. Upham, whom he described as "a federalist, a good lawyer, &

a man of a fair irreproachable character." All three Republicans opposed him, but by the next meeting of the Council, Plumer had persuaded one of the three to change his vote. Upham was appointed.[21]

When the legislative session ended, Plumer went to Portsmouth to talk with Richardson about further judicial appointments. The new chief justice told him that "he was much gratified with his own appointment, & especially so that Arthur Livermore was not appointed for he had no confidence in him." That comment should not be passed over without due attention. It may tell us little about Richardson's judicial values and legal principles, but it should weigh on how we evaluate the place and the success of Smith in the story of legal change in the early republic and the common law's reception into American jurisprudence. Some students of New Hampshire judicial history have wondered whether Smith has been accorded too much credit as a legal reformer. During both his terms as chief justice, Livermore sat beside him on the bench, shared with him the work of the court, and therefore must be due some of the praise always lavished on Smith. That may be a reasonable historical assumption, but it certainly is not what was thought by the lawyers who knew Livermore and who had to experience his personalized method of judging.[22]

We can be certain we know what Richardson thought. He told Plumer that Livermore "would have afforded him no aid on the bench." Livermore, Richardson explained, "was so fickle & has so little legal information [i.e., education], that if he agreed with him in an opinion it would not confirm his own, & if he disagreed it would not excite doubts, or induce him to reexamine the subject." That is surely as clear a statement as we can ever expect to get. Both he and the state of New Hampshire, Richardson told the governor, "were under great obligation to me for my firmness in declining to appoint Livermore, it had relieved him from much anxiety."[23]

Plumer did not have to be told why lawyers had doubts about Livermore. Seven years earlier, when Livermore had been named chief justice, Plumer thought the appointment a mistake. "In that office he will neither acquire or promote the public interest." Some reasons why, Plumer told himself, were that Livermore "has not a clear discriminating mind or a quick apprehension—he is whimsical & capricious, impatient & fretful." After leaving Richardson and making the social rounds of Portsmouth, Plumer spent the day chalking up more congratulations for not appointing Livermore. Edward Cutts, a practitioner, "expressed his satisfaction that Livermore was not reappointed." So did former governor John Langdon. Peyton R. Freeman, the attorney whom Livermore had ordered not to practice in his court and who had petitioned the General Court to impeach Livermore, "observed" to Plumer that "when information first reached Portsmouth that Arthur Livermore was not appointed judge, an attempt was made to incite censure upon the executive; but the best men of both parties approved the omission, & . . . men whom he did not expect condemned & censured Livermore."[24]

The new associate justice, Samuel Bell, strongly agreed with his chief justice. Two years after Richardson and Bell had been appointed to the Superior Court, Plumer decided not to run for reelection. He told Bell that he wanted him to be the next governor. When Bell hesitated, Plumer ran down the various other men who were likely candidates, ending with Livermore. "[T]he government in the hands of Arthur Livermore," Plumer assured Bell, "would be plunged into an ocean of uncertainty, subject to whim & caprice, & . . . if republicans elected him it would be only for one year." Bell replied that Livermore was too unpredictable and, though a man of more talents than the other potential candidates whom Plumer had named, "was more dangerous—for no man, not even himself, could for a single day know what course he would pursue." "Arthur Livermore is too whimsical to be trusted," Bell concluded.[25]

In October Livermore was nominated to run as the Republican candidate for Congress from Grafton County. Party members from Rockingham County announced that they would not support him. They would not, the *Concord Gazette* reported, "in any manner aid or assist the election of such an inconsistent, double minded man as the Hon. Arthur Livermore, who looks one way and rows another."[26] This statement more than any other summed up how many New Hampshirites thought of Livermore. It may safely be concluded that there were few other aspects that legitimated in the minds of leading citizens the court that Plumer was creating than the fact that Arthur Livermore was not to be a member.

After Upham declined the appointment to the high court, Richardson advised Plumer about whom next to appoint. He named three Republicans, but Plumer insisted that he still wanted a Federalist. Interestingly, Richardson replied that if Mason could be persuaded to be a judge, he would resign as chief justice and serve under him. But he would not do the same for Smith. "He would not accept a subordinate seat on the bench under Smith," he told the governor. Richardson had little enthusiasm for Federalist appointments and considered them only because Plumer wanted them. He remained a faithful Republican for at least his earliest years on the bench, even publishing anonymously an article in the *Patriot* six months after becoming chief justice, criticizing Republicans "who came for offices, and who have gone, when offices could not be gained." It was an attack on the Claggetts, who were still demanding the third seat on the high bench.[27]

Plumer succeeded in persuading the Republican councilors to make one more try at appointing a Federalist judge. The candidate he nominated was John Harris, a Concord attorney, who was respected by members of both parties and recommended to Plumer by Richardson, Bell, and Levi Woodbury. Harris had indicated to the governor that he would accept, but after some hesitation he returned the commission. Plumer was bitterly disappointed. "This is an unpleasant circumstance," he wrote his son. "I thot I had made judges enough for one year." Now he had to make another and was "really embarrassed who to select," especially because he felt that the Council was becoming resistant and would not consider another Federalist. He blamed the "talents" of New Hampshire lawyers when he should have blamed the compensation. "There are some young men who are promising but they want character & influence," he observed. Again his son told him to forget about Federalists, and the governor finally agreed.[28]

No one was angrier when Plumer kept nominating Federalists to the Superior Court than the Claggetts, father and son. From their perspective he was placing political enemies into an office that by right belonged to Clifton Claggett. Early in the legislative session Claggett told Plumer that he had to be reappointed to the court "to convince the world that he possessed the confidence of the republicans." He was then a leading candidate to succeed Mason as United States senator but still said he needed to be named judge. It was, Plumer concluded, "proof of the littleness of his mind. Men of small talents are the most zealous, & the most anxious for public notice."[29]

Claggett became obsessed with the notion that his reputation could be restored if he got a multiple of offices. That summer he was a candidate for both the federal Senate and the federal House of Representatives. Once elected to congress he still sought appointments to be clerk of two courts in Hillsborough County and to be judge of probate. Richardson visited him in October and found him unhappy in being only a congressman. "He will agree I believe to be satisfied if he can be appointed clerk of both courts in this county & judge of Probate. Whether the people will agree that one man should be thus *loaded* with offices I know not. He however seems to insist on it." And that was not all. "I wish you to inform your Father particularly," Claggett wrote the younger Plumer, "that my nomination in this County for Mem[ber] of Cong[ress] is understood as not *interfering* with any *appointments* to be made." He still expected to sit on the Superior Court.[30]

When he first suspected that Harris might not accept the judgeship, the younger Plumer began to fear that Claggett would have to be reappointed. He consulted with Richardson, who answered that Claggett was "so weak a man, that if he is appointed, he (Richardson) should feel himself compelled to resign, that both he & Bell had much rather do the business alone than have such an associate." Four days later, he reported Richardson as saying that it was "better to appoint nobody for the present than to appoint a man who is unfit for the office." Three days after that, when it began to appear that no desirable prospect was likely to accept appointment, Richardson relented somewhat, as the younger Plumer told his father. If Claggett "is really & truly disposed to take an open & manly part in support of the administration, he should not object, if you see fit, to his being appointed Judge, though at the same time he thinks his talents hardly equal to the place."[31]

Most likely, Richardson had not changed his mind. What probably happened was that the younger Plumer told him that he was advising his father that he might have to appoint Claggett. Possibly the son even told the chief justice of the anxiety that the governor was experiencing because of his daughter's marital predicament, and Richardson decided that it was unreasonable for him to threaten resignation if Claggett was appointed. That threat had put Plumer in too difficult a spot. Moreover, Richardson, like every other Republican in the state, knew that the daughter's husband, William Claggett, was becoming more and more belligerent. As early as July, he had told his brother-in-law that he and other Republicans working with him could no longer support the Plumer administration, that they were forming a coalition "to restore" the party and would publish a newspaper that would end William Plumer's political career. And surprising as it seems today, he raised the financing and actually implemented one part of his threat. He and some other disgruntled Republicans founded and financed a newspaper that they named the *People's Advocate*, edited at Portsmouth, which defies description even by the rough and bitter politics of those times. "The term 'newspaper' is hardly appropriate," Lynn Turner observed, "it was devoted solely to political invective," all of which was directed against Governor Plumer.[32]

Richardson need not have been concerned that his threat to resign would make the Claggett problem impossible for Plumer to resolve. The governor simply was not going to put Claggett back on the court, no matter the personal and political pressure. At the November session of the legislature, both Claggetts appeared in Concord, making the governor uncomfortable, especially as he and the former judge were in the same boardinghouse. Claggett told him that "he ought to have been appointed judge, but as I did not appoint him, he should no longer support me." Then, when he had heard that Harris had declined his commission, Claggett went to Plumer and said he expected "to succeed him." "[B]ut," Plumer wrote his wife, he "will not be appointed." That statement tells us everything we have to know about the importance to Plumer of this judicial appointment. He was not saying to his wife that Clifton Claggett was never going to be reappointed a judge. He was warning her to expect trouble with her son-in-law and that she might not be seeing her daughter as much as she would like.[33]

As it became more evident that no amount of political pressure would get Claggett back on the bench, his son lost all caution. Plumer, William Claggett told Levi Woodbury, had "forfeited public confidence." It was, he added, "well known that should the present governor even succeed in getting another nomination, most true republicans will not give him their support." A month later, after Harris had refused to serve, Richardson was in despair, doubting "whether any republican could be found who was fit for it [the judgeship], unless it might be Woodbury, whose age he though[t] was some objection, but not conclusive." Woodbury was twenty-six years old. The younger Plumer had also been thinking of Woodbury, believing that he had all the qualities needed for judicial success. Though only ten months older, Plumer, Jr. also feared that Woodbury was too young. "It would hardly be prudent to appoint a young man," he wrote his father. "Such men, if they have other qualifications want the weight of character & influence necessary for the office of a judge."[34]

Levi Woodbury had been at the bar only four years. A Dartmouth graduate, he had studied law at the Litchfield, Connecticut, school of Tapping Reeve and James Gould, destining him to become the first member of New Hampshire's highest court and the first justice of the United States Supreme Court to attend a law school. He later studied at a law office in Boston and with Jeremiah Smith at Exeter. He was serving as secretary of the state senate at the June 1816 session, and as Plumer's militia aide-de-camp, rooming at the same boardinghouse as the governor, Isaac Hill's home in Concord.[35]

Plumer was very impressed with Woodbury, and when he received Harris's rejection, he may have already determined that Woodbury should be the next appointee. "I frankly informed Levi Woodbury that I thot of nominating him a judge of the Superior court," the governor noted. "He said he did not wish it, but if the present judges approved of it, he would accept it, for three or four years, tho he would make a great sacrifice of interest. His object he said was political life." He had never wanted to be a judge, he told Plumer, and even though he had been in practice only four years, accepting the office would "subject me to peculiar pecuniary sacrifices." He had only recently raised his income somewhat above subsistence and believed he was ready for the vocation for which he had been preparing—politics.[36]

The three Republicans on the executive Council, grateful that Plumer had not nominated another Federalist, quickly accepted Woodbury. It was the most satisfying hour of Plumer's governorship. "The question that gave me most anxiety was yesterday settled to my entire satisfaction," he explained. Woodbury had not wanted "the office of judge," he admitted, "but I thot the office wanted him." As everyone knew, "[n]o other man in the state of half his worth would have accepted the office." New Hampshire now had "judges of whom I am proud in saying they derived their office from my authority."[37] Plumer may not have realized it, but he was fulfilling the reforms he had worked for as a young lawyer at the Constitutional Convention of 1791–1792. He was doing in 1816 what he had hoped to do then, give New Hampshire a strong judicial base on which the law of tomorrow would be built, by competent, learned judges and not by Jeffersonian legislators. It was a triumph for which he had always worked, spending endless hours planning, plotting, and dreaming with his friend of those early years, Jeremiah Smith. The tragedy of 1816 was that he did it without Smith to lend it the luster of a truly great jurisprudence. The legacy he would bequeath to New Hampshire was a court to match the stature of Jeremiah Smith, but without Smith presiding.

As with all changes judicial in New Hampshire during the first half of the nineteenth century, there was a good deal of opposition. Some observers said Woodbury was "*guilty of being young in years*," and newspapers in Boston as well as New Hampshire referred to him as the "baby judge." Woodbury himself, according to his biographer, thought that the outcry against him "contributed to the growth of Republican factionalism."[38] The better view is that Republican divisions were caused by dissenters and malcontents such as the Claggetts. Astonishingly, Clifton Claggett, who less than a month earlier had been elected to Congress, outpolling Jeremiah Smith, who led the Federalist ticket,[39] still had expected he could get a judgeship. On hearing of Woodbury's appointment, he went immediately to see Plumer, telling him that this event was the ultimate insult and would bring retribution at the next election. "To prevent my re-election, you & your son may injure yourselves," the governor replied, "but cannot effect my reputation or inflict new wounds to my feelings."[40] That night Claggett told the Republican caucus that he would petition the legislature to pay his salary from the day he was legislated out of office in 1813 to the day he was addressed out at that last June session. Surprisingly, the Claggetts still had sympathy in the party. The committee appointed to consider his petition reported that "he [should] have and receive out of the treasury one thousand dollars in full of his salary as justice of the Superior Court—which report was not accepted." Too bad—we could almost wish that the money had been appropriated so that we could know whether Plumer would have signed the bill for compensation. To have done so would have contradicted his brilliant coup of addressing out of office all the judges of the state. But then, he also had to consider that the money was for his daughter's father-in-law.[41]

The most overt factionalizing of the Republicans was caused by William Claggett's newspaper, although only for three or four months. Woodbury noted in his diary that, when the November session of the General Court convened in Concord, the main topic of conversation was the *People's Advocate*. William Claggett had announced that he expected to lose a thousand dollars on the publication, but no matter, he would have the pleasure of driving Plumer from office. The *People's Advocate*, in Turner's judgment, "became more vicious than any Federalist journal in its slander of the administration." Still, the journalism was so inept and the attacks on Plumer so overstated that they almost never hit the mark.[42]

Governor Plumer was more than satisfied. His expressions of pleasure indicate that he was prouder of his court than of any other accomplishment of his public career. "I feel a conscious pride in reflecting that better judges have been commissioned by me than ever before existed at one time in the state," he told his son. He may well have been right. Even Jeremiah Smith did not preside over a court as strong as the first bench presided over by William Merchant Richardson. "Our courts of law were never before filled by men so well qualified for their places as are the present judges," Plumer boasted. He repeated that claim to the man he had hoped to make chief justice, the Federalist Jeremiah Mason. "I feel a conscious pride that the court contains so much talent, legal science, & integrity as it does," he told Mason. "This single circumstance is more than a reward for all the calumny that has been heaped on my administration. No man estimates the importance of an able & upright judiciary higher than I do. I look to it as the bulwark & support of our rights."[43]

The strength of the new court came mainly from Richardson. Very quickly he proved he was worthy of serving as head of the judiciary between the memorable and distinguished chief justiceships of Jeremiah Smith and Joel Parker. He was by no means the accomplished student of jurisprudence that they each were, but as chief justice he was their equal as the leader of both bench and bar. One reason was his length of service. Smith was chief justice for almost ten years before being legislated out by Plumer, and Parker held the position just about the same amount of time before leaving New Hampshire to become Royall Professor of Law in Harvard. A few weeks before he was voted off the court, Smith told the grand jury of Grafton that "[u]pon average our Chief Justices have not continued in office more than five years, and our other Judges not more than six." He believed that the recent death of his colleague Caleb Ellis was "the first instance of the death of a Judge of the Supreme Court, while in office, since . . . the revolution."[44]

Richardson not only became the first New Hampshire chief justice to die in office, he was the first to preside over the court for more than a decade. He served for nearly twenty-two years, more than any other chief justice in the nineteenth century. It was a remarkably longer term than his first two colleagues. Samuel Bell was a judge for just a little more than two years before becoming governor, succeeding Plumer. Woodbury was on the bench six years before leaving the court to succeed Bell.

It was Richardson's length of service that marked his judicial career and provided reason for Governor Charles H. Bell to conclude that, "[w]ith the exception of Judge Jeremiah Smith, perhaps no occupant of the judicial bench has done so much to shape the jurisprudence of New Hampshire" as Richardson.[45] He became the leader of the law, providing the direction, the integrity, and the dedication to principle that Governor Plumer had been looking for and that Chief Justice Smith had hoped for. Long before he died, the antagonisms and animosities that had dogged Smith had ended, and so had the supervision of the legislature. The judiciary was, as yet, far from becoming the dominant branch of government, but it was at least becoming an equal. And the law that the courts were pronouncing was being accepted as legitimate for New Hampshire—not surprising and not unusual, but still a bit ironic as it was a receptionist law in a politically Jeffersonian state.

*Chapter Thirteen*

# Judicial Legacy

After appointing the three judges of the new Superior Court, Governor Plumer surely had the right to expect that his problems with the judiciary were behind him. With his party in absolute control of the government, there was no chance that lawyers could bring back any reforms of Smith's that had been introduced by the Judicial Act of 1813 and repealed by the act of 1816. Law terms and single-judge trials would now be but memories of a failed experiment at judicial efficiency and, Plumer could hope, would not be raised again as political issues. Unfortunately for the governor, events did not unfold as he might have expected.

One of Plumer's hallmarks as a civic leader and as a pacesetter of public mores was his frugality. Even during his younger days as a Federalist, he had been vocal on the question of state salaries. New Hampshire officials, he opined, should be appointed or elected for the virtue of serving the people, not to obtain a living. Public office was a high civic good, not an occupation. It sounds platitudinous to make the claim, but truly, Plumer practiced his ideals. In 1814 he had pledged that if elected governor he would "serve the *people*, for half the stated salary, which has been for years given to the *Governor*." The Federalists heaped sarcasm on the promise. Plumer, the *Constitutionalist* smirked, "says, we give our public officers too high salaries; he says no man ought to have more than six hundred dollars salary in the highest office, in this little contemptible state."[1]

After the election of 1816, Plumer had no difficulty persuading the legislature to implement his pledge. Members of the General Court were delighted to lower salaries, and his own compensation was quickly reduced. The *Patriot* reported that the salary paid to the governor of Pennsylvania was "more than *five times* as much as the Governor of New-Hampshire receives," a fact that did not embarrass New Hampshirites. More likely, it pleased them. The legislature reduced other pay as well, including that of the justices, leading the *Portsmouth Oracle*, a Federalist newspaper, to complain of "Cheap Judges." "Chief Justice RICHARDSON, and Mr. Justice BELL, have accepted seats on the Bench, upon the *half-pay system*, which Gov. PLUMER has established," the *Oracle* remarked. "Perhaps a little experience will satisfy the people, that when Judges are too *cheap*, Justice is too *dear*." It did not take Plumer long to learn that, high-minded as he believed his frugality ideal to be, civic virtue was no substitute for adequate judicial pay. The salaries that had been paid to Smith's court had been too high, he told Jeremiah Mason, but now he realized that the compensation he had negotiated for Richardson's court was too low. "A medium between both appear to me the most proper, & . . . it will be an object with me to increase their salaries."[2]

The governor had begun the year of 1817 recommending what the *Patriot* described as "a system of economy and retrenchment, by the reduction of salaries, where they are too high." Isaac Hill said that Plumer's parsimony demonstrated the difference between Federalists and Republicans. Federalists wanted office not to serve the people but to obtain high emoluments.[3] Just three days after the *Patriot* had claimed that Plumer had seized the moral high ground from the Federalists, Judge Bell visited the governor to warn that at least the chief justice, if not the other judges, had to have more money. "[H]e feared if the salary was not raised judge Richardson would resign." Plumer then realized that he would have to jettison one element of his principles of frugal government or he might lose his chief justice. He had been convinced, he wrote his son, that the coming political year would be harmonious. "There is however one difficulty to be encountered, which is that respecting the salaries of the Judges of the Superior Court. They must be raised; or the Court will be no longer composed of its present members," he explained just before the election of 1817. "[S]hould I be placed at the head of the government for the year ensuing, I contemplate recommending it to the legislature." He gave a quite lame excuse for reversing a policy in which he had taken so much pride. "When I recommended in June 1816, a reduction of the salaries of the justices of the superior court," he explained, "their duties were small compared with those of the present time; then only one judge was necessary to hold two thirds of the courts, but no term can be holden by less than two, indeed all three judges are expected to attend every court." Plumer concocted some rather foolish explanations over his long career, but even he must have wondered at this reasoning. After all, he was responsible for the additional duties of the justices. They had come about because of his Judiciary Act of 1816, and at the time he had asked the legislature to lower judicial salaries, he had known the Act of 1816 would certainly become law. And when they accepted their commissions, the three judges had known that their duties were being extensively enlarged over the work of the Smith court. After all, the act had already been passed. It was law. By going from one-judge trials to three-judge trials, Richardson expected that their work load would be substantially increased. They started their first term presiding at three-judge trials and understood that all three of them had to attend every circuit. Plumer knew very well that the judges were not complaining about his low salaries because they had to preside at trials more often than Jeremiah Smith and his associates had presided. They were unhappy with their pay because not only was it low, it was *too low*. When Plumer had set the salaries, his measure of compensation had been what he thought virtuous New Hampshire officials should be willing to accept, not what New Hampshire's leading lawyers were making at the bar. It was what they might have earned in private practice that made the judges' salaries low.[4]

By the time that the June 1817 session of the General Court began, Plumer had decided to raise judicial salaries, but the leaders of the legislature were not in a generous mood. "An act for establishing salaries of the Justices of the Superior Court" was introduced in the House of Representatives, fixing the salary for the chief justice at $1,500, a surprisingly large sum as it was the highest amount that Smith had ever received as chief justice.[5] It was far too much for members of the lower house, and by a vote reported as "47 yeas, nays 125," it was rejected. The legislators then started a process they had run through several times over the past quarter of a century. A motion was made to strike the sum $1,500 from the bill and insert $1,350. When that failed to obtain a majority of votes, it was moved to strike $1,350 and insert $1,200 and then to strike $1,200 and insert $1,100. When $1,100 passed in the negative, "yeas 66, nays 106," the lawmakers gave up and voted to postpone the bill "indefinitely," meaning there would be no salary increases that year.[6]

Disappointed, Woodbury wrote Plumer that the "parsimony" of the legislators might cause the state to "lose the services" of Richardson and Samuel Bell. If that happened, "the conduct of the Legislature will prove a source of lasting regret." Then he made an interesting although somewhat obscure observation. "The old delay and uncertainty of justice," he said, "would not only operate as a direct evil, in numerous particulars, but would indirectly double perhaps the profits of the Bar."[7]

Fortunately for Plumer, both Richardson and Bell made do with the low salaries and stayed on the court. To get them raises at the June 1818 session of the legislature, the governor adopted a new strategy. He asked the two houses to give the Superior Court exclusive jurisdiction of all real and personal actions of $50 or more. "And as a compensation for the additional duty thus imposed upon the justices of the superior court, grant them an additional salary, equal to the fees of entry of those actions (except a certain portion to the clerks) which would increase the compensation of the judges without taxing the public treasury." The lawmakers may not have been able to figure whether the treasury gained or lost on that deal, for they did not take it up. Instead, they solved the salary problem by addressing it directly. The chief justice was voted $1,400 annually and the associate justices $1,200 each. But any fees they were paid they could not keep. "[T]he fees which said justices may receive in the discharge of the duties of their office, shall be severally accounted for and deducted from their salaries."[8] And, as a result, Jeremiah Smith remained the judge who had been the highest paid in New Hampshire history.

Plumer did not plan to run again for governor after 1818, which may explain why his address to the June session of the General Court that year was most unusual. Except for his message urging support for James Madison and the federal military forces fighting the War of 1812, this speech of 1818 was the most important and memorable of his lifetime of public service. Lynn Turner asserts that Plumer devoted the "entire" address to "remodeling of judicial practices," but that estimate depends on whether such matters as relieving debtors from house arrest or regulating clerks of court are considered "judicial practices." The speech was published as a separate pamphlet, a printing that for New Hampshire governors was quite unusual, and a close count of its eleven pages shows that at least seven or eight of them deal with judicial matters, the court system, and questions of procedure.[9] Plumer proposed several changes in New Hampshire's justice system that, Turner marveled, were "remarkably liberal, if not actually socialist." What both Turner and he termed "natural justice," Plumer cautioned, "was being thwarted by the vast amount of trivial litigation in the state, which fell with peculiar weight upon the poorest people, bringing ruin to the individual and economic burdens of society."[10]

> A spirit of litigation, instead of being repressed, appears to meet with encouragement in various parts of the State. The great number of law-suits, (many of which are trivial) and their expense and delay ruin many of the suitors, who after being relieved from imprisonment, by taking the poor debtor's oath, become a burthen to society. The annual expense of suits in this State is immense, and the tax, levied in this way, falls with oppressive weight upon a class of people least able to bear it. . . . And has not the government some reason to apprehend that evil consequences may

> result from the vast number, and expense attending those suits? If states are secure, only in proportion as the great body of the people are contented with their situation, and attached to the laws and institutions of their country, it is surely our interest as well as our duty to render the people happy, by diminishing their burthens and thus increasing their attachment to the laws and to the government.[11]

It should be emphasized that Plumer was the legal reformer who had once rallied many of his fellow young lawyers to attend the Constitutional Convention in 1791, hoping they would make the judiciary independent and autonomous—especially independent and autonomous from the legislature. Now, at the late date of 1818, he was, as governor, doing the opposite. For he was asking that the legislature take the initiative in remaking the judiciary, implying it was the lawmakers, not the judges, who should correct abuses in litigation, reduce the costliness of jury trials, especially as they bore on the poorer people, and discourage unnecessary law suits. Remember too, that Plumer was the lawyer-governor who, just two years earlier, in 1816, had engineered a total reform of the judiciary of New Hampshire. Yet here he was before the General Court in 1818 outlining a surprisingly lengthy list of further changes he said should be made in the jurisdictions of both the Superior Court and the Common Pleas court. Intending to diminish unnecessary suits, capricious motions for new trials, and mounting costs, he recommended reforming rules governing the recovery of damages, assessment of costs, collection of fees, and determination of forfeitures.[12]

It is a telling fact that there was only one rule of the court, developed and strengthened by Chief Justice Smith, that Plumer asked the legislature to abolish. It was the Superior Court's authority "to grant new trials, in the nature of a review, in cases where it appears to them that substantial justice has not been done." Although there is little evidence, it is a fairly safe conjecture that Plumer once supported this judicial procedure. Now he was decidedly opposed to it. "[T]he policy and expediency of allowing a review in all civil cases, appears to me doubtful," he explained. "It is not only attended with great expence and long delay, but encourages litigation, if not false swearing. The losing party having discovered what testimony his case requires, is under inducements to procure it."[13] It is extraordinary that Plumer ever made this argument—even more so that he made it in public. Any Rockingham County lawyer who had been at the bar for fifteen years could have remembered when he expressed ideas exactly the opposite. It is most unlikely that litigants, after losing a jury trial, moved for review because they now knew what evidence they should have introduced to win. Possibly there was some "false swearing" at trials *de novo*, but it could not have been a serious problem. It is true that perjury was more common at that time than it would be in later decades, but it was not a problem peculiar to second trials. Then, parties, either defendants or plaintiffs, could not testify; hence, any false swearing would have been committed by witnesses who were not parties, when at the new trial they would have been under oath, subject to cross examination. A certain question they would have been asked was why they had not testified at the first trial as they now testified. Plumer's reasoning is quite unpersuasive, but then, he may have been speaking politically, not about law, that is, he may have been acting the part of a good Jeffersonian. Quite likely he was defending the right to trial by jury, intending to make only a single important point—that the verdict in a jury trial should not be subject to review.

There was one more major change in the law that occurred during Plumer's administration, and it is more than likely that he was instrumental in instigating the process that brought the change about. It challenged the legislative practice that Plumer had very much opposed when he was a young lawyer and, most likely, still did: the General Court's authority to enact legislation restoring litigants, defeated in a jury trial to their "law" by ordering a new jury trial, that is, a new trial in a cause that had been fully adjudicated, with a promulgated final ruling. The legality of the process had been challenged several times in court and had been declared unconstitutional by Superior Court judges more than once. But the legislature had paid no attention to what the judges held.[14] In fact, the procedure may not have been questioned by the lawmakers until the June 1818 session of the legislature, when the two houses passed a joint resolution, asking the Superior Court for an opinion as to whether the legislature had the legal authority to restore private citizens to their law. "Resolved by the Senate and House of Representatives in General Court convened," the resolution provided, "That the Justices of the Superior Court of Judicature be requested to express to the Legislature at their next session, an opinion in writing on the following question, viz:—Has the Legislature a right to grant new trials or restoration to law in any case; and if so, in what case or cases?"[15]

The suggestion is merely conjecture, but perhaps we should not take the resolution on its face. It appears to be a straightforward, unencumbered order for an Opinion of the Justices, a procedure of the New Hampshire Constitution, authorizing "[e]ach branch of the legislature as well as the governor and council . . . to require the opinions of the justices of the superior court, upon important questions of law, upon solemn occasions."[16] It could be a grave mistake to interpret the resolution from the perspective of the twenty-first century. Today for the General Court or the executive branch to request an Opinion of the Justices is to ask an opinion on the constitutionality of contemplated legislation or a projected state action. It is doubtful whether legislators in 1818 would have questioned the court about constitutionality. They might not have considered themselves as competent as were the judges about issues of private law, but they did feel themselves as able to interpret the constitution, and they knew that they were as authorized to make constitutional rulings as were the justices. Most likely, they had reached the limits of their tolerance for the time-consuming procedures they followed when restoring to law. Petitions praying to be restored to law took up much legislative time. In both 1816 and 1818 the House of Representatives and the Senate had each appointed a "standing committee on new trials or restoration to law." As recently as the previous June session, the General Court had granted a new trial and relief to two litigants praying to be restored to their law.[17]

So, what was occurring in 1819? If the legislators were annoyed by the time they had to devote to restorations to law, why not just end the practice? Why not just announce that the General Court would no longer restore disappointed litigants to their law? The moral persuasion of a ruling by the Superior Court is one obvious answer. An Opinion of the Justices, holding that restorations to law were either illegal or unconstitutional, certainly could be expected to strengthen the arguments of legislative leaders seeking to dissuade members from taking up valuable legislative time by filing restoring legislation. Lawmakers, pressured by constituents for acts relieving them from judicial judgments and granting them new jury trials, could tell those constituents that the judges would not allow retrials, that even if the two houses passed bills restoring them to their law and the governor signed the bills into acts, the judges would not obey. They would, instead, quash the action for a new trial.

The judges did not answer the legislature as they had been expected to, that is directly, with a specially drafted and issue-specific *Opinion of the Justices*. When they received the official notice from Governor Plumer that the General Court wanted their opinion, the judges explained, "an action was pending before us, which appeared to involve most of the questions proposed in the resolve. That action has since been decided, and the report of it hereto annexed, forms a part of our reply to those questions."[18] That is, they submitted to the Senate and House of Representatives a decision of an actual litigation: the legal issue in dispute was a motion on which they passed judgment, the opinion for which they had drafted in the regular course of their docket. As with most judicial decisions it dealt with the facts of the case and the legal issue presented by the motion, explained how the court had resolved the controversy, and presented the justices' reasoning.

It is a matter of some historical regret that the court chose to file the decision in *Merrill v. Sherburne*, rather than prepare an Opinion of the Justices. Richardson had been of counsel in the case and therefore "did not sit." That meant he did not write the reply, as he most likely would have had a separate Opinion been drafted. Only the other two judges participated in the decision, and the writing had been assigned to Woodbury. Although one of his earliest attempts at judicial composition, it is very much an example of the opinions he would become known for: overlong, filled with simplicities,[19] irrelevancies,[20] and even sloppy work.[21] Samuel Bell was the second judge, joining Woodbury in the decision. By the time that *Merrill v. Sherburne* was submitted to the General Court, Bell had become governor, thus signing the opinion as an associate justice and signing as governor the communication that sent it to the two houses.[22]

*Merrill v. Sherburne* was a factually simple case of restoring a litigant to law. Benjamin Merrill had lost a will contest in the probate court of Rockingham County. He died, and the administratrix, his widow, petitioned to be restored to her law. The two houses voted to restore her,[23] authorizing her "to enter the cause anew at the superior court," directing "that said cause have a day in said court, and shall be heard, tried and determined in said court upon pleadings had in the former trial," that is, by having a jury trial de novo on the pleadings of the original trial and empowering the Superior Court "to affirm or reverse the former judgment or decree, . . . as the said trial may terminate for or against either party."[24] Joseph Sherburne, one of the plaintiffs in the original lawsuit, served with a copy of the restoring legislation and ordered to appear in the Superior Court for a new trial, moved to quash "on the ground that the act of the legislature was unconstitutional." It was that motion to quash that Woodbury and Bell had ruled on, and it was their opinion explaining why they ordered "the proceedings in this case to be quashed"[25] that they submitted to the legislature.

Twenty-seven years earlier, William Plumer had convinced Chief Justice John Pickering that legislation restoring a losing litigant to her law was unconstitutional on the grounds that it deprived the plaintiff of his right to trial by jury.[26] It was a striking argument. It is possible that Plumer thought it his only plausible winning argument, even possible that he did not think of contending that it would violate either the principle of judicial independence or the doctrine of separation of powers for the two legislative houses to restore the defendant to her law. But it may also be that he argued that restoring to law deprived the plaintiff of his right to a trial by jury because that argument was quite persuasive at that time and the one best calculated not to irritate New Hampshire legislators. Woodbury, who was less an original thinker than was Plumer, spun no new theories and announced no dramatic breakthrough in constitutional principle. His reasoning rested squarely on the doctrine of separation of powers, introduced into New Hampshire law by the Constitution of 1784, the constitution written by Pickering. By reversing an adjudicated probate-court judgment and restoring Merrill to her law, the legislature, Woodbury contended, was exercising a judicial power beyond the bounds of its constitutional legislative authority and violating the doctrine of separation of powers.[27]

Woodbury may have been less legally adventuresome than Plumer, but his argument was more calculated to impress lawyers, and as time went on and as the principle of trial by jury as the chief guardian of liberty lost much of its constitutional vogue, the separation-of-powers theory became the one that impressed law school graduates. The sequence is by no means certain, but from what existing research tells us, it does seem that the *Merrill* decision did not take on its latter-day prestige until lawyers in the twentieth century elevated it as one of New Hampshire's leading constitutional opinions, establishing, in state law, the power in the courts of judicial review.[28] That interpretation is pure legal anachronism. Woodbury certainly had judicial review in mind, though it is doubtful that he foresaw any of its twentieth- and twenty-first century nuances when he wrote of the separation of powers: "That clause which confers upon the 'general court' the authority 'to make laws,' provides, at the same time, that they must not be 'repugnant or contrary to the constitution,'" he pointed out. Then Woodbury explained to New Hampshire lawyers the constitutional possibilities of judicial review. "One prominent reason for creating the judicial, distinct from the legislative department, was, that the former might determine when laws were thus 'repugnant,' and so operate as a check upon the latter, as a safeguard to the people against its mistakes or encroachments." In the next two sentences he may have intended to rule unconstitutional the legislative authority of restoring losing litigants to their law. He was writing in 1818, however, and like most New Hampshire judges at that time, he may have felt the need to be cautious in challenging the two houses directly and so avoided stating the issue emphatically: "But the judiciary would in every respect cease to be a check on the legislature, if the legislature could at pleasure revise or alter any of the judgments of the judiciary. The legislature, too, would thus become the court of last resort, 'the superior court,' or 'supreme judicial' tribunal of the state; and those expressions so often applied to this court in the constitution would become gross misnomers."[29]

It is true that Woodbury was not quite saying that New Hampshire courts had the authority to review the constitutionality of legislation. He was claiming that as long as the General Court could interfere in the judicial process by restoring litigants to their law, the Superior Court could not effectively question the constitutionality of enacted legislation. But no matter. Lawyers being lawyers, his words were easily spun into a broader interpretation. Lawyers of a later era, after the era of legislative supremacy, that is, lawyers of an era of judicial supremacy, could easily convert them into a claim of judicial review. Even a graduate student writing on the separation of powers could conclude that "Woodbury claimed in *Merrill* the 'unquestionable' power to void clearly unconstitutional laws,"[30] which he did, because looking back we know that is the way the law developed, and so that must have been what he meant.

What usually goes unnoticed by twentieth- and twenty-first century observers, as that graduate student in history noted, is that Woodbury "refused to offer an absolute statement of the legislature's authority." A likely reason is that he did not want to upset those in the General Court sensitive about the legislature's constitutional authority, even though they probably constituted a slight minority of the membership. And besides, a ruling on the legislative authority was not relevant to the holding he wrote. It was a holding for the law of his day, not for ours. Members of the legislature could not be sure what he intended about their authority, and they probably did not ask. As Plumer wrote five years later, after *Merrill* "the legislature continued to hear petitions and pass bills directing new trials, without vacating the former judgments; but the courts of law decided these were also unconstitutional and dismissed the process." Eventually, the legislators realized that they no longer were absolutely supreme over the judiciary and vested the judges of the Superior Court with authority "to grant new trials in such cases as in their opinion justice and equity required." And so, Plumer concluded in 1823, "it now appears to be settled that the legislature have no authority to interfere in the trial of *suits between* individuals."[31]

Thinking as lawyers, we may continue to say that Woodbury, in *Merrill v. Sherburne*, wrote into New Hampshire law the doctrine of judicial review. But if we think as historians, it would be better to say that the legacy of *Merrill* is that it created a "new relationship between New Hampshire's judiciary and the legislature." With Woodbury's decision the judiciary obtained a further degree of independent legitimacy, and the principle of legislative supremacy began to pass from New Hampshire constitutional law. "Woodbury's theory," Lawrie has pointed out, "did not established the court 'supreme' arbiter of the constitution, as some have suggested. Rather, it provided judges an independent part in the political functions of government."[32] Although judiciary supremacy lay more than a half century in the future, legislative supremacy was beginning to recede into the past.

It was a moment of transition but not of immediate change. Even the election of 1819 did not mark the change in New Hampshire politics that might have been expected. William Plumer did not run that year for reelection as governor. He was finished with elective politics forever. Departing from the political scene, he ended an era of public leadership in which he had, at first, furnished most of the intellectual momentum and later was the dominate officeholder. Yet his passing was marked as much by continuity as by change. The new governor was his personal protégé, his own chosen successor, Associate Superior Court Justice Samuel Bell. Three of the six candidates that the Republicans nominated for Congress that year were men that he had helped to make well known throughout the state: Clifton Claggett, Arthur Livermore, and William Plumer, Jr. They were all elected. Most Republicans were elected. Plumer, with the *Patriot*'s printer, Isaac Hill, had created a remarkably united party, and it was poised to win elections for many years to come. In fact, there was very little that changed from the gubernatorial administration of Plumer to Bell except perhaps for one reversal that probably even Plumer foresaw. Bell had been governor only a week or so when he persuaded the two houses to raise his salary to $1,200. He was perfectly happy to inherit Plumer's party but not Plumer's income.[33]

Some of the people and some of the events remained familiar. On 8 June 1819, the widow of Richard Evans petitioned "for arrearages of her late husband's salary as judge." On the twelfth she was voted leave "to be heard on the floor of the House on her petition," and on the fifteenth her brother-in-law appeared and "addressed the Convention in a speech of about two hours in behalf of the petitioner." Next day the House of Representatives voted "*Leave to withdraw petition granted* to . . . Ann W. Evans, 164 to 1." That vote brought to a close the farce of Evans and Clifton Claggett seeking their former judgeships and their claim to back pay.[34]

Other issues died harder. The next year, at the June 1820 session of the General Court, the House of Representatives received the petition of Thomas Carlisle, praying that he be restored to law. The supposedly precedent-shattering and seminal decision by Justice Woodbury in *Merrill v. Sherburne* apparently was of little account to the legislators. They voted that the petition be committed to the standing committee on restorations to law and asked the committee to report on its merits.[35]

The most excruciating hold that the legislators had over the judges as individuals, at that time, was the authority to address them from office. The unrestricted power of addressing out judges would remain unaltered in the New Hampshire Constitution for another century and a half. It would never again be exercised against the judiciary in such a wholesale way as it had been in 1816, when every nonprobate judge, whether then sitting or previously legislated from office, was addressed out. Although Article 73 of the New Hampshire Constitution, defining the authority to address from office, was in the section defining the powers of the judiciary, it was, after 1816, primarily employed to terminate nonjudicial state officials. Perhaps most frequently, addresses were voted to cancel the commissions of militia officers who had moved from their military districts and officials such as coroners who were incompetent or incurably sick.[36] The most extensive addressing from office of judicial personnel after 1816, occurred in 1855 and 1856, following seminal elections, when a coalition of Know-Nothings, Whigs, Free Soilers, and the second Republican Party for the first time ousted from control of the state government the previously invincible Democratic machine that had been built by William Plumer and Isaac Hill. The victors, upon address of both houses of the General Court to the Governor and Council, removed from office sheriffs, county officers such as registers of deeds, probate judges, clerks of court, justices of the peace, and other officials, including, most memorable judicially, the young solicitor of Strafford County, Charles Doe, just out of Harvard Law School and destined to become New Hampshire's greatest jurist.[37]

It should be noted that, unlike legislating a court from office, addressing out was never a political weapon used by the New Hampshire legislature to keep the judiciary subordinate or to open up judgeships for members of the majority party. Even so, as long as Article 73 remained in the state constitution, it had the appearance of a threat hanging over the judges, causing some uneasiness, or at least annoyance. It was not, however, until 1966 that the article was amended, and some of the potential sting of legislative supremacy over the judiciary was removed from the constitution. Though it still remained among the "Judiciary Power" articles, it no longer specifically referred to judges as the officers who could be addressed out. Rather, the governor with consent of the Council was empowered to "remove any commissioned officer for reasonable cause upon address of both houses of the legislature, provided nevertheless that the cause for removal shall be stated fully and substantially in the address and shall not be a cause with a sufficient ground for impeachment, and provided further that no officer shall be so removed unless he shall have an opportunity to be heard in his defense by a joint committee of both houses of the legislature."[38] Although the purpose of the authority to address out, as originally intended, was mutilated by this substitute, it did satisfy the felt need of twentieth-century American lawyers for what a New Hampshire attorney termed a "little due process."[39]

Legislating out, not addressing out, was the authority exercised by the New Hampshire legislature when asserting supremacy over the judiciary in the nineteenth century. In 1855 the coalition of Know Nothings, Whigs, and Free Soilers that now had become the second Republican Party legislated out the Superior Court of Judicature that Plumer had reformed in 1816 and created a new tribunal called the Supreme Judicial Court. Again, all the justices lost their tenure at good behavior, and new appointments were made by the Republican governor.[40] In 1859 the then-existing Court of Common Pleas was abolished by a statute providing that "the Court of Common Pleas shall be and hereby is abolished, and all laws establishing such court and providing for the justices thereof shall be and hereby are repealed." This provision, Richard Upton pointed out, was sufficient "to legislate the members of the Court from office."[41]

The Republicans were the dominant political party in New Hampshire from 1856 to 1874. Then in 1874 the Democrats gained control of the government, addressing from office many Republican officeholders and legislating out the Supreme Judicial Court. Two years later, in 1876, the Republicans were returned to power, and together with addressing all the new Democratic officials from office, they legislated out the Democrats' Superior Court of Judicature and created yet another tribunal, the Supreme Court. All the judges were removed, and in their place Republicans were appointed, including Charles Doe as chief justice.[42] To that extent the legislature retained supremacy over the judiciary.

Employing his prestige as chief justice, which was much greater than Jeremiah Smith's had been, Doe sought to end the cycle of legislating out, but change moves so slowly in New Hampshire that he obtained no results during his lifetime. Five years after he died—that is, in the first year of the twentieth century—the last restructuring of New Hampshire's high court occurred. It was much different from all the previous occurrences of legislating out. It was effected by a compact between the two major political parties, agreeing to divide the state's highest court into two separate tribunals, an appellate court and a trial court. None of the judges were to be left out of office. What Upton termed a "gentlemen's agreement" was negotiated. In the future all judicial appointments would alternate in turn between them, with the party in power retaining only one more seat on the bench than its opponent. "Since 1901," Upton summarized, "this agreement has been substantially complied with, down to the present day."[43]

Actually, it was complied with down to 1966. That year another amended clause was inserted into the constitution of New Hampshire, providing that "[t]he judicial power of the state shall be vested in the supreme court, a trial court of general jurisdiction known as the superior court, and such lower courts as the legislature may establish." The friends of an independent judiciary had finally accomplished what Plumer and

Smith had been unable to bring about at the Constitutional Convention in 1791–1792. They entrenched in the state constitution the appellate court and the highest trial court or, to use the words of twentieth-century New Hampshire lawyers, they gave the two courts "constitutional status."[44] Even if New Hampshire politicians were to return to their nineteenth-century policy of legislative supremacy, they could not legislate the judges of these courts from office. The judges could refuse to go.

It would not do to end this study with twentieth-century constitutional amendments protecting the judiciary from threats such as addressing out and legislating out, which no legislators would today use to suppress either the courts or the judges with tenure, even if they knew what was meant by "addressing out" and "legislating out." Better to consider a much more compelling question of history. Once the political party and the Jeffersonian legal policy of William Plumer had triumphed in 1816, what was left of the judicial reforms to the development and promotion of which Jeremiah Smith had devoted so much of his professional life?

Plumer, together with Isaac Hill of the *Patriot*, had built a political machine that would dominate New Hampshire government for thirty-nine years, or two generations as Thomas Jefferson calculated time. With the Judiciary Act of 1816, Plumer not only took control of the courts, he intended to expunge from the law and the judiciary system most of the reforms of Jeremiah Smith. He should have succeeded, for he had the political power and the support of the people.

We cannot know whether many New Hampshire voters understood the nature and purpose of Jeremiah Smith's substantive and procedural reforms. What we do know is that many, especially Republicans and non-lawyers in general, strongly and vocally objected to some of them. One that has been referred to but not thoroughly discussed in this book was his program to professionalize the high court,[45] which was opposed by some Federalists as well as most Republicans, mainly because of the dislike of lawyers then prevailing among New Hampshirites. This was the major element of Smith's objectives on which Plumer did not reverse the jurisprudence of his early years and which he did not turn against. Rather, he was the governor who can be credited with professionalizing the high court as Smith had intended. His appointment of Richardson, Bell, and Woodbury was in the image of Smith. After Plumer, there would no longer be laymen appointed to New Hampshire's highest court.

Another of Smith's reforms not discussed in this book, the one Smith cared deeply about implementing, was to write and publish judicial opinions, if possible in official state volumes, produced at public expense and edited by a reporter who would be a government employee. He could obtain nothing. The Republicans in the legislature just would not allow judges to publish their decisions officially. Expense was one reason. Lawmakers did not care to vote money for such activities, even though Smith's plans would have paid the costs of publication by taxing every lawyer $5.00 a year, for which the attorney would have received a copy of each volume of the *New Hampshire Reports.* A more compelling reason was that many Republicans, even those who knew little and cared less about the law of the lawyers, understood that if the judges published their decisions and their reasoning became legal precedent used by other judges to resolve future law suits, the judges and not the legislature would be writing and formulating some, if not most, of New Hampshire law. Every scheme that Smith came up with was voted down in one or both houses.[46]

Another fact we can no longer learn is whether Smith was responsible for having the Federalist Party, sometime before 1813, become more or less committed to creating a reporter system in New Hampshire. Several schemes were advanced, generally surreptitiously, all to be voted down by the Republican majority. The most open and well-publicized proposal for a reporter was in the Thompson-Webster bill of 1812, that puzzling draft of a judicial act that Daniel Webster and Thomas Thompson wrote. Their purpose is difficult to explain, unless just possibly it was a clever preview, a preparing of Federalist legislators for the introduction in the next year of the Judicial Act of 1813. Quite unexpectedly, it contained a provision for a court reporter, which cannot be accounted for unless it was demanded by Smith. Webster surely knew it would never be enacted, but then, its inclusion may not have mattered to him, as he undoubtedly expected the bill would not become law in 1812.

The next year the Federalists, returning to power, drafted and passed the Judicial Act of 1813, codifying several of Smith's projected reforms, but there was no mention, either in any statute or in any Federalist newspaper, of reporting judicial decisions or of a court reporter. Just why there was none is not certain. The obvious explanation is that simply too many legislators were against it. We get an indication of how much opposition existed by considering the next year, 1814, when there was not only a concerted effort to create the office of court reporter but there was strong evidence that the Federalists intended to make Smith the reporter, in addition to remaining as chief justice, with an additional salary of $500 a year. The legislation failed in the House of Representatives by a vote of 63 to 97. That is a large negative vote when we consider that the Federalists, Smith's party, were in the majority. The plurality of 34 votes out of 160 is as adequate a measure as we will ever discover of the opposition that existed to judicial reporters and the reporting of judges' opinions. It was not just Jeffersonians who were opposed to reporting. There must have been substantial numbers of Federalists who were against it as well.[47]

At the June session of the General Court the next year, Smith's friends enacted the bill for which he had been working for well over a decade. They passed into law "An act to provide for publishing Reports of the decisions of the Supreme Judicial Court." The statute gave the judges authority to appoint a reporter, which they did. With their choice, however, they miscalculated how easy it was to anger people when they gave the appearance of granting public money to one of their own. Instead of appointing as reporter the clerk of court or some competent lawyer in need, the three judges—Smith, Arthur Livermore, and Caleb Ellis—appointed Smith. It was not a politically wise appointment and one particularly difficult to explain to the voters. It made Smith both chief judge of the court and the reporter for the court. Of course, it could be defended on one premise. There was no lawyer more qualified than he or one who could perform the tasks of reporting better. But that was not what New Hampshirites would think about. Their first impressions were that the appointment was made to solve Smith's salary needs. He had asked the legislature for more money, the two houses had refused, and so he had invented and accepted a second office. That was how the Republican press presented the facts: a nebulous, mostly useless office, never before known in New Hampshire, had been created with the enormous salary of $500 a year to satisfy, in part, the greed of the chief justice. As a consequence, opposition to court reporting grew even stronger.[48]

Accepting the office of court reporter hurt Smith's reputation without doing a thing to help his finances. He never produced a single volume of the *New Hampshire Reports*. He was legislated out of office before he could even begin to edit judicial opinions. At the December 1816 session of the General Court, shortly after legislating Chief Justice Smith from office, the Republicans repealed the statute authorizing a reporter. An impartial observer would have reasonably concluded that with Plumer's judicial appointees—Richardson, Bell, and Woodbury—in office, there would be no further mention of reporting and reporters. But it is indicative of the merits of Jeremiah Smith's jurisprudence and of how his objectives conformed to the legal theories that receptionist jurists in other states had been establishing that eventually all of Smith's reforms were incorporated into New Hampshire law. What is amazing about reporting and publishing opinions is the speed with which the process was adopted in New Hampshire once Smith was off the court. He had gotten absolutely nowhere: all his various proposals for reporting had been rejected by the General Court; and when he began any project to report and publish, he not only had to terminate, he had been vilified by the Republican press. Yet within two years of taking office, the court of Richardson, Bell, and Woodbury let the governor know that all three judges wanted to publish their opinions. In 1818 their clerk of court announced that he would publish their decisions, and rather than being attacked by Republican newspapers as Smith had been, incredibly he was praised by the *New-Hampshire Patriot*. Isaac Hill completely reversed himself, not only assuring his readers that reports would be "valuable" to everybody, not just lawyers, but even urging legislators to have the treasury buy at least one copy of the *Reports* for every town government in the state. At the next June session, in 1819, the legislature voted that the treasury purchase 150 copies, relieving the clerk of most of his financial gamble and making the *New Hampshire Reports* at least semiofficial.[49]

To say that reporting was "official" at that time is to say much. It shows how the Republicans of New Hampshire, even the more committed Jeffersonians such as Plumer and Hill, were willing to abandon republicanist jurisprudential theory. They did not even make an issue of the fact that Richardson and his colleagues did not write their opinions seriatim, as Jeffersonian legal theory required. Instead they adopted the receptionist method of one judge speaking for the court—the single opinion as perfected by Lord Mansfield and Chief Justice Marshall—the two judges and the judicial method that Jefferson himself detested.[50]

One legacy of the opposition to Smith and reporting may have lingered on. New Hampshire's General Court would not authorize an official state reporter until 1850. It is possible that the ridicule flung by the Republicans at Smith's double officeholding—court reporter as well as chief justice—had created so strong a prejudice against the office of reporter that the legislators wanted nothing to do with it. The result was that, after Adams reported the first volume, the three judges became the reporters. They did all the work: collected the briefs from the lawyers, edited them, wrote the decisions, made the contracts with the printers to produce and bind the volumes, and then proofread the text. It is uncertain but likely that they received the remuneration, which could not have been much, but considering their low salaries, this may have been one of the reasons that they accepted the extra burden of reporting.[51]

There is one other major legacy of Smith's program that the Republicans thought they had buried in 1816, but that the Richardson court would try to resurrect, partly because it was so practically useful, but mostly because, although they were Republicans, they were not judges of the republicanist or Jeffersonian school. It was the most successful of the legal changes that Smith had introduced and also the most opposed: law terms.

It was previously mentioned that the evidence is not clear just why such a large part of the New Hampshire population had opposed law terms when Smith was the chief justice. It cannot be assumed that law terms were misunderstood. Most Republicans quite likely did not understand the functions of judicial reports or of a court reporter, even while strongly opposing them. Laymen may have appreciated vaguely that judicial reports were a means by which judges could make law and felt that was undesirable, especially if they believed that law should come from their elected legislators, not from legal custom or the precedent of written judicial decisions. But it is unlikely that many understood more than that—not how decisions, written by judges, were employed as precedents of legal principles and how other judges treated these precedents as binding authority to promulgate more law. Opposition to law terms in New Hampshire during Jeremiah Smith's tenure on the high court was based on more concrete grounds. No doubt, most people misunderstood their purpose, thinking, as they were told by the more committed Republicans, that Smith would use law terms to undermine the right to trial by jury. That was a possibility, but it was not Smith's intention. The purpose of law terms was to provide the court with relatively leisurely time to consider reserved cases, demurrers, writs of error, and other motions in the nature of appeals and to study the law of the case at bar in order to reach a decision based on precedents and pronounced legal principles. One consequence of the process, of course, was that at law terms the judges were examining, even reviewing, verdicts reached by juries. They were, in those cases, undermining the finality of jury trials. True, they were not questioning the right to a jury trial, but in the politics of America at that time, just to question jury verdicts could be argued to the public as a direct attack on the people's right to trial by jury. That was how Republicans understood law terms and, therefore, why they opposed them.[52]

A political promise that Plumer's followers had made to voters in the election of 1816 was to abolish law terms, and that was what they did, by passing a well-publicized provision of the judicial repeal act of that year. Surely, when Richardson and his colleagues accepted their commissions it was with at least the implication that they could and would be a successful court without law terms. Within a year they decided they needed them. "I think," Woodbury wrote Plumer in August 1817, "the public interest would be subserved by the creation of a Law term to be holden annually in June at Concord." He even boldly went contrary to every argument the Republicans had been making since 1806 and claimed that most litigants would not object to having their causes reserved to a law term, "as the convenience of arguing them at length and when access can readily be had to books will more than counterbalance the delay." That was exactly what Smith had wanted, to schedule the terms in one or two towns only, where books could be collected into a permanent law library.[53]

Plumer may not have been surprised or even disappointed that his judges wanted him to repudiate the Republicans' policy on law terms. During his years working with Smith he had been a supporter of law terms, but after rebuilding the party that won the election of 1816, he must have been astonished to discover that political opinion could so swiftly be reversed on an issue that had been very controversial as little as three years before. He came to the conclusion that law terms were no longer the volatile issue they had been.[54] He did not hesitate to ask the legislators of his party to abandon a major component of their campaign against Smith. At the June 1819 session of the General Court, he advised the two houses to reinstitute law terms. "The number of questions of law, which the superior court are bound to decide," he pointed out, "often renders it necessary to continue the suits in which those questions arise from term to term, and occasions considerable delay in the trial of other causes by the jury. To remedy this evil, I recommend to your consideration the propriety of establishing a law term annually in some central and convenient part of the State."[55]

Plumer may have had a purpose not to mention that law terms should be held in one community so that a permanent law library could be gathered. He may have expected that to say anything about legal treatises or study or searching for precedents would spur renewed opposition to law terms if Democrats were reminded that the judges would use them to write judicial opinions while reviewing jury trials. As it was, the opposition was still too strong. The apprehension that the right to trial by jury would be jeopardized or undermined if judges were encouraged to scrutinize verdicts persisted among members of the General Court. They refused to bring back law terms.

It was only a matter of time—a short amount of time—before the judges had their way. The legislators gave in, and law terms were authorized, held on a regular schedule at the courthouse in Concord. In fact, before either he or William Plumer had died, all of Jeremiah Smith's proposed legal reforms had been incorporated into New Hampshire's judicial system. Along with law terms and the official reporting of the high court's decisions, New Hampshire litigations were presided over by one judge sitting alone except for specified criminal actions. Civil trials were governed by the rule that only the judge, and not any of the attorneys in a case, could charge the jury. Rigid, certain forms of procedure crept in, though generally mitigated by rights of amendment. At first in criminal cases, and soon after in civil, judges began to exercise the authority to overturn jury verdicts that were contrary to instructions. And by a slow process of evolving expansion, the high court developed the practice of reviewing jury verdicts on questions of the correctness of the law applied in a litigation, on errors in the trial judge's instructions, and on the misreception of evidence at a trial.[56] Two decades earlier Plumer had been the chief supporter of this jurisprudence. He had schemed to make Smith chief justice, knowing he was the best hope for instilling predictability and a measurable degree of certainty into New Hampshire law. Later, he had turned against the chief justice for personal reasons, embraced some but not all of the jurisprudence of Thomas Jefferson, and rejected some but not all of the judicial leadership of Lord Mansfield and John Marshall. Because of the triumphs of the Republican Party that Plumer had built with Isaac Hill, Smith was clearly the man on the outside of New Hampshire government in 1818, while Plumer was New Hampshire's innermost man. In the rivalry that Plumer had commenced and had continued against Smith, Plumer was clearly the winner, but Smith was not the loser. The politics of that day belonged to William Plumer, but the law of the future would lie in the jurisprudence of Jeremiah Smith.

# Notes

## Chapter One—The Arena of the Giants

1. Nelson, *Common Law in Colonial America.*

2. Nelson, *Americanization.*

3. *Controlling the Law*; *Legislating the Courts.*

4. There is one biography of a very important jurist that emphasizes his jurisprudence, but the interpretation is so political (New Deal) as to date the study. See Horton, *James Kent.*

5. Kentucky, Tachau, *Federal Courts.* Rhode Island, Graham, *To Bring Law Home*; there is discussion of Rhode Island legal business at 24–68.

6. Ireland, *County Courts in Kentucky.*

7. Roeber, *Faithful Magistrates and Republican Lawyers.*

8. *Legislating the Courts*, 15–17; "Resolution of 29 November 1815," 132–33; Almand, "Supreme Court of Georgia."

9. Rowe, *Thomas McKean*; Rowe, *Embattled Bench*; Marietta and Rowe, *Troubled Experiment.*

10. Carpenter, *Judicial Tenure*, 128–30; Carrington, "Judicial Independence," 89.

11. Nelson, "Cases of the Judges," 256–57; Mays, *Edmund Pendleton*, 274, 396n2; Anon., *Friend to Constitution*, 28–29, 31; also see *Legislating the Courts*, 14.

12. They were the "Midnight Judges" of 1802. Preyer, "Federalist Policy"; Preyer, "Midnight Judges"; *Legislating the Courts*, 71–89.

13. In some states the method of choice for removing judges was impeachment. Pennsylvania, Rowe, *Embattled Bench*; Ohio, Melhorn, *Lest We Be Marshall'd*, 31–33, 95–118.

14. Corning, "Highest Courts of Law," 469; Bell, *In Memory of Ira Perley*, 14.

15. Brandeis, "Harvard Law School," 16; Holmes, "Use of Law Schools," 43. Governor Bell claimed that Parker "was admittedly one of the most able and

learned of a sequence of jurists rarely equaled in the annals of any State." Bell, *Bench and Bar*, 88.

16. Paludan, *Covenant With Death*, 121–63; Streichler, "Parker, Joel," 31; Bell, *Bench and Bar*, 89–90.

17. Bell, *In Memory of Ira Perley*, 12 (quoting Choate).

18. White, *American Judicial Tradition*, 122; Pound, *Formative Era*, 4, 30n2.

19. For more details, see "Arena of the Giants."

20. Rantoul, *Eulogy on Woodbury*, 8.

21. Fuess, *Daniel Webster*, 113–14.

22. Plumer, *Plumer*, 236.

23. Shirley, *Dartmouth College Causes*, 153–54.

24. As is detailed in a companion study to this book. See *Controlling the Law*.

25. Fuess, *Daniel Webster*, 107.

26. Plumer, *Plumer*, 212.

27. Gray, "Jeremiah Mason," 3.

28. Ibid., 27.

29. Ibid., 31.

30. Robinson, "Bartlett, Ichabod," 6 (quoting Rantoul, *Eulogy on Woodbury*).

31. Bell, *Bench and Bar*, 176.

32. Gray, "Jeremiah Mason," 26.

33. Fuess, *Daniel Webster*, 90.

34. Ibid., 91.

35. *Memoirs of Jeremiah Mason*, 42.

36. Plumer, *Plumer*, 179.

37. Gray, "Jeremiah Mason," 25n6. Mason treated his two friends with impartiality. In a closet of his Portsmouth home, he kept two pairs of slippers, a red pair for Webster and a green pair for Story.

38. "Arena of the Giants," 214; Kutler, *Charles River Bridge Case*, 37ff.

39. At his death Haven was honored with a 351-page study of his writings and a memoir written by George Ticknor. See *Remains of Haven*. Also see "The Remains of Nathaniel Appleton Haven," *North American Review* 27 (July 1828): 154–66.

40. Who need not be introduced here as we will meet him in the later chapters of this book.

41. Plumer, *Plumer*, 219.

42. Bell, *Bench and Bar*, 63.

43. Gray, "Jeremiah Mason," 3.

44. *Speak for Yourself, Daniel*, 42.

45. Plumer, *Plumer*, 179.

46. Ibid.

47. *Legislating the Courts*, 71–89.

48. *Controlling the Law*, 26.

49. For the most extensive discussion, see ibid., 18–32.

50. Morison, *Life of Smith*, 209–10 (reprinting Mason).

51. For elaboration on the jurisprudential dichotomy, see *Controlling the Law*, 33–55.

52. These incidents have also been discussed in a companion volume, *Controlling the Law*, 95–179.

53. Plumer, *Plumer*, 178–79.

54. See *Legislating the Courts*, 40–52.

## Chapter Two—An Unschooled Judge

1. Morison, *Life of Smith*, 141n1.

2. A FRIEND TO TRUTH, "On the Judicial Act—No. 11," in *New Hampshire Gazette*, 20 July 1813, p. 2, col. 4. For discussion of the salary problem, see *Controlling the Law*, 71–82.

3. Turner, *Plumer*; Turner, *Ninth State*.

4. Turner, *Ninth State*, 159.

5. Letter of 27 February 1798, quoted in Stearns, "Livermore," 445. For Smith's candidacy, see Turner, *Ninth State*, 162.

6. Turner, *Ninth State*, 161. Also, Governor Gilman was not friendly with the Livermores. Ibid., 162.

7. Letter of 5 April 1798, quoted in Stearns, "Livermore," 445; Plumer quoted in Turner, *Ninth State*, 161.

8. Plumer to Smith, 25 January 1797, in First Plumer Letterbook; Turner, *Ninth State*, 101–02.

9. Federalist newspapers: *Concord Gazette*, 1 November 1808, p. 3, col. 1; QUERIST, "A Few Plain Questions," in *Farmer's Cabinet*, 23 August 1808, p. 2, col. 3; ROCKINGHAM, in *New Hampshire Gazette*, 1 November 1808, p. 3, col. 2; RATTLE, "The Tory Lawyers in an Uproar," in *New Hampshire Gazette*, 6 March 1810, p. 2, col. 4.

10. *New-Hampshire Patriot*, 11 July 1809, p. 3, col. 4; *New Hampshire Gazette*, 10 December 1805, p. 2, col. 1.

11. *New-Hampshire Patriot*, 30 July 1816, p. 2, col. 5.

12. *New-Hampshire Patriot*, 18 July 1809, p. 3, col. 3, and 12 July 1814, p. 2, col. 5.

13. DECIUS, "British Influence—Letter VII," in *New-Hampshire Patriot*, 6 February 1810, p. 1, col. 3, reprinted in *New Hampshire Gazette*, 6 March 1810, Supplement, p. 1, col. 2. A Federalist newspaper asserted, "Two articles in the Jefferson creed are to denounce Lawyers and Merchants. Lawyers because they read English law-books, and merchants because they trade with England." *Portsmouth Oracle*, 24 February 1810, p. 3, col. 3.

14. *New Hampshire Gazette*, 1 November 1808, p. 3, col. 2.

15. A DOVER FARMER, "Farmers of New-Hampshire," in *New Hampshire Gazette*, 1 November 1808, p. 2, col. 2; VERITAS, in *Concord Gazette*, 31 July 1810, p. 4, cols. 3–4. Plumer's home was in Epping.

16. *People's Advocate*, 28 December 1816, p. 2, col. 3.

17. *Concord Gazette*, 31 July 1810, p. 2, col. 1; *New Hampshire Gazette*,

14 September 1802, p. 2, col. 1; Lucius, "To the Independent Electors of New-Hampshire," in *New Hampshire Gazette*, 2 March 1802, p. 2, col. 3.

18. Circular, "Legislative and State Concerns," in *New Hampshire Gazette*, 10 December 1805, p. 2, col. 1.

19. *American Patriot*, 25 October 1809, p. 3, col. 3; "pettifogger," Robinson, *Isaac Hill*, 24–25; *New-Hampshire Patriot*, 25 February 1817, p. 1, col. 3, and 11 July 1809, p. 3, col. 4.

20. A Dover Farmer, "Farmers of New-Hampshire," in *New Hampshire Gazette*, 1 November 1808, p. 2, col. 2.

21. As has been explained for neighboring Massachusetts. Nelson, *Americanization*, 13–65.

22. *New-Hampshire Patriot*, 3 May 1814, p. 1, col. 3. Also see Lambert, *Ten Pound Act*, 29–30.

23. *New-Hampshire Patriot*, 25 December 1810, p. 3, col. 3. Plumer, writing as Aristides, reported that there were 130 lawyers. Ibid., 27 February 1810, p. 1, col. 4.

24. Publicola, *New Vade Mecum*, 85–86; "Government," Cincinnatus No. 87 [Plumer], in *Portsmouth Journal*, 31 May 1823, p. 2, col. 2.

25. Phocion, in *New-Hampshire Patriot*, 1 March 1814, p. 1, col. 4.

26. Arbitration, in *New-Hampshire Patriot*, 25 December 1810, p. 2, col. 3; Plumer to Smith, 25 January 1797, quoted in Turner, *Plumer*, 69; Junius, in *New-Hampshire Patriot*, 4 June 1811, p. 1, cols. 4–5. For efforts to regulate admission, see *General Regulations for Bar*, 4–5; Report of Rockingham County Bar Committee, 20 January 1812, *Webster Legal Papers* 1: 237–40.

27. *New-Hampshire Patriot*, 27 June 1809, p. 3, col. 4. For the text of Smith's address, see Morison, *Life of Smith*, 246–49. The address is discussed below, chapter 11.

28. Parker, *Courts and Lawyers*, 555; *New Hampshire Gazette*, 3 September 1816, p. 1, col. 5; Plumer, "Richard Evans," 10.

29. Elected, *New Hampshire Gazette*, 15 October 1805, p. 3, col. 1, and *Farmer's Cabinet*, 29 October 1805, p. 3, col. 3; Plumer to Evans, 4 February 1809, *Plumer Papers* (promising to contribute to the *Patriot*).

30. Speech of 14 June 1809, Morison, *Life of Smith*, 247; Answer of the House of Representatives, *Portsmouth Oracle*, 1 July 1809, p. 3, col. 4.

31. *New-Hampshire Patriot*, 27 June 1809, p. 3. col. 4, and 11 July 1809, p. 3, col. 4.

32. *New Hampshire Gazette*, 3 September 1816, p. 1, col. 5.

33. Morison, *Life of Smith*, 247; *New-Hampshire Patriot*, 28 November 1809, p. 3, col. 2, and 11 July 1809, p. 3, col. 4.

34. *Portsmouth Oracle*, 17 June 1809, p. 3, col. 1; Turner, *Ninth State*, 256.

35. Citizen, in *Concord Gazette*, 20 February 1810, p. 3, col. 1; ibid., 18 July 1809, p. 3, col. 3; *Portsmouth Oracle*, 23 October 1813, p. 1, col. 2. Also see Enquirer (from the Dover *Sun*), in *Concord Gazette*, 14 March 1809, p. 2, cols. 1–2; A Yankee, in *Concord Gazette*, 6 March 1810, p. 3, col. 1; Z, in *Concord Gazette*, 3 April 1810, p. 3, col. 3; Phil Laos, "To the Hon. Judge Evans," in *Constitutionalist*, 25 June 1810, p. 3, col. 3, and 2 July 1810, p. 2, col. 5.

36. Address of Governor Jeremiah Smith, 14 June 1809, *Senate Journal* (June 1809), 32.

37. AN IMPARTIAL CITIZEN, "The Judiciary," in *Portsmouth Oracle*, 31 July 1813, p. 1, col. 2; RESTORATOR, "To John Langdon," ibid., 30 June 1810, p. 2, col. 2 (reprinted in *Concord Gazette*, 7 August 1810, p. 4, col. 3); *Portsmouth Oracle*, 5 May 1810, p. 3, col. 2.

38. *New-Hampshire Patriot*, 27 June 1809, p. 3, col. 3.

39. *New Hampshire Gazette*, 6 November 1810, p. 3, col. 3.

40. Plumer, "Richard Evans," 11; ARISTIDES [Plumer], "To the Citizens of New-Hampshire," in *New Hampshire Gazette*, 18 July 1809, p. 3, col. 1; PHIL LAOS, "Letter to Hon. Judge Evans," in *Constitutionalist*, 25 June 1810, p. 3, col. 4.

41. Bell, *Bench and Bar*, 66–67; ARISTIDES [Plumer], "To the Citizens of New-Hampshire," in *New Hampshire Gazette*, 18 July 1809, p. 3, col. 1.

42. RESTORATOR, "To the Citizens of New-Hampshire," in *Portsmouth Oracle*, 30 June 1810, p. 2, col. 2; *New-Hampshire Patriot*, 3 October 1809, p. 3, col. 4, and 11 July 1809, p. 3, col. 4.

43. Evans, *Appeal to People*, 26–27 (quoting memorial to General Court praying that Evans's salary be paid for 1813–1816). Also see Plumer, "Richard Evans," 11; Bell, *Bench and Bar*, 67.

44. *Concord Gazette*, 27 June 1809, p. 3, col. 3. The "many judges" refers to the Court of Common Pleas.

45. Turner, *Ninth State*, 254.

46. *New-Hampshire Patriot*, 28 November 1809, p. 3, col. 2; *Concord Gazette*, 20 February 1810, p. 2, col. 1.

47. Turner, *Ninth State*, 254; ARISTIDES [Plumer], "To the Citizens of New-Hampshire," in *New Hampshire Gazette*, 25 July 1809, p. 2, col. 1; Plumer, *Autobiography*, 246.

48. *New Hampshire Gazette*, 6 November 1810, p. 3, col. 3; RESTORATOR, "To His Excellency John Langdon," in *Concord Gazette*, 7 August 1810, p. 4, col. 4.

49. Bell, *Bench and Bar*, 68.

50. ARISTIDES [Plumer], "To the Citizens of New-Hampshire," in *New Hampshire Gazette*, 25 July 1809, p. 2, col. 1; Plumer, *Autobiography*, quoted in Turner, *Ninth State*, 254; Plumer, "Richard Evans," 11.

## Chapter Three—Federalist Indian Summer

1. Plumer to Smith, 4 January 1793, First Plumer Letterbook; Webster quoted in Holmes, "Address," 46. For Plumer's support of Smith's appointment, see *Controlling the Law*, 56–61.

2. Turner, *Ninth State*, 160 (also 160–63); Plumer, *Autobiography*, 68.

3. Turner, *Ninth State*, 144, 163, 167, 229.

4. *Controlling the Law*, 8, 40–41, 45–48.

5. Plumer to William Gordon, 5 February 1798, Turner, *Ninth State*, 152; Smith to William Gordon, 17 December 1794, Morison, *Life of Smith*, 66; Plumer

to Daniel Plumer, 10 January 1803, *Plumer Letters to his Brother.*

6. Plumer to William Gordon, 5 February 1798, First Plumer Letterbook; Smith to Robert Fletcher, 12 February 1794, Morison, *Life of Smith,* 61; Smith to Plumer, 25 December 1793, *Plumer Documents;* Plumer quoted in Turner, *Plumer,* 66.

7. Plumer to William Gordon, 29 May 1797, *Historical Society Correspondence* (frame 9); Smith to Plumer, 4 April 1795, *Plumer Documents.* Smith was opposing James Madison's resolutions restricting British trade. For Plumer's opposition to war in general, see Cincinnatus [Plumer], No. 163 and No. 164, *Portsmouth Journal,* 29 March 1828, p. 2, cols. 3–4, and 28 April 1828, p. 1, cols. 3–4.

8. "Virginia," 26 December 1803, Plumer, Repository V (frame 504); "Anecdotes," *Plumer Documents* (reel 13, frame 504).

9. Smith to John Smith, 30 October 1791, Morison, *Life of Smith,* 46; Smith to Plumer, 16 November 1791, *Plumer Documents;* Plumer to unidentified, 2 February 1804, *Historical Society Correspondence* (frame 37).

10. Turner, *Plumer,* 107; Plumer, *Autobiography,* 108; Plumer to David Lawrence, 27 December 1802, Turner, *Plumer,* 107. Also see Plumer to Isaac Lyman, 17 March 1804, Fourth Plumer Letterbook; Plumer to Peter Holt, 2 February 1804, *Historical Society Correspondence* (frame 36).

11. Smith to Plumer in Turner, *Ninth State,* 145; Smith to Robert Fletcher, 3 January 1795, Morison, *Life of Smith,* 67–68; Mayo, *John Langdon,* 250–51.

12. Plumer to Edward St. Loe Livermore, 24 December 1803, Turner, "Jefferson Through Plumer," 208; Plumer to Smith, 18 December 1803, and 27 January 1803, ibid., 206, 207.

13. Conversation, Turner, "Jefferson Through Plumer," 207; Turner, *Ninth State,* 210.

14. Plumer to Thomas W. Thompson, 28 January 1804, Turner, *Plumer,* 138–39; Plumer to Smith, 10 February 1804, Fourth Plumer Letterbook.

15. Plumer, *Autobiography,* 130; Plumer to Smith, 11 March 1809 [1804?], Fourth Plumer Letterbook, 191; Plumer to Thompson, 19 March 1804, Turner, *Ninth State,* 215. For Pickering's impeachment and Plumer's defense of the judge, see *Legislating the Courts,* 90–105.

16. For an excellent and detailed account of Plumer's involvement, see Gannon, "Escaping Jefferson's Plan," 434; for the letters, see 435–36, 438–39, 441–42.

17. Turner, *Ninth State,* 215; Turner, "Jefferson Through Plumer," 209–10; Plumer, *Memorandum,* 453–54.

18. Mayo, *John Langdon,* 245–46; Richard Upton, "John Langdon and John Sullivan," in *New Hampshire the State,* 223; *New Hampshire Gazette,* 9 November 1802, p. 3, col. 2, and (from the *Baltimore American*) 5 October 1802, p. 2, col. 3. Plumer attributed Langdon's Republicanism to Jay's Treaty. Plumer, "John Langdon," 197.

19. *Newhampshire Sentinel,* 19 February 1803, p. 2, col. 2; Turner, *Ninth State,* 216; *Courier of New Hampshire,* 13 June 1804, p. 2, col. 4, (speaker elected and Message of Governor Gilman, 7 June 1804) p. 3, col. 1.

20. Notice from Philip Carrigan to Republicans, 10 January 1804, *Ports-*

*mouth Oracle*, 25 February 1804, p. 3, cols. 1–2; Smith to Plumer, 22 February 1804, Turner, *Ninth State*, 215.

21. Turner, *Ninth State*, 215, 216–17; Plumer, "A Private confidential Narrative," 21 October 1804, *Plumer Documents* (reel 13, frame 132). The pamphlet Plumer wrote is Plumer, *Address to Electors.*

22. Plumer, Jr. to Plumer, 3 March 1804, *Plumer Documents* (reel 14, frame 405).

23. Opal, "Politics of Industry," 669; Smith to Plumer, 18 March 1804, and Plumer to Uriah Tracy, 2 May 1804, Turner, *Ninth State*, 216, 219.

24. [Webster,] *Appeal to Old Whigs*, 7, 8–9.

25. Entry for 22 February 1805, Plumer, *Memorandum*, 299; *New Hampshire Gazette*, 11 June 1805, p. 3, col. 2; *Farmer's Cabinet*, 11 June 1805, p. 3, col. 1; entry for 25 June 1805, Plumer, *Memorandum*, 323, 324; *New Hampshire Gazette*, 2 December 1806, p. 3, col. 2.

26. For an account of Smith being "legislated" from the federal bench, see *Legislating the Courts*, 71–89.

## Chapter Four—Federalist Apostate

1. A VOTER, in *Concord Gazette*, 1 November 1808, p. 3, cols. 3–4.

2. Parker, Plumer, *Autobiography*, 223; Atkinson, Smith to Plumer, 7 March 1804, Fourth Plumer Letterbook, 153–54; Bell, *Bench and Bar*, 65.

3. Smith to Plumer, 7 March 1804, Fourth Plumer Letterbook, 155.

4. Morison, *Life of Smith*, 39. Smith was then writing as a member of the House of Representatives and serving as a manager for the house of the impeachment trial of a Superior Court judge. To prepare for the trial, Smith had drawn a picture of a competent, conscientious jurist and had singled out the holding of multiple offices as the one offense that a good judge had to avoid. A judge, he had written, "must especially disengage himself from all other business and employment, and devote himself to the duties of the office" (ibid.). For details of the impeachment, see *Legislating the Courts*, 33–39.

5. Plumer to Smith, 27 January 1803, *Plumer Documents.*

6. Plumer to John Norris, 7 November 1804, Fourth Plumer Letterbook; Turner, "Jefferson Through Plumer," 210; Plumer, *Autobiography*, 179.

7. "A private confidential narrative of the proceedings of the Federalists in New Hampshire," 21 October 1804, Plumer, Repository I (frame 134); Plumer to Plumer, Jr., 20 November 1804, Fourth Plumer Letterbook; entry for 14 January 1807, Plumer, *Register I*; IN PORTSMOUTH, entry for 28 March 1807, Plumer, *Register I*; REELECTION, entry for 25 June 1806, Plumer, *Memorandum*, 506 (also see entry for 15 December 1805, 352).

8. Entry for 7 February 1805, Plumer, *Memorandum*, 277–78. Also see Plumer to Congressman Samuel Taggart, 1 January 1808, and 3 February 1808, *Plumer Papers.*

9. Plumer to Congressman Clement Storer, 19 April 1808, *Plumer Papers.* Also see Plumer to Jefferson, 22 July 1808, Third Plumer Letterbook; Plumer to

John Langdon, 15 October 1808, *Plumer Documents*; John Langdon to Plumer, 22 October 1808, *Plumer Papers*. Years earlier Plumer had opposed a Federalist embargo against the French. "It would materially injure our commerce & greatly affect the revenue." Plumer to Congressman William Gordon, 29 May 1797, *Historical Society Correspondence* (frame 9).

10. Turner, "Jefferson Through Plumer," 212. For explanations of Plumer's new politics, see Plumer to Plumer, Jr., 28 March 1809, *Plumer Papers*; Plumer to Henry Dearborn, 3 February 1809, and to John Quincy Adams, 22 December 1807, *Plumer Documents*; Leidtker, *Political Development*, 41; Turner, *Ninth State*, 264; Wait, "William Plumer," 130–31.

11. *New-Hampshire Patriot*, 16 January 1810, p. 3, col. 5. For VERITAS, see Plumer to Richard Evans, 7 and 15 November 1808, *Plumer Papers*. Plumer also had solicited public offices from Republicans as, e.g., postmaster of Epping (which he received), see Plumer to Gideon Granger, 25 March 1808, *Plumer Papers*; Granger to Plumer, 14 November 1808, *Plumer Documents*; and as a judge of Common Pleas (which he did not), see Plumer to John Langdon, 7 December 1806, Fourth Plumer Letterbook; Plumer to Langdon, 7 November 1808, *Plumer Papers*.

12. ARISTIDES [Plumer], in *New-Hampshire Patriot*, 6 March 1810, p. 1, col. 4.

13. Plumer to Mason, 21 December 1805, Fourth Plumer Letterbook.

14. *Legislating the Courts*, 71–89.

15. ARISTIDES [Plumer], in *New-Hampshire Patriot*, 13 February 1810, p. 1, col. 1; ARISTIDES [Plumer], "The Pretensions of Gov. Smith Examined," in *New Hampshire Gazette*, 27 February 1810, Supplement, p. 2, col. 2.

16. *Controlling the Law*, 83–94.

17. Plumer, *Autobiography*, 158.

18. Ibid., 197.

19. For details of the litigation, see *Controlling the Law*, 83–88.

20. ARISTIDES [Plumer], "The Pretensions of Gov. Smith Examined," in *New-Hampshire Patriot*, 20 February 1810, p. 1, col. 3.

21. Plumer, *Autobiography*, 239–40; VERITAS, "For the N. H. Gazette," in *New Hampshire Gazette*, 11 October 1808, p. 2, col. 5. Similarly, see ARISTIDES [Plumer], "The Pretensions of Gov. Smith Examined," in *New-Hampshire Patriot*, 20 February 1810, p. 1, col. 3.

22. Plumer to Thomas W. Thompson, 23 December 1804, Fourth Plumer Letterbook.

23. *Portsmouth Oracle*, 8 October 1808, p, 1, col. 2 (quoting Dover *Sun*); *Farmer's Cabinet*, 6 December 1808, p. 3, col. 3.

24. ARISTIDES [Plumer], "The Pretensions of Gov. Smith Examined," *New-Hampshire Patriot*, 20 February 1810, p. 1, col. 3.

25. CINCINNATUS [Plumer], No. 128, *Grafton Journal*, 21 January 1826, p. 2, col. 4, and pp. 2–3.

26. CINCINNATUS [Plumer], No. 93, *Portsmouth Journal*, 13 September 1823, p. 1, cols. 1–2. Plumer wrote these words after all but one of the states were publishing judicial decisions, some for almost twenty years.

27. Cincinnatus [Plumer], No. 128, *Grafton Journal*, 21 January 1826, p. 2, col. 1. Yet Plumer, like Smith, was critical of legislation. "[T]oo many of our statutes are replete with prolixity, verbosity, and tautology; and instead of expressing their meaning with utmost clearness, they are involved in Great obscurity; and abound with technical terms and hard words, which the people cannot understand." Cincinnatus [Plumer], No. 96, *Collections Historical* 2: 278–79.

28. Cincinnatus [Plumer], No. 128, *Grafton Journal*, 21 January 1826, p. 2, col. 1.

29. Aristides [Plumer], "The Pretensions of Gov. Smith Examined," *New-Hampshire Patriot*, 20 February 1801, p. 1, col. 3.

30. "Observations on Government, Laws & offenses," 18 May 1801, Plumer, Repository I (frames 19 and 20). For rule of law, see *Rule of Law*, 3–9.

31. "Observations on Government, Laws & offenses," 18 May 1801, Plumer, Repository I (frame 20); Aristides [Plumer], "The Pretensions of Gov. Smith Examined," in *New Hampshire Gazette* (Supplement), 6 March 1810, p. 1, col. 4.

32. Aristides [Plumer], "The Pretensions of Gov. Smith Examined," *New-Hampshire Patriot*, 20 February 1810, p. 1, col. 3.

33. Plumer to Isaac Hill, 21 January 1810, Third Plumer Letterbook, 71; Plumer, Repository II, 43.

34. Plumer, *Autobiography*, 309.

## Chapter Five—A "Law" Governor

1. Stories, *Newhampshire Sentinel*, 19 February 1803, p. 3, cols. 2–3; Langdon, Taishoff, "State Politics," 35.

2. Turner, *Ninth State*, 241–42; Taishoff, "State Politics," 36; Plumer to Daniel Meserve Durell, 7 February 1809, *Plumer Documents*.

3. Turner, *Ninth State*, 249; XYZ, "The Cloven Foot of Federalism," in *New Hampshire Gazette*, 1 November 1808, p. 2, col. 1.

4. *Portsmouth Oracle*, 11 February 1809, p. 3, col. 2; *Concord Gazette*, 28 February 1809, p. 1, col. 2; Strafford, "Communication," in *New Hampshire Gazette*, 14 February 1809, p. 3, col. 3.

5. Turner, *Ninth State*, 250.

6. Union, in *Farmer's Museum*, 20 February 1809, p. 3, col. 2; ibid., 13 February 1809, p. 2, col. 4; An Elector, "From the Concord Gazette," ibid., 20 February 1809, p. 3, col. 3; *Portsmouth Oracle*, EXTRA, 1 March 1809, p. 2, col. 4 (quoting *Dartmouth Gazette*).

7. Turner, *Plumer*, 188; *New-Hampshire Patriot*, 27 June 1809, p. 3, col. 4; An Injured People, *New-Hampshire Patriot*, 9 November 1813, p. 1, col. 3. "The lawyers wish to *lift* Judge Smith from the *bench* because they say, he is too arbitrary!" *American Patriot*, 7 March 1809, p. 1, col. 1.

8. Thousands, "Our Next Governor," in *Farmer's Cabinet*, 14 February 1809, p. 2, col. 2; Philo, *Farmer's Cabinet*, 6 March 1810, p. 2, col. 1.

9. "In his diary Smith reminisced that his civic duty compelled him to

comply with his associates, who urged him to oppose Langdon in 1809," Taishoff, "State Politics," 37. This statement cannot be relied on. The author cites no page, and there is no known Smith diary.

10. Morison, *Life of Smith*, 244–45.

11. Ibid., 245.

12. Ibid., 245–46.

13. Civis, in *Portsmouth Oracle*, 4 February 1809, p. 3, col. 2; An Elector, ibid., 25 February 1809, p. 3, col. 1; *American Patriot*, 28 February 1809, p. 2, col. 3; Taishoff, "State Politics," 36.

14. Cato, in *New Hampshire Gazette*, 28 February 1809, p. 3, col. 2.

15. *Portsmouth Oracle*, 11 February 1809, p. 3, cols. 2 and 3; Franklin, ibid., 25 February 1809, p. 1, col. 3.

16. *New Hampshire Gazette*, 14 March 1809, p. 3, col. 2.

17. Thousands, "Our Next Governor," in *Farmer's Cabinet*, 14 February 1809, p. 2, col. 2; *Portsmouth Oracle*, 4 March 1809, p. 3, cols. 1 and 2.

18. "One of the strongest objections to the views of the democratic party is their contempt for judicial decisions and their *systemic endeavours* to controul the judiciary and reduce it to subserviency to their will." *Portsmouth Oracle*, 18 February 1809, p. 3, col. 1.

19. Taishoff, "State Politics," 36; *New-Hampshire Patriot*, 1 August 1809, p. 3, col. 3.

20. Plumer, *Autobiography*, 248.

21. *Portsmouth Oracle*, 1 April 1809, p. 3, col. 1; *Concord Gazette*, 23 May 1809, p. 3, col. 1, and 13 June 1809, p. 3, col. 4; *New Hampshire Gazette*, 13 June 1809, p. 3, col. 4; Turner, *Ninth State*, 250. When the legislature met and officially counted the votes, Federalists newspapers reported that Smith had won by 396 votes, and the Republican press said the margin was only 118 votes. *Portsmouth Oracle*, 17 June 1809, p. 2, col. 2; *New-Hampshire Patriot*, 13 June 1809, p. 3, col. 3.

22. Plumer to Nahum Parker, 16 June 1809, Third Plumer Letterbook. He apparently was confident of his facts for he made the charge publicly, writing that every Republican in the legislature believed some votes to be illegal. Aristides [Plumer], "The Pretensions of Gov. Smith Examined," *New-Hampshire Patriot*, 20 February 1810, p. 1, col. 3. The Republican press wrote of "supernumerary votes and illegal returns." *New-Hampshire Patriot*, 13 June 1809, p. 3, col. 2.

23. Plumer, *Autobiography*, 248.

24. Plumer to Nahum Parker, 16 June 1809, Third Plumer Letterbook, 59.

25. Cincinnatus [Plumer], No. 101, in *Collections Historical* 3: 207; *Portsmouth Oracle*, 10 June 1809, p. 3, col. 4; *Farmer's Cabinet*, 20 June 1809, p. 3, col. 2.

26. Plumer, Repository II, 50–51, 58; *Portsmouth Oracle*, 17 June 1809, p. 3, cols. 2–3.

27. *Portsmouth Oracle*, 17 June 1809, p. 3, col. 1; *Concord Gazette*, 18 July 1809, p. 3, cols. 2–4; An Impartial Citizen, in *Constitutionalist*, 10 August 1813, p. 2, col. 2.

28. Aristides [Plumer], "To the Citizens of New-Hampshire," in *New*

*Hampshire Gazette,* 11 July 1809, p. 2, col. 3, and 18 July 1809, p. 2, col. 5.

29. Turner, *Plumer,* 189.

30. Address of Governor Smith, 14 June 1809, *Senate Journal* (June 1809), 29; Morison, *Life of Smith,* 247–48.

31. See *Legislating the Courts.*

32. Morison, *Life of Smith,* 248. The quotation is from Article 35 of the New Hampshire bill of rights.

33. Morison, *Life of Smith,* 249.

34. Turner, *Ninth State,* 255.

35. Address of the Senate to Governor Smith, 20 June 1809, *Concord Gazette,* 27 June 1809, p. 2, col. 3.

36. Address of Governor Smith, 14 June 1809, *Portsmouth Oracle,* 24 June 1809, p. 1, col. 1.

37. *New-Hampshire Patriot,* 1 August 1809, p. 3, cols. 3 and 4.

38. Ibid., 11 July 1809, p. 3, col. 4.

39. Ibid., 3 October 1809, p. 3, col. 4.

40. Morison, *Life of Smith,* 247, 248.

41. *New-Hampshire Patriot,* 28 November 1809, p. 3, col. 2; *New Hampshire Gazette,* 12 December 1809, p. 2, col. 2 (reprinting "Hon. Richard Evans" from the *Patriot*).

42. Morison, *Life of Smith,* 249–50.

43. Plumer, Repository II, 87; Hill to Plumer, 20 February 1810, Eighth Plumer Letterbook, 37.

44. Aristides [Plumer], "The Pretensions of Gov. Smith Examined," No. IV, in *New-Hampshire Patriot,* 27 February 1810, p. 1, col. 4.

45. Ibid., p. 1, cols. 3–4. "The duties of a judge require he should be thoroughly acquainted with the law and its principles, the voluminous treatises upon the laws, and the numerous reports of adjudicated cases. This requires much study and close application for a long time." Cincinnatus [Plumer],—No. 126, in *Grafton Journal,* 25 November 1825, p. 191, col. 1.

46. Cincinnatus [Plumer], No. 100, in *Collections Historical* 3:163.

47. *New-Hampshire Patriot,* 26 September 1809, p. 3, col. 4; Turner, *Ninth State,* 256. Livermore apparently hesitated before accepting. Plumer wrote in December, "Report says Arthur Livermore has not yet accepted the office of chief justice; & that Jeremiah Smith regrets that he resigned that office for one of so uncertain tenure as that of governor." Plumer to Nahum Parker, 22 December 1809, Third Plumer Letterbook, 68.

48. Morison, *Life of Smith,* 251.

49. Ibid., 251–52 (quotation at 252); Turner, *Plumer,* 190; Turner, *Ninth State,* 256; *New-Hampshire Patriot,* 20 February 1810, p. 3, col. 5.

50. Elector, *Newhampshire Sentinel,* 10 November 1804, p. 3, col. 2; Plumer, "Jonathan Steele," 13; *Farmer's Cabinet,* 6 March 1810, p. 3, col. 2; "violent Federalist," Plumer, *Autobiography,* 253.

51. Plumer, "Jonathan Steele," 11, 13; Plumer, *Autobiography,* 253. Plumer

scolded a Republican councilor for supporting Steele: "[H]e is not a moderate but an *outrageous bitter partizan*—a man of strong passions & violent prejudices." Plumer to Samuel Bell, 6 April 1810, Third Plumer Letterbook, 92.

52. Plumer, *Autobiography*, 253; Plumer, "Jonathan Steele," 12, 13.

53. Plumer, "Jonathan Steele," 11, 13.

54. Turner, *Ninth State*, 253; Morison, *Life of Smith*, 246.

55. Turner, *Ninth State*, 256; *Constitutionalist*, 20 August 1810, p. 3, cols. 2–3; *New Hampshire Gazette*, 6 March 1810, p. 2, col. 5, and 27 February 1810, p. 2, col. 5.

56. Morison, *Life of Smith*, 254–55.

57. *Farmer's Cabinet*, 11 July 1809, p. 3, col. 1; *New-Hampshire Patriot*, 18 July 1809, p. 3, col. 4.

58. *Portsmouth Oracle*, 27 January 1810, p. 3, col. 2; Junius, "Citizens of New-Hampshire," in *Farmer's Cabinet*, 27 February 1810, p. 2, col. 3; Mayo, *John Langdon*, 283; minutes of 7 June 1810, *Senate Journal* (June 1810), 10.

59. *New Hampshire Gazette*, 6 March 1810, p. 2, col. 5; "Governor Smith," *New-Hampshire Patriot*, 9 January 1810, p. 2, cols. 2–3 (from *New Hampshire Gazette).*

60. *New-Hampshire Patriot*, 1 January 1811, p. 3, col. 2, and 19 February 1811, p. 3, col. 3.

## Chapter Six—In Judicial Depths

1. *Constitutionalist*, 11 June 1810, p. 2, col. 4; Turner, *Plumer*, 192–93; Turner, *Ninth State*, 257. The articles were entitled, "The Pretensions of Gov. Smith Examined." Some contemporaries attributed to Smith the answers by Brutus, describing Plumer's articles as a "long column of drivelling folly and base misrepresentations." "It would be absurd for the Federalists to accuse you of changing your *principles*. The accusation would *imply* something which they in no wise credit. They do you the justice to believe, that in your *adherence* to *principles, you are as uniform, as in your adherence* to parties." Brutus, "To the Hon. William Plumer," in *Portsmouth Oracle*, 4 August 1810, p. 1, col. 4, and 18 August 1810, p. 1, col. 4.

2. Plumer, *Autobiography*, 259; Turner, *Ninth State*, 258–59.

3. Caius Julius, "His Excellency Jeremiah Smith," in *New Hampshire Gazette*, 22 May 1810, p. 2, col. 3.

4. For legislative restoring to law, see *Legislating the Courts*, 53–70.

5. *Controlling the Law*, 115–30.

6. Speech of Governor Langdon, 7 June 1810, *Senate Journal* (June 1810), 12–13.

7. Turner, *Ninth State*, 259.

8. Answer of the House to Governor Langdon, 13 June 1810, *House Journal* (June 1810), 50.

9. Answer of the Senate to Governor Langdon, 12 June 1810, *Senate Journal* (June 1810), 29.

10. Plumer to Plumer, Jr., 9 June 1810, and Nahum Parker to Plumer, 14 April 1810, Eighth Plumer Letterbook, 67–68, 53.

11. Plumer, "Jonathan Steele," 15.

12. Justus, "To the People of New-Hampshire," in *New-Hampshire Patriot*, 22 October 1811, p. 3, cols. 2 and 3.

13. Ibid., col. 3.

14. *New-Hampshire Patriot*, 14 January 1817, p. 3, col. 1, and 13 February 1810, p. 3, col. 3.

15. Ibid., 9 January 1810, p. 2, col. 1, and 13 February 1810, p. 3, col. 2.

16. Ibid., 29 August 1809, p. 3, col. 2, and 5 September 1809, p. 3, col. 2; Bell, *Answer to Petition*, 6–24.

17. For discussion of Smith's objectives, see *Controlling the Law*, 131–42.

18. *New-Hampshire Patriot*, 30 April 1811, p. 3, col. 2.

19. Ibid.

20. *Controlling the Law*, 131–39.

21. *New Hampshire Gazette*, 6 November 1810, p. 3, col. 3 (quoting the Boston *Gazette* and the *Newhampshire Sentinel*).

22. Plumer to Senator Stephen R. Bradley, 31 January 1811, Eighth Plumer Letterbook, 115.

23. *Farmer's Cabinet*, 11 June 1811, p. 3, col. 1; *Concord Gazette*, 11 June 1811, p. 2, col. 5; Turner, *Ninth State*, 257.

24. *Concord Gazette*, 31 December 1811, p. 3, col. 5.

25. Turner, *Ninth State*, 264–65.

26. Ibid., 261; No Party Man, in *Portsmouth Oracle*, 29 February 1812, p. 3, col. 2.

27. Plumer to Harper, 28 January 1812, Third Plumer Letterbook; Harper to Plumer, 6 February 1812, Eighth Plumer Letterbook, 190. Harper studied law with Smith.

28. Egan, "Path to War," 156n20; *Farmer's Cabinet*, 2 March 1812, p. 2, col. 3; *New-Hampshire Patriot*, 11 February 1812, p. 3, col. 1; Turner, *Ninth State*, 265.

29. Plumer to Harper, 14 February 1812, Third Plumer Letterbook; 166. Also see Plumer to Harper, 2 March 1812, Eighth Plumer Letterbook, 194.

30. Rumors, *Portsmouth Oracle*, 22 February 1812, p. 2, col. 3; Smith withdrew, *New-Hampshire Patriot*, 25 February 1812, p. 3, col. 4; election, *Portsmouth Oracle*, 6 June 1812, p. 3, col. 2; *Farmer's Cabinet*, 8 June 1812, p. 3, col. 3, and 15 June 1812, p. 1, col. 3; *House Journal* (June 1812), p. 11.

31. Plumer, *Autobiography*, 264; Turner, *Plumer*, 202.

32. Turner, *Plumer*, 217n55; Plumer, "Jonathan Steele," 14.

33. Message to the General Court, 25 November 1812, Plumer, *Proclamations and Writings*, 115; Plumer, "Jonathan Steele," 14–15.

34. Jonathan Steele, "Letter to the Printer," 3 July 1813, in *Portsmouth Oracle*, 10 July 1813, p. 3, col. 3.

35. Ibid., col. 4. Also see Jonathan Steele, "Letter to the Printer," 29 July 1813, *Portsmouth Oracle*, 7 August 1813, p. 1, cols. 2–3.

36. Plumer, "Clifton Clagett," 460.

37. Bell, *Bench and Bar*, 80.

38. Claggett was spelled several ways by people quoted in this study, e.g., Clagett, Clagget, Claget.

39. Turner, *Ninth State*, 277; Plumer, "Clifton Clagett," 460.

40. Turner, *Plumer*, 217; Stearns, "Livermore," 435 (quoting Plumer); Turner, *Ninth State*, 278. Smith's biographer says that he "repeatedly refused to nominate [Claggett] for the bench." Morison, *Life of Smith*, 265. But it may be that Claggett was appointed probate judge for Hillsborough County while Smith was governor. *Farmer's Cabinet*, 29 May 1810, p. 3, col. 2.

41. Entry for 15 September 1812, Plumer, *Register II*; Plumer, "Clifton Clagett," 460.

42. Plumer to Congressman John A. Harper, 2 March 1812, Eighth Plumer Letterbook, 198; Turner, *Plumer*, 217.

43. Entry for 19 May 1813, Plumer, *Register II.*

44. Plumer, *Autobiography*, 292; Plumer, "Richard Evans," 12.

45. Plumer, *Autobiography*, 279.

46. *Constitutionalist*, 22 December 1812, p. 1, col. 4; *Farmer's Cabinet*, 21 December 1812, p. 3, col. 1; Motion of Address, 11 December 1812, *House Journal* (November 1812), 110; *Concord Gazette*, 15 December 1812, p. 2, col. 3; *Democratic Republican*, 21 December 1812, p. 3, col. 3.

47. Plumer, *Autobiography*, 281; *Constitutionalist*, 30 June 1812, p. 1, col. 2.

48. At that time the Common Pleas was experiencing one of its periods of intense criticism. See, e.g., "P," "The Judiciary," in *Concord Gazette*, 3 June 1812, p. 2, cols. 1–2 (from the Keene *Sentinel*).

49. *Controlling the Law*, 171–79.

50. *New-Hampshire Patriot*, 24 November 1812, p. 3, col. 2.

51. *Legislating the Courts*, 40–52.

52. "Copy of Governor Plumer's objections to the Proposed Judiciary Bill," 13 November 1812, *Plumer Documents* (reel 13, frame 388).

53. Ibid., (reel 13, frame 389).

54. Plumer, *Autobiography*, 294 ( 2 June 1813). Five years later he was still brooding about Claggett's appointment, ibid., 361 (May 1818).

## Chapter Seven—Legislative Hegemony

1. *New Hampshire Gazette*, 1 June 1813, p. 3, col. 4; Evans, *Appeal to People*, 23–24; *Farmer's Cabinet*, 25 October 1813, p. 1, col. 2 (from the *Portsmouth Oracle*); Plumer, *Plumer*, 396; Edward St. Loe Livermore to Edward Cutts, 1 September 1813, Edward St. Loe Livermore Papers (file 2), New Hampshire Historical Society.

2. Plumer to John Adams Harper, 2 March 1812, Eighth Plumer Letterbook, 198.

3. The Voice Of New-Hampshire, "To Arthur Livermore, Esq." in *People's Advocate*, 29 October 1816, p. 1, col. 4.

4. Ibid., col. 3.

5. Bell, *Bench and Bar,* 380; *Farmer's Cabinet,* 22 June 1816, p. 3, col. 3.

6. *New-Hampshire Patriot,* 16 June 1812, p. 2, col. 2.

7. Entry for 18 June 1812, Plumer, *Register II.* Livermore that year was complimented at the Republican Fourth of July celebration in Portsmouth with the toast: "Hon. Arthur Livermore, chief justice of N. Hampshire, maintaining the dignity and independence of the Judiciary, he will not fear to do right, though assailed by the shafts of faction." *New Hampshire Gazette,* 7 July 1812, p. 3, col. 1.

8. *New-Hampshire Patriot,* 23 June 1812, p. 3, col. 2; *Farmer's Cabinet,* 6 July 1812, p. 2, col. 3.

9. Entry for 18 June 1812, Plumer, *Register II.*

10. *New-Hampshire Patriot,* 23 June 1812, p. 3, col. 3; *Farmer's Cabinet,* 6 July 1812, p. 2, col. 3.

11. Entry for 18 June 1812, Plumer, *Register II*; *Constitutionalist,* 30 June 1812, p. 1, col. 2.

12. *Democratic Republican,* 21 December 1812, p. 2, col. 1; *Portsmouth Oracle,* 12 December 1812, p. 1, cols. 3–4.

13. Minutes of 17 December 1812, *House Journal* (November 1812), 157–58.

14. Cato [Plumer], *New-Hampshire Patriot,* 22 February 1814, p. 1, col. 1. The example set by President Jefferson and the national Republicans is discussed in *Legislating the Courts,* 71–89.

15. *Concord Gazette,* 8 February 1814, p. 2, col. 5; *Portsmouth Oracle,* 14 March 1812, p. 3, col. 1; Turner, *Ninth State,* 280–81.

16. Turner, *Ninth State,* 278; Message of Governor Plumer, 18 November 1812, *House Journal* (November 1812), 11–12; Plumer, *Speech on War,* 4.

17. Protest of the Minority of the House of Representatives, 18 December 1812, *House Journal* (November 1812), 160.

18. Sullivan, *Speech at Rockingham Convention,* 4, 11–12; Cooke, *Oration at Keene,* 11; Gates, *Oration at Bedford,* 8; Worcester, *Fast Day Sermon at Salisbury,* 15–32; "Passive Obedience and Non-Resistence," *Portsmouth Oracle,* 26 December 1812, p. 2, col. 1.

19. Gilman to Harrison Gray Otis, 31 October 1814, Morison, *Life and Letters of Otis* 2:182, also 107.

20. Turner, *Ninth State,* 284.

21. A Friend To Justice, "On the Judicial Act," in *Portsmouth Oracle,* 10 July 1813, p. 2, col. 4.

22. Plumer, *Plumer,* 158.

23. For example, Samuel Livermore. *Controlling the Law,* 21–22.

24. A Friend To Justice, "On the Judicial Act," in *Portsmouth Oracle,* 10 July 1813, p. 2, col. 4.

25. Address of John Taylor Gilman, 5 June 1813, *Senate Journal* (June 1813), 27; *Democratic Republican,* 14 June 1813, p. 2, col. 4.

26. *Farmer's Cabinet,* 14 June 1813, p. 2, cols. 1 and 2, p. 3, col. 3, and 21 June 1813, p. 2, col. 1. Some reports referred to it as the "new judiciary bill." "The

new Judiciary bill it is thought will not be got through this session." Ibid., 21 June 1813, p. 3, col. 3.

27. *Constitutionalist*, 6 July 1813, p. 1, col. 1.

28. *Portsmouth Oracle*, 24 July 1813, p. 1, cols. 1–5; *New-Hampshire Patriot*, 6 July 1813, p. 1, cols. 1–5. For the Judicial Act, see *Public Laws June 1813*, 5–19.

29. *Controlling the Law*, 11.

30. *Judicial Act of 1813*, 6–7 (section 2) and 7 (section 3).

31. Ibid., 9–10; *Constitutionalist*, 13 July 1813, p. 1, col. 2.

32. *Constitutionalist*, 13 July 1813, p. 1, col. 4. An amendment of the act passed at the following November session allowed single-judge civil trials in what otherwise would have been two-judge trials "in consequence of any legal disqualification of one or more of the Justices. . . ." *Constitutionalist*, 29 November 1813, p. 1, col. 5.

33. Section 5, *Judicial Act of 1813*, 8–9; Smith, "Preface," *Smith's Reports*, vii.

34. Section 9, *Judicial Act of 1813*, *New-Hampshire Patriot*, 6 July 1813, p. 1, col. 2.

35. E.g., "The new system provides, that . . . there shall be two sessions annually, holden by one Judge of the trial of questions of fact, and one session annually, holden by the whole Court, for the trial of questions of law." The Voice Of The People, "To the Majority of the Legislature of New Hampshire," in *New-Hampshire Patriot*, 17 August 1813, p. 1, col. 2.

36. "An Act in addition to an act," *Constitutionalist*, 20 November 1813, p. 1, col. 4.

37. Turner, *Ninth State*, 288; The People, "The Administration of Gov. Gilman," in *New Hampshire Gazette*, 15 February 1814, EXTRA, p. 2, col. 4.

38. Section 12, Act of 1813, *Public Laws, June 1813*, 12; *New-Hampshire Patriot*, 6 July 1813, p. 1, col. 2.

39. Cato, "To Governor Gilman," in *New-Hampshire Patriot*, 25 January 1814, p. 3, col. 3. For Plumer's saying he was Cato, see Plumer, *Essays and Writings*, 95–96.

40. Turner, *Plumer*, 49n51.

41. Report of House Committee on Judiciary, *New-Hampshire Patriot*, 25 June 1816, p. 2, col. 5.

42. Morison, *Life of Smith*, 265.

43. See chapter one.

## Chapter Eight—Dependent Court, Reluctant Chief

1. *New-Hampshire Patriot*, 29 June 1813, p. 3, cols. 1–2; *New Hampshire Gazette*, 29 June 1813, p. 3, col. 3.

2. Turner, *Ninth State*, 285–86; Morison, *Life of Smith*, 265–66.

3. A Friend To Justice, "On the Judicial Act. No. II," in *Constitutionalist*, 13 July 1813, p. 3, col. 4; An Impartial Citizen, "The Judiciary," in *Portsmouth Oracle*, 31 July 1813, p. 1, col. 2.

4. MARCELLUS, "To the Federal Farmers and Mechanics of New-Hampshire," in *New-Hampshire Patriot,* 5 March 1816, p. 2, col. 2.

5. Turner, *Ninth State,* 284.

6. The later campaigns by Senator William Eaton Chandler to rouse public opposition to the jurisprudence of Chief Justice Charles Doe were not successful. *Chief Justice,* 265–66, 324–25, 422–24.

7. PHOCION, "To the Candid Citizens of New Hampshire," in *Farmer's Cabinet,* 20 September 1813, p. 2, col. 1; *Constitutionalist,* 3 August 1813, p. 2, col. 1; Report on Memorials, 83; A FRIEND TO JUSTICE, "On the Judicial Act," in *Constitutionalist,* 6 July 1813, p. 3, col. 4; Webster to Edward Cutts, Jr., 26 May 1813, *Webster Papers* 1:138. For defects of the Common Pleas, see *Constitutionalist,* 10 August 1813, p. 2, col. 2.

8. *New-Hampshire Patriot,* 29 June 1813, p. 1, col. 2.

9. As was suggested by the judiciary bill of 1812 drafted by Thompson and Webster. Supra, 130–32.

10. *Controlling the Law,* 108–14 (single-judge trials), and 143–56 (law terms).

11. "We . . . understand it is pretty much a transcript of the Massachusetts system . . . a good model." *Farmer's Cabinet,* 5 July 1813, p. 2, col. 1.

12. *Controlling the Law,* 157–70.

13. Ibid., 173.

14. Turner, *Plumer,* 226; entry for 8 August 1813, Plumer, *Register II.*

15. *Controlling the Law,* 102; entry for 8 August 1813, Plumer, *Register II.*

16. Report of the General Court Committee on Memorials, *Portsmouth Oracle,* 5 February 1814, p. 1, col. 5.

17. A FRIEND TO JUSTICE, "On the Judicial Act. No. III," in *Constitutionalist,* 27 July 1813, p. 3, col. 2; Report on Memorials, 79; A FRIEND TO JUSTICE, "On the Judicial Act. No. IV," in *Constitutionalist,* 3 August 1813, p. 3, col. 1. The memorials the committee reported on were petitions demanding repeal of the Judicial Act of 1813.

18. DEFENDER OF THE CONSTITUTION, "The Judiciary No. 3," in *New Hampshire Gazette,* 13 July 1813, p. 2, col. 1; CINCINNATUS [Plumer], No. 130, in *Portsmouth Journal,* 13 May 1826, p. 2, col. 6.

19. *Farmer's Cabinet,* 27 September 1813, p. 1, col. 3 (from the *Constitutionalist*); A FRIEND TO JUSTICE, "On the Judicial Act," in *Portsmouth Oracle,* 21 August 1813, p. 2, col. 1. Although these New Hampshire commentators drew analogies to the federal law legislating out of office the midnight judges, they drew none from other states' law, convincing evidence that they did not know of another state legislating judges out of office.

20. *Constitutionalist,* 3 August 1813, p. 2, col. 1 (from the *NewHampshire Sentinel*); Report on Memorials, 77; A FRIEND TO TRUTH, "On Judicial Act," in *New Hampshire Gazette,* 17 August 1813, p. 1, cols. 4–5.

21. *Portsmouth Oracle,* 7 August 1813, p. 2, col. 4; A FRIEND TO JUSTICE, "On the Judicial Act," in *Portsmouth Oracle,* 14 August 1813, p. 2, col. 1; CINCINNATUS

[Plumer], No. 126, in *Grafton Journal*, 25 November 1825, p. 191, col. 2.

22. *Farmer's Cabinet*, 27 September 1813, p. 1, col. 2.

23. Report on Memorials, 78.

24. *Legislating the Courts*, 43–44, 51.

25. *Portsmouth Oracle*, 17 July 1813, p. 3, col. 2. For an argument that the Superior Court had been entrenched, see Claggett, *Speech in House*, 19–20.

26. Report on Memorials, 81.

27. Report on Memorials, 82.

28. Defender Of The Constitution, "The Judiciary No. 3," in *New Hampshire Gazette*, 13 July 1813, p. 2, col. 1.

29. *New-Hampshire Patriot*, 28 September 1813, p. 3, col. 4; similarly, see Hillsborough, ibid., p. 2, col. 2.

30. *Farmer's Cabinet*, 1 November 1813, p. 3, col. 2 (quoting the *Patriot*).

31. A Friend To Justice, "On the Judicial Act," in *Portsmouth Oracle*, 21 August 1813, p. 1, col. 5. Also see Batchellor, "Tenure of Judges," 546.

32. In 1816, 1855, 1874, 1876, and 1901. Upton, "Independence of Judiciary," 38.

33. New Hampshire's highest court upheld legislating judges out of office, even though legislating out affected the remedies of litigants. *Cummings v. White Mountain Railroad*, 43 N.H. 114 (1861); Upton, "Independence of Judiciary," 39.

34. Cincinnatus [Plumer], No. 126, in *Grafton Journal*, 25 November 1825, p. 191, col. 2; Defender Of The Constitution, "No. 7," in *New Hampshire Gazette*, 31 August 1813, p. 2, col. 3; An American, "Judiciary—No. 2," in *New Hampshire Gazette*, 27 February 1816, p. 3, col. 1.

35. E.g., The People, "The Administration of Gov. Gilman," in *New Hampshire Gazette*, 25 January 1814, p. 2, col. 2; *New-Hampshire Patriot*, 15 June 1813, p. 2, col. 4; Turner, *Ninth State*, 286–87 (quoting Vox Populi); Claggett, *Speech in House*, 5, 6, 24.

36. *New Hampshire Gazette*, 25 September 1813, p. 3, col. 2.

37. Morison, *Life of Smith*, 267.

38. Smith to Farrar, 26 July 1813, Morison, *Life of Smith*, 271. Plumer apparently believed that Smith's denial was sincere. In his biography of his father, Plumer's son said that Smith was opposed to the law. Plumer, *Plumer*, 412–13.

39. Morison, *Life of Smith*, 267; *New Hampshire Gazette*, 21 September 1813, p. 2, col. 4.

40. Compensation, Morison, *Life of Smith*, 267; *New Hampshire Gazette*, 24 August 1813, p. 1, col. 4 (reprinting the *Patriot*); Turner, *Ninth State*, 286. Memorial, *Legislating the Courts*, 88. Also see Claggett, *Speech in House*, 23.

41. Turner, *Ninth State*, 286. Smith "was so deeply committed to the reforms written into the new system that he accepted appointment." Turner, *Plumer*, 226.

42. Mason to Smith, 6 July 1813, and same to same, no date, Morison, *Life of Smith*, 267–68.

43. Smith to Mason, 26 July 1813, ibid., 268–69.

44. Smith to Farrar, 26 July 1813, ibid., 269–71.

45. Smith to Farrar, 26 July 1813, ibid., 271–72; *Controlling the Law,* 81–82.

46. Appointment, *New-Hampshire Patriot,* 20 July 1813, p. 3, col. 4; *New Hampshire Gazette,* 24 August 1813, p. 1, col. 3 (reprinting from *Patriot*).

47. *Controlling the Law,* 82.

48. An Injured People, in *New-Hampshire Patriot,* 9 November 1813, p. 1, col. 3; Phocion, in *New-Hampshire Patriot,* 8 March 1814, p. 1, col. 2; A Friend To Truth, "On the Judicial Act," in *New Hampshire Gazette,* 13 July 1813, p. 2, col. 2.

49. Morison, *Life of Smith,* 267; *Webster Legal Papers,* 246, 247.

## Chapter Nine—Contesting Courts

1. Letter of Livermore to House of Representatives Committee, *Portsmouth Oracle,* 23 October 1813, p. 2, col. 2; entry for 1 July 1813, Plumer, *Register II.*

2. The Voice Of New-Hampshire, "To Arthur Livermore, Esq.," in *People's Advocate,* 29 October 1816, p. 2, col. 1; entry for 15 September 1812, Plumer, *Register II.*

3. "Attornies in the County of Cheshire," *Collections Historical* 3:53; Plumer, "Caleb Ellis," 32.

4. Smith, *Sketch of Ellis,* 10; Smith, "Hon. Caleb Ellis," *Collections Historical* 2:277.

5. *Farmer's Cabinet,* 22 June 1816, p. 1, col. 4; *Portsmouth Oracle,* 1 June 1816, p. 2, col. 5; entry for 13 July 1816, Plumer, *Register II,* 112. Also see "Hon. Judge Ellis" (Funeral Sermon by Reverend Farley), in *Portsmouth Oracle,* 14 September 1816, p. 2, col. 4; *Farmer's Cabinet,* 7 September 1816, p. 3, col. 2; Plumer, "Caleb Ellis," 32; entry for 13 July 1813 [1816?], Plumer, *Register II.*

6. The People, "The Administration of Gov. Gilman," in *New Hampshire Gazette,* 25 January 1814, p. 2, col. 1; A Farmer, "Solemn Inquiry," in *New Hampshire Gazette,* 28 September 1813, p. 3, col. 2; Defender Of The Constitution, in *New Hampshire Gazette,* 17 August 1813, p. 3, col. 1; "Thoughts upon the new Court," *New Hampshire Gazette,* 21 September 1813, p. 2, col. 4; *New Hampshire Gazette,* 23 November 1813, p. 3, col. 3.

7. *Farmer's Cabinet,* 4 October 1813, p. 3, col. 2; sheriffs, A Friend To Justice, "On the Judicial Act," in *Constitutionalist,* 27 July 1813, p. 3, col. 1; *New-Hampshire Patriot,* 2 November 1813, p. 3, col. 4; gag Order, *New Hampshire Gazette,* 28 June 1814, pp. 2–3.

8. *Portsmouth Oracle,* 5 February 1814, p. 1, col. 1.

9. Report on Memorials, 76; "Portsmouth Memorial," *New-Hampshire Patriot,* 23 November 1813, p. 2, col. 2.

10. "Chester Memorial to the Gen. Ct., 27 October 1813," *New-Hampshire Patriot,* 7 December 1813, p. 1, col. 2; Upton, "Independence of Judiciary," 31.

11. Entry for 13 July 1813, Plumer, *Register II;* Cato, "To Governor Gilman," Plumer, *Essays and Writings,* 99; Turner, *Ninth State,* 285.

12. Entry for 13 July 1813, Plumer, *Register II,* 112 (also see same date, Plumer, *Register II*).

13. Richard Evans, "To the Printer of the Oracle," in *Portsmouth Oracle*, 14 August 1813, p. 2, col. 3; Judge Evans's Opinion, *Opinions of Clagett and Evans*, 19, 21.

14. Judge Claggett's Opinion, *Opinions of Clagett and Evans*, 10, 5, 12. For entrenching the high court, see *Legislating the Courts*, 40–52.

15. *New-Hampshire Patriot*, 26 October 1813, p. 3, col. 2; DEFENDER OF THE CONSTITUTION, "The Judiciary No. 1," in *New Hampshire Gazette*, 6 July 1813, p. 1, col. 1. Also see *New-Hampshire Patriot*, 31 August 1813, p. 3, col. 4, and 23 November 1813, p. 2, col. 3.

16. Stearns, "Livermore," 440; Morison, *Life of Smith*, 373–74.

17. Stearns, "Livermore," 439–41; Morison, *Life of Smith*, 274.

18. *Portsmouth Oracle*, 23 October 1813, p. 2, col. 4 (from the *New Hampshire Gazette*, 11 September). Also see *New-Hampshire Patriot*, 21 September 1813, p. 2, col. 5, and p. 3, col. 1. Plumer heard that Livermore had told Claggett "he was resolved to do every thing in his power to prevent the reelection of every man who voted for that law." Plumer, *Autobiography*, 298.

19. *Portsmouth Oracle*, 23 October 1813, p. 2, col. 4, and FAIR PLAY, p. 3, col. 3; *Farmer's Cabinet*, 25 October 1813, p. 3, col. 2. Also see *Farmer's Cabinet*, 11 October 1813, p. 3, col. 2.

20. *Legislating the Courts*, 140–48.

21. "Judge Livermore's Letter," *Constitutionalist*, 9 November 1813, p. 3, col. 1; *New-Hampshire Patriot*, 19 October 1813, p. 3, cols. 3–4.

22. *New-Hampshire Patriot*, 19 October 1813, p. 3, col. 4; *Farmer's Cabinet*, 25 October 1813, p. 2, col. 1. Also see Stearns, "Livermore," 442. "Having been *turned out* of one office and accepted a new appointment in the Judiciary, he thinks *in his conscience* it would be wrong to turn him *out* again!" *Farmer's Cabinet*, 1 November 1813, p. 3, col. 3.

23. JUNIUS, in *New-Hampshire Patriot*, 9 November 1813, p. 1, col. 5.

24. *Portsmouth Oracle*, 23 October 1813, p. 2, col. 4. "The Judge thinks the act, so far as it . . . empowers *one* Judge to hold a court alone, is constitutional. But so far as it effects the tenure of the offices of the Judges of the Superior Court, or goes to abolish the Court, that it is unconstitutional." *New Hampshire Gazette*, 26 October 1813, p. 2, col. 4.

25. Interpreting the clause in the state constitution that no person may be arrested or property be confiscated "but by lawful judgment of his peers, or by the law of the land," the high court ruled that "all statutes, not repugnant to any other clauses in the constitution" are to be "considered as 'the law of the land.'" *Dartmouth College v. Woodward*, 1 N.H. 111, 129, 130 (1817). Therefore, there was no concept of due process in New Hampshire constitutionalism.

26. *Farmer's Cabinet*, 23 October 1813, p. 3, col. 2; *Portsmouth Oracle*, 30 October 1813, p. 1, col. 2.

27. Webster to Moses Paul Payson, 16 September 1813, Stearns, "Livermore," 441–42; *Webster Legal Papers*, 225. The quotation follows the wording in Stearns's article. *Webster Legal Papers* reads "excited," rather than "existed."

28. Peabody to Plumer, 11 September 1813, *Plumer Documents*; William Claggett to Woodbury, 12 September 1813, Capowski, *Making of Democrat*, 42.

29. Justice, "To the Sheriffs of the several counties in this State," in *New Hampshire Gazette*, 2 August 1813, p. 3, col. 4; A Friend To Justice, "On the Judiciary Act," in *Portsmouth Oracle*, 31 July 1813, p. 2, col. 2; Voice Of The People, "To the Sheriffs," in *New Hampshire Gazette*, 29 June 1813, p. 3, col. 3.

30. Z, "The Judiciary," in *New Hampshire Gazette*, 20 July 1813, p. 1, col. 3.

31. Morison, *Life of Smith*, 274–75; *New Hampshire Gazette*, 28 September 1813, p. 2, col. 4.

32. *New Hampshire Gazette*, 28 September 1813, p. 2, col. 4; *New-Hampshire Patriot*, 28 September 1813, p. 3, col. 3.

33. *Portsmouth Oracle*, 9 October 1813, p. 1, col. 2; Morison, *Life of Smith*, 275; *New Hampshire Gazette*, 28 September 1813, p. 2, col. 4.

34. *New-Hampshire Patriot*, 28 September 1813, p. 3, col. 3. Also see Report of the Special Committee, 3 November 1813, *House Journal* (October 1813), 43–44.

35. Anon., "To the Editor of the Concord Gazette," in *Farmer's Cabinet*, 11 October 1813, p. 1, col. 3.

36. Ibid., 25 October 1813, p. 1, col. 2 (reprinting the *Oracle*); Turner, *Ninth State*, 287.

37. *Farmer's Cabinet*, 11 October 1813, p. 1, col. 2, and 25 October 1813, p. 1, col. 2.

38. Ibid., 11 October 1813, p. 3, col. 1; *Constitutionalist*, 12 October 1813, p. 3, cols. 3–4.

39. *New Hampshire Gazette*, 19 October 1813, p. 2, col. 5; *Farmer's Cabinet*, 11 October 1813, p. 3, col. 1.

40. *New Hampshire Gazette*, 19 October 1813, p. 2, col. 5.

41. Ibid.

42. *Farmer's Cabinet*, 11 October 1813, p. 3, col. 2.

43. *New Hampshire Gazette*, 19 October 1813, p. 2, col. 5.

44. *Constitutionalist*, 26 October 1813, p. 3, col. 3.

45. *New-Hampshire Patriot*, 12 October 1813, p. 2, col. 5; *Constitutionalist*, 26 October 1813, p. 3, col. 3; *New Hampshire Gazette*, 23 November 1813, p. 2, col. 4.

## Chapter Ten—Judicial Interregnum

1. *New Hampshire Gazette*, 28 September 1813, p. 2, col. 4.

2. Edward St. Loe Livermore to Edward Cutts, 13 September 1813, Edward St. Loe Livermore Papers (file 3), New Hampshire Historical Society.

3. Memorial of Richard Evans to General Court, *New-Hampshire Patriot*, 20 August 1816, p. 3, col. 4; Evans, *Appeal to People*, 24.

4. Memorial of Richard Evans to the General Court, *New-Hampshire Patriot*, 20 August 1816, p. 3, col. 4; Turner, *Ninth State*, 287; *Constitutionalist*, 12 October 1813, p. 3, col. 3 (from the *Portsmouth Oracle*).

5. Speech of Governor Gilman, 27 October 1813, *New-Hampshire Patriot*, 2 November 1813, p. 3, col. 3.

6. "[I]s there not something more wanting to substantiate the facts so the Legislature may act on them, than a mere 'it is said' from Governor Gilman," ibid., p. 3, col. 2.

7. Turner, *Ninth State*, 287–88; THE PEOPLE, in *New-Hampshire Patriot*, 14 December 1813, p. 1, col. 2.

8. HONESTUS, in *New-Hampshire Patriot*, 14 December 1813, p. 1, col. 2.

9. "We also protest against the vote which excluded Sheriff Butler from being heard on the floor of the House, agreeably to his written request. . . . Had he been impeached, he would have enjoyed this right, before the Senate; but as the House has voted his removal from office, by address, and refused to hear him make his defence, he has been completely deprived of this constitutional right." Protest of Dissenters, Minutes of 5 November 1813, *House Journal* (October 1813), 70, also 67.

10. The issue was settled in 1816 when the General Court addressed out the judges who had been legislated out that term. See *post*, 238–41.

11. "Had Justices Evans and Clagett been arraigned at the bar for robbery and murder, they could not have appeared more criminal than this speech would have them appear." "Governor's Speech," *New-Hampshire Patriot*, 2 November 1813, p. 3, col. 3.

12. Report of Committee, 3 November 1813, *House Journal* (October 1813), 35.

13. Ibid., 36; *Constitutionalist*, 16 November 1813, p. 2, cols. 1–2. The report is printed separately as *Proceedings on Important Subjects.*

14. Report of Committee, *Portsmouth Oracle*, 13 November 1813, p. 2, col. 3.

15. Turner, *Plumer*, 226; *Farmer's Cabinet*, 27 September 1813, p. 3, col. 3; entry for 2 November 1813, Plumer, *Register* II, 118. The pamphlet's short title is *Opinions of Clagett and Evans.*

16. For a political (not a judicial) evaluation of public esteem, see Turner, *Ninth State*, 287.

17. Morison, *Life of Smith*, 276–77.

18. *Portsmouth Oracle*, 30 October 1813, p. 1, col. 2; *Farmer's Cabinet*, 1 November 1813, p. 3, col. 3; Report on Memorials, 84.

19. ARISTIDES [Plumer], "The Glory and Excellence of the New Judiciary System," in *New-Hampshire Patriot*, 26 October 1813, p. 2, cols. 1–2.

20. Ibid., col. 2.

21. For the Jeffersonian argument against law terms, see *Controlling the Law*, 143–56.

22. A FRIEND TO JUSTICE, "On the Judicial Act. No. III," in *Constitutionalist*, 27 July 1813, p. 3, col. 2; *Concord Gazette*, 10 August 1813, p. 1, col. 2.

23. *Portsmouth Oracle*, 17 July 1813, p. 3, col. 2.

24. Morison, *Life of Smith*, 277.

25. Mason to Smith, 10 July 1814, Morison, *Life of Smith*, 277–78.

26. Morison, *Life of Smith*, 279; Report of House Committee on Judiciary, *New-Hampshire Patriot*, 25 June 1816, p. 2, col. 5.

27. Minutes of 5 November 1813, *Senate Journal* (October 1813), 53. The committee was voted powers not usually accorded recess committees: "to send for such persons and papers, as, in their judgment, will afford light on the subject of their enquiry." Ibid.

28. Phocion, *New-Hampshire Patriot,* 15 February 1814, p. 1, col. 5. The authority that Phocion was specifically discussing was the power of addressing from office, not directly legislating out.

29. Report of Joint Committee on Judiciary Bill, 5 November 1813, *Proceedings of the Legislature,* 27–28.

30. Plumer to Mason, 25 February 1814, Mason Papers, box 11, folder 28, New Hampshire Historical Society. Shortly before the election Henry Clay and his delegation to the peace negotiations set sail for Europe. *Farmer's Cabinet,* 7 March 1814, p. 3, col. 3.

31. Republican editorial, *New-Hampshire Patriot,* 8 February 1814, p. 3, cols. 1–2; Federalist editorial, *Constitutionalist,* 7 March 1814, p. 3, col. 3.

32. A Citizen, *Constitutionalist,* 7 March 1814, p. 2, col. 2; *Farmer's Cabinet,* 7 February 1814, p. 3, col. 1. Also see A Voter, "The Question," in *Farmer's Cabinet,* 21 February 1814, p. 2, col. 3. The *Cabinet* article is evidence of Smith's regained prestige. *Farmer's Cabinet,* 31 January 1814, p. 3, col. 3; Rusticus, ibid., 21 February 1814, p. 2, col. 2.

33. *New Hampshire Gazette,* 22 February 1814, p. 1, col. 5. For a Federalist answer, see *Portsmouth Oracle,* 26 February 1814, p. 3, col. 2.

34. *Constitutionalist,* 5 March 1811, p. 1, col. 3.

35. *New-Hampshire Patriot,* 8 March 1814, p. 3, col. 2; *New Hampshire Gazette,* 1 March 1814, p. 3, col. 4.

36. Calculator, "Governor Gilman's Indirect Tax," in *New Hampshire Gazette,* 22 February 1814, p. 1, col. 5.

37. *Farmer's Cabinet,* 25 October 1813, p. 3, col. 1; *New-Hampshire Patriot,* 26 April 1814, p. 3, col. 2. Also see "The New Court," *New Hampshire Gazette,* 13 December 1814, p. 3, cols. 1–2.

38. *Constitutionalist,* 29 March 1814, p. 2, col. 5.

39. *House Journal* (June 1814), 9; *New-Hampshire Patriot,* 7 June 1814, p. 3, col. 1; *Farmer's Cabinet,* 6 June 1814, p. 3, col. 1.

40. *Constitutionalist,* 2 March 1813, p. 3, col. 3.

41. *Portsmouth Oracle,* 28 May 1814, p. 3, col. 2.

42. *New-Hampshire Patriot,* 28 June 1814, p. 3, col. 2; Report of Joint Committee on Judiciary Bill, 5 November 1813, *House Journal* (October 1813), 85; Report of the Joint Committee on Petitions for Repeal of the Judicial Act, *Portsmouth Oracle,* 5 February 1814, p. 2, col. 1.

43. *Portsmouth Oracle,* 2 July 1814, p. 3, col. 2; letter from C. S., *New-Hampshire Patriot,* 9 August 1814, p. 2, col. 3.

44. *Farmer's Cabinet,* 20 February 1815, p. 3, col. 3; *New Hampshire Gazette,* 21 February 1815, p. 3, col. 2; *Concord Gazette,* 21 February 1815, p. 2, col. 4, and p. 3, cols. 1–3.

45. *New Hampshire Gazette*, 11 March 1815, p. 1, col. 3; *New-Hampshire Patriot*, 7 March 1815, p. 3, col. 1.

46. *Farmer's Cabinet*, 10 June 1815, p. 3, col. 3.

47. Claggett, *New Hampshire Gazette*, 27 June 1815, p. 1, col. 1; *Farmer's Cabinet*, 24 June 1815, p. 2, col. 2; Morison, *Life of Smith*, 278–79.

48. *New-Hampshire Patriot*, 11 July 1815, p. 2, col. 5. For Smith's assignment, see minutes of 11 June 1814, *House Journal* (June 1814), 87.

49. Gilman, *Concord Gazette*, 12 December 1815, p. 3, col. 2; Sheafe, Capowski, *Making of Democrat*, 65–66.

50. Johnson, "Dartmouth College Case," 46.

51. *Farmer's Cabinet*, 24 February 1816, p. 3, col. 3. The *Cabinet* described the "Judiciary" as the "great question of the election." Ibid., 9 March 1816, p. 3, col. 3.

52. *Portsmouth Oracle*, 9 March 1816, p. 1, col. 4 (also *Farmer's Cabinet*, 9 March 1816, p. 3, col. 1) (reprinting the *Concord Gazette*). But see Lynn Turner: "The gradual accretion in his [Plumer's] favor—from 48.44 per cent of the total in 1812, to 49.12 per cent in 1815—would probably have brought success in 1816 without help from any unusual quarter. The Dartmouth issue, however, turned what might have been a moderate conquest into a rout. Plumer received 52.95 per cent of the second largest total ever cast in a New Hampshire election, and defeated Sheafe by more than 2,300 votes" (Turner, *Plumer*, 238).

53. Washington, "Freemen of Newhampshire," in *New Hampshire Gazette*, 13 February 1816, p. 2, col. 5; Junius, "To the Honorable Jeremiah Smith," in *New-Hampshire Patriot*, 27 February 1816, p. 2, col. 1.

54. A Friend To Justice, "To the Sentinels of Liberty, and Men yet Free," in *New Hampshire Gazette*, 30 January 1816, p. 4, col. 1, and 27 February 1816, p. 1, col. 5.

55. *New-Hampshire Patriot*, 6 February 1816, p. 2, col. 5; A Friend To Justice, "To the Sentinels of Liberty, and Men yet Free," in *New Hampshire Gazette*, 30 January 1816, p. 3, col. 4; Leonidas, "To Members of the Society of Friends," in *New Hampshire Gazette*, 5 March 1816, p. 2, col. 2.

56. *Portsmouth Oracle*, 3 February 1816, p. 2, col. 5; Plain Truth, "Electors of New-Hampshire," ibid., 9 March 1816, p. 2, col. 5; A Citizen, *Constitutionalist*, 7 March 1814, p. 2, col. 2. Also see *Portsmouth Oracle*, 3 February 1816, p. 2, col. 5, and 10 February 1816, p. 2, col. 3; *Concord Gazette*, 27 February 1816, p. 1, col. 3. One correspondent claimed he had computed the figures and that Evans and Claggett would collect more than $1,500. *Portsmouth Oracle*, 9 March 1816, p. 1, col. 5.

57. *Farmer's Cabinet*, 2 March 1816, p. 1, col. 2 (from the *Keene Sentinel*), p. 3, col. 1 (from the *Portsmouth Oracle)*, and 9 March 1816, p. 3, col. 1 (from the *Concord Gazette*).

58. *Farmer's Cabinet*, 10 February 1816, p. 1, col. 1, and 2 March 1816, p. 3, col. 1 (also see p. 2, col. 4).

59. Junius, "To the Honorable Jeremiah Smith," in *New Hampshire Gazette*, 5 March 1816, p. 1, col. 5; Calculator, "Fees of Lawyers," ibid., 20 February

1816, p. 1, col. 3. Similarly, see ibid., 13 February 1816, p. 3, col. 1.

60. *Portsmouth Oracle*, 3 February 1816, p. 2, col. 5, and 10 February 1816, p. 3, col. 1. Three hundred sixty-five cases were said to have been pending in Rockingham County in 1813, and fifty-two were pending just before the 1816 election. *Farmer's Cabinet*, 2 March 1816, pp. 2–3.

61. HILLSBOROUGH, "The Election," *Farmer's Cabinet*, 2 March 1816, p. 2, col. 4. Also see WASHINGTON, "To the Electors of Newhampshire," in *New Hampshire Gazette*, 5 March 1816, p. 2, col. 4; *Portsmouth Oracle*, 10 February 1816, p. 3, col. 1.

62. *Farmer's Cabinet*, 1 June 1816, p. 3, col. 2.

63. Hill to Plumer, Jr., 22 April 1816, *Plumer Papers*; *Concord Gazette*, 30 April 1816, p. 3, col. 3 (reprinting the *New Hampshire Gazette*); *Portsmouth Oracle*, 22 June 1816, pp. 2–3.

## Chapter Eleven—Addressing Out the Judges

1. *Portsmouth Oracle*, 8 June 1816, p. 3, col. 2, and 15 June 1816, p. 1, col. 4.

2. Capowski, "Era of Good Feelings," 4; Cole, *Jacksonian Democracy*, 30–31.

3. Turner, *Plumer*, 244; *Portsmouth Oracle*, 15 June 1816, p. 3, col. 1.

4. Capowski, *Making of Democrat*, 69; Turner, *Plumer*, 244.

5. Plumer, "Address," 6 June 1816, in *New-Hampshire Patriot*, 11 June 1816, p. 2, cols. 2–3.

6. Turner, *Plumer*, 244.

7. Turner, *Ninth State*, 310–11; Answer of the Senate to Governor's Address, 13 June 1816, *Portsmouth Oracle*, 22 June 1816, p. 1, col. 5. For an argument that judicial tenure was "a limitation upon the power of the legislature over the courts, and that an attempt to remove judges by replacing all laws giving them jurisdiction, is unconstitutional," see Report of House Committee on Judiciary, 20 June 1816, *New-Hampshire Patriot*, 25 June 1816, p. 2, col. 4 (also see col. 5).

8. *Concord Gazette*, 23 July 1816, p. 1, col. 4; Section 1, Act of 27 June 1816, *Laws of the State of New-Hampshire. June Session, 1816* [Exeter, New Hampshire: Norris, 1816].

9. Turner, *Ninth State*, 311; Plumer to Plumer, Jr., 24 June 1816, *Plumer Documents.*

10. The third Supreme Judicial Court judge, Caleb Ellis, had recently died.

11. Turner, *Ninth State*, 311–12.

12. Evans, *Appeal to People*, 14.

13. Plumer, *Plumer*, 437–38.

14. Report of Committee on Judiciary, 20 June 1816, *New-Hampshire Patriot*, 25 June 1816, p. 2, col. 4. Also see CINCINNATUS [Plumer],–No. 93, "Government," in *Portsmouth Journal*, 13 September 1823, p. 1, col. 2.

15. Resolve of Senate and House, 27 June 1816, Gubernatorial Papers I (frame 134); Address to the Executive from a "Committee of both branches of the Legislature," 27 June 1816, ibid. (frames 136–37); "I do therefore remove the said

Jeremiah Smith and Arthur Livermore from their respective offices. . . ." Order of 29 June 1816, ibid. (frame 138).

16. Evans, *Appeal to People*, 14, 20.

17. Ibid., 21, 9.

18. *New Hampshire Gazette*, 2 November 1813, p. 2, col. 5; *Concord Gazette*, 27 February 1816, p. 1, col. 3; *Portsmouth Oracle*, 9 March 1816, p. 1, col. 3.

19. See, e.g., Speech of Virginia's William Giles, Senate Debates, n.d., *Newhampshire Sentinel*, 10 April 1801, p. 1, col. 1; "The Judiciary Question Laid Open," *Portsmouth Oracle*, 22 June 1816, p. 2, col. 5; "The Judges of the Old Court," *Farmer's Cabinet*, 1 November 1813, p. 3, col. 2.

20. Chase to Marshall, 24 April 1802, *Papers of Marshall* 6:113. For the midnight judges controversy, see *Legislating the Courts*, chapter 4; *New Hampshire Gazette*, 24 August 1813, p. 1, col. 3 (from "Judge Smith," *New-Hampshire Patriot*).

21. Act of 28 June 1816, Gubernatorial Papers I (frames 136–37); message House of Representatives to Governor Plumer, 25 June 1816, ibid. (frames 138–39). See *Concord Gazette*, 9 July 1816, p. 3, col. 2; *New Hampshire Gazette*, 9 July 1816, p. 2, col. 4.

22. Plumer, *Autobiography*, 338–39.

23. Stearns, "Livermore," 442; Turner termed the two addresses "comic." Turner, *Plumer*, 256n74.

## Chapter Twelve—A Receptionist Court

1. Plumer, *Autobiography*, 324.

2. *Legislating the Courts*, 42–52.

3. That May, between the election and the legislative session. "Her choice was different from the one I wished, but as it was hers I consented." Plumer, *Autobiography*, 317.

4. Sara Plumer to Plumer, Jr., 13 July 1816, *Plumer Papers*.

5. Plumer, Jr. to Thomas Whipple, 27 January 1819, *Plumer Documents* (reel 7, frame 810).

6. Turner, *Plumer*, 262.

7. William Claggett to Plumer, Jr., 30 July 1816, and Plumer, Jr., to Plumer, 30 August 1816, *Plumer Papers*. For William Claggett's first public discussion of the appointment, see "Political Ingratitude," *New Hampshire Gazette*, 16 July 1816, p. 3, col. 1.

8. Plumer to Plumer, Jr., 1 July 1816, *Plumer Papers*. Also Turner, *Plumer*, 258.

9. Plumer, *Autobiography*, 264, 318; Mason to Plumer, 18 August 1816, *Plumer Papers*.

10. Plumer, Jr., to Plumer, 30 August 1816, *Plumer Papers*. Newspapers, ONE OF THE PEOPLE, "The Policy of Appointing Federalists to Office," in *New Hampshire Gazette*, 20 August 1816, p. 3, col. 3; Turner, *Plumer*, 261. Of course, Isaac Hill's newspaper was not supportive. *New-Hampshire Patriot*, 14 January 1817, p. 2, col. 5.

11. Turner, *Plumer*, 258–59; Turner, *Ninth State*, 314, 316.

12. H. W. Gordon to Plumer, 24 July 1816, and Plumer to Gordon, 27 July 1816, *Plumer Papers*; *New-Hampshire Patriot*, 13 August 1816, p. 3, col. 2; Turner, *Plumer*, 260–61; Plumer, *Autobiography*, 327.

13. Turner, *Ninth State*, 315; Bell, *Bench and Bar*, 700; Plumer, *Autobiography*, 330–31. In fact, all but one of Plumer's Federalist appointees to the Court of Common Pleas were persuaded to decline. Turner, *Plumer*, 261–62.

14. Plumer, Jr., to Plumer, 14 August 1816 and 30 August 1816. *Plumer Papers*; Turner, *Plumer*, 267.

15. Clement, *Discourse on Richardson*, 4–5; Parker, *Courts and Lawyers* 3:556–57; Richardson to Charles Humphrey Atherton, 20 June 1812, Atherton Papers, folder 4, New Hampshire Historical Society.

16. Bell, *Life of Richardson*, 32–33; Richardson, *Oration at Groton*, 13–15 (he spoke of "a monster, not of *seven heads and ten horns*, but of seven thousand heads and ten thousand horns" and said he was referring to "the new philosophy," that is, "the blasphemous publications of Thomas Paine," the "worship of reason" rather than of God, 14–16).

17. Parker, *Charge to Grand Jury*, 25–26.

18. Ibid.

19. Plumer, *Autobiography*, 176–78.

20. Ibid., 317; Bell to Plumer, 5 August 1816, *Plumer Documents*.

21. Entries for 1 and 2 July 1816, Plumer, *Autobiography*, 325; Turner, *Ninth State*, 314; Turner, *Plumer*, 259–60.

22. Plumer, *Autobiography*, 327.

23. Ibid.

24. Ibid., 250, 327.

25. Ibid., 363.

26. *Concord Gazette*, 15 October 1816, p. 3, col. 2.

27. Plumer, *Autobiography*, 327; Plumer, Jr., to Plumer, 27 November 1816, and 1 December 1816, *Plumer Papers;* [William Merchant Richardson,] A Farmer Of Hillsborough County, in *New-Hampshire Patriot*, 14 January 1817, p. 3, col. 1. In a letter dated 12 January 1817, Plumer, Jr., told his father that Richardson was the author.

28. Turner, *Plumer*, 268–69; Turner, *Ninth State*, 321; Plumer to Plumer, Jr., 28 November 1816, *Plumer Papers*; Plumer, Jr., to Plumer, 1 December 1816, *Plumer Papers*.

29. Plumer, *Autobiography*, 320; Plumer, "Clifton Clagett," 460.

30. Turner, *Plumer*, 262n13; Richardson to Plumer, Jr., 6 October 1816, *Plumer Papers;* Claggett to Plumer, Jr., 12 September 1816, *Plumer Papers*.

31. Plumer, Jr., to Plumer, 27 November 1816, 1 December 1816, and 4 December 1816, *Plumer Papers*.

32. William Claggett to Plumer, Jr., 30 July 1816, *Plumer Documents*; Turner, *Plumer*, 268.

33. Plumer, *Autobiography*, 338; Plumer to his wife, 1 December 1816, *Plumer Papers*.

34. William Claggett to Woodbury, 21 October 1816, Capowski, *Making of Democrat*, 80; Plumer, Jr., to Plumer, 27 November 1816, and 1 December 1816, *Plumer Papers.*

35. Rantoul, *Eulogy on Woodbury*, 6, 7; Cole, *Jacksonian Democracy*, 9; Woodbury, *Memoir of Woodbury*, 5; Turner, *Ninth State*, 321; Capowski, *Making of Democrat*, 67–68.

36. Plumer, *Autobiography*, 333; Woodbury to Plumer, 18 January 1817, *Plumer Documents*; Capowski, *Making of Democrat*, 64; Turner, *Plumer*, 269–70.

37. Capowski, *Making of Democrat*, 83; Plumer to Plumer, Jr., 6 December 1816 and 14 December 1816, and Plumer to George Washington Plumer, 11 December 1816, *Plumer Papers.*

38. Plumer to Plumer, Jr., 8 December 1816, *Plumer Papers*; Bell, *Bench and Bar*, 82; Capowski, "Era of Good Feelings," 5.

39. *Portsmouth Oracle*, 21 September 1816, p. 3, col. 1, and 16 November 1816, p. 3, col. 2; *New-Hampshire Patriot*, 2 November 1816, p. 1, col. 3.

40. Turner, *Plumer*, 270.

41. Plumer, *Autobiography*, 340; *Farmer's Cabinet*, 16 November 1816, p. 3, col. 4.

42. Capowski, *Making of Democrat*, 80; Turner, *Ninth State*, 454n62, 322. For *Advocate*'s comments on Plumer's judicial appointments, see *People's Advocate*, 21 December 1816, p. 3, col. 3, 28 December 1816, p. 2, col. 4, and 11 January 1817, p. 2, col. 2.

43. Plumer to Plumer, Jr., 14 December 1816, *Plumer Papers;* Wait, "William Plumer," 135; Plumer to Mason, 22 December 1816, *Plumer Papers.*

44. Smith, *Sketch of Ellis*, 4, 3.

45. [Bell], *Life of Richardson*, 75.

## Chapter Thirteen—Judicial Legacy

1. *Portsmouth Oracle*, 12 February 1814, p. 2, col. 3; *Constitutionalist*, 8 February 1814, p. 3, col. 2.

2. *New-Hampshire Patriot*, 4 February 1817, p. 1, col. 5; *Portsmouth Oracle*, 17 August 1816, p. 3, col. 1; Plumer to Mason, 22 December 1816, *Plumer Documents.*

3. *New-Hampshire Patriot*, 14 January 1817, p. 2, col. 5, and 11 February 1817, p. 2, col. 2.

4. Plumer, *Autobiography*, 346; Plumer to Plumer, Jr., 29 March 1817, and 1 April 1817, *Plumer Documents*; Plumer to Richard Rush, 30 July 1817, *Historical Society Correspondence* (frame 129).

5. *Controlling the Law,* 71–82.

6. *New Hampshire Gazette*, 1 July 1817, p. 2, col. 2; *New-Hampshire Patriot*, 24 June 1817, p. 2, col. 3.

7. Woodbury to Plumer, 12 July 1817, *Plumer Documents.*

8. Plumer to General Court, 4 June 1818, *Concord Gazette*, 9 June 1818, p.

2, col. 4; *New Hampshire Gazette*, 7 July 1818, p. 3, col. 1, and 29 September 1818, p. 1, col. 5.

9. Turner, *Ninth State*, 343. The pamphlet is [Plumer,] *Message from His Excellency*. Parts of the speech are also printed in Publicola, *New Vade Mecum*.

10. Turner, *Ninth State*, 346, 347.

11. Address of Governor, 4 June 1818, *House Journal* (June 1818), 15–16.

12. Turner, *Ninth State*, 347.

13. Ibid., 17–18.

14. *Legislating the Courts*, 53–70.

15. Minutes of 24 June 1818, *House Journal* (June 1818), 239.

16. New Hampshire Constitution, Article 74. For Plumer's interpretation of and objections to this authority, see CINCINNATUS [Plumer]—No. 125, *Grafton Journal*, 12 November 1825, p. 185, col. 2.

17. Minutes of 27 November 1816, *Senate Journal* (November 1816), 42; Committee "On Petitions for new trials and restoration to law," *New Hampshire Gazette*, 16 June 1818, p. 2, col. 2; *New Hampshire Gazette*, 8 July 1817, p. 2, col. 1 (new trial for Dolly Merrill) and col. 2 (relief for Isaac Hodadon).

18. Superior Court to Senate and House, 31 May 1819, *Communication from Governor*, 5. The opinion did not form "part," but all of the reply. The justices had nothing else to say.

19. E.g., "[T]he very nature and effect of a new law is a rule for future cases. They must, too, in general, be rules prescribed for civil conduct to the whole community, and not a 'transient, sudden order from a superior to, or concerning a particular person.[']" *Merrill v. Sherburne*, 1 N.H. 199, 212 (1818).

20. E.g., "The legislative power is surely one of the most honorable and useful in all governments." Ibid.

21. E.g., the House of Representatives "are the tribunal to try impeachments." Ibid., 210.

22. Bell to Senate and House, 24 June 1819, *Communication from Governor*, 4.

23. *New Hampshire Gazette*, 8 July 1817, p. 2, col. 1.

24. *Merrill v. Sherburne*, 202.

25. Ibid., 217.

26. For discussion of Plumer's constitutional theory, see *Legislating the Courts*, 63–64.

27. *Merrill v. Sherburne*, 206–11; Hesse, "Legislature, Court and Constitution," 43; Murphy and Van Oot, "Judicial Independence," 12; McNamara, "Separation of Powers," 71, 84.

28. Douglas, "Judicial Review," 262–63; Carpenter, *Judicial Tenure*, 159–60; Lawrie, "Interpretation and Authority," 327, 310.

29. *Merrill v. Sherburne*, 210.

30. Lawrie, "Interpretation and Authority," 327.

31. Ibid., 326; CINCINNATUS [Plumer], No. 92, in *Portsmouth Journal*, 23 August 1823, p. 2, col. 2.

32. Lawrie, "Interpretation and Authority," 326.

33. *New Hampshire Gazette*, 9 February 1819, p. 2, col. 5, 18 May 1819, p. 3, col. 1, and 29 June 1819, p. 3, col. 1.

34. Ibid., 22 June 1819, p. 2, cols. 2, 4, and 29 June 1819, p. 1, col. 4 and p. 2, col. 2.

35. Ibid., 20 June 1820, p. 2, col. 1.

36. On one occasion the House of Representatives addressed the governor and Council to remove twenty-one "persons from military office." Ibid., 1 July 1817, p. 2, col. 3; e.g., "An address to remove Jonathan Noyes, one of the Coroners for the county of Grafton." *Farmer's Cabinet*, 28 June 1817, p. 2, col. 3.

37. Upton, "Independence of Judiciary," 32–33; for Doe, see minutes for 11 July 1856, *Senate Journal* (June 1856), 251, 284–85.

38. New Hampshire Constitution, Article 73.

39. Batchelder, "Independence of Judiciary," 64–65.

40. A few of the removed judges were reappointed. Upton, "Independence of Judiciary," 32–33; Batchellor, "Tenure of Judges," 534–35.

41. The Circuit Court was also abolished that year and its judges removed. Upton, "Independence of Judiciary," 33.

42. Ibid., 34.

43. Batchelder, "Independence of Judiciary," 62 (quoting Upton).

44. New Hampshire Constitution, Article 73; Batchelder, "Independence of Judiciary," 64.

45. See *Controlling the Law*, 131–42.

46. Ibid., 157–79.

47. Shirley, "Reporter's Note," 7.

48. *Controlling the Law*, 175–79; Shirley, "Reporter's Note," 7–8.

49. *Controlling the Law*, 190–92.

50. Ibid., 192.

51. Shirley, "Reporter's Note," 8.

52. For opposition to law terms in New Hampshire, see *Controlling the Law*, 143–56.

53. Woodbury to Plumer, 18 August 1817, *Plumer Documents*. Five years later a Massachusetts lawyer urged limiting law terms to just two cities: Boston and somewhere "in the interior." Anon., "Review of Collection of Cases," 69.

54. Telling Woodbury he would recommend that law terms be reintroduced, he wrote: "It appears to me that it would be a real improvement in the system: & I do not think any substantial objection can be made to it." Plumer to Woodbury, 7 March 1818, Ninth Plumer Letterbook, 49.

55. Address of Governor Plumer to General Court, 4 June 1818, *New-Hampshire Patriot*, 9 June 1818, p. 2, col. 5.

56. The expansion soon went beyond anything that Smith had dared to propose or probably ever thought of.

# Short Titles

Almand, "Supreme Court of Georgia"
Bond Almand. "The Supreme Court of Georgia: An Account of Its Delayed Birth." In *A History of the Supreme Court of Georgia: A Centennial Volume*, edited by John B. Harris, 1–18. Macon, GA: J. W. Burke, 1948.

American Patriot
*The American Patriot.* Weekly newspaper published in Concord, New Hampshire (became *New-Hampshire Patriot*).

Anon., *Friend to Constitution*
Anonymous. *A Friend to the Constitution.* N.p., 1801.

Anon., "Review of Collection of Cases"
Anonymous [Theron Metcalf]. Book Review, *North American Review* 15 (July 1822): 65–72 (reviewing Simon Greenleaf, *A Collection of Cases Overruled, or Limited in Their Application. Taken from American and English Reports* [1821]).

"Arena of the Giants"
John Reid. "The Arena of the Giants: Rockingham County, New Hampshire." *American Bar Association Journal* 46 (January 1960): 163–66, 214–16.

Batchelder, "Independence of Judiciary"
William F. Batchelder. "The Independence of the Judiciary in New Hampshire Revisited." *New Hampshire Bar Journal* 39, no. 2 (June 1998): 62–70.

Batchellor, "Tenure of Judges"
Albert S. Batchellor. "President's Address: The Tenure of Office of the Judges of the Supreme Court of the State Under the Constitution." *Proceedings of the Bar Association of the State of New Hampshire.* Vol. 1—Old Series, Vol. 6 (1900–1903): 523–56.

Bell, *Answer to Petition*
Samuel Bell. *An Answer to the Petition of Eli Brown, Complaining of Misconduct, &c. &c. of the Directors and Agents of the Hillsborough Bank.* Amherst, NH: R. Boylston, [1811].

Bell, *Bench and Bar*
Charles H. Bell. *The Bench and Bar of New Hampshire: Including Biographical Notices of Deceased Judges of the Highest Court, and Lawyers of the*

*Province and State and a List of Names of Those now Living*. Boston: Houghton, Mifflin, 1894.

Bell, *In Memory of Ira Perley*
Charles H. Bell. *Address in Memory of Hon. Ira Perley, LL.D., Late Chief-Justice of the Supreme Judicial Court of New Hampshire. Pronounced Before the Alumni Association of Dartmouth College, June 23, 1880*. Concord, NH: Republican Press Association, 1881.

[Bell,] *Life of Richardson*
[Charles Henry Bell.] *The Life of William M. Richardson, LL.D. Late Chief Justice of the Superior Court of New Hampshire*. Concord, NH: 1839.

Brandeis, "Harvard Law School"
Louis D. Brandeis. "The Harvard Law School." *Green Bag* 1 (1889): 10–25.

Capowski, "Era of Good Feelings"
Vincent J. Capowski. "The Era of Good Feelings in New Hampshire: The Gubernatorial Campaigns of Levi Woodbury, 1823, 1824." *Historical New Hampshire* 21 (Winter 1966): 3–30.

Capowski, *Making of Democrat*
Vincent Julian Capowski. *The Making of a Jacksonian Democrat: Levi Woodbury, 1789–1831* (Ph.D. diss., Fordham University, 1966).

Carpenter, *Judicial Tenure*
William S. Carpenter. *Judicial Tenure in the United States With Especial Reference to the Tenure of Federal Judges*. New Haven, CT: Yale University Press, 1918.

Carrington, "Judicial Independence"
Paul D. Carrington. "Judicial Independence and Democratic Accountability in Highest State Courts." *Law and Contemporary Problems* 61 (Summer 1998): 79–126.

Chief Justice
John Phillip Reid. *Chief Justice: The Judicial World of Charles Doe*. Cambridge, MA: Harvard University Press, 1967.

Claggett, *Speech in House*
William Claggett. *Speech of William Claggett, Esq. in the House of Representatives of N. H. June Session, 1814*. Concord, NH: Isaac and W. R. Hill, 1814.

Clement, *Discourse on Richardson*
Jonathan Clement. *Discourse Delivered at the Funeral of Hon. William M. Richardson, on the 26th Day of March, A. D., 1838*. Concord, NH: 1838.

Cole, *Jacksonian Democracy*
Donald B. Cole. *Jacksonian Democracy in New Hampshire, 1800–1851*. Cambridge, MA: Harvard University Press, 1970.

*Collections Historical*
*Collections Historical and Miscellaneous; and Monthly Literary Journal*. Volumes 1, 2, and 3. Concord, NH: J. B. Moore, 1824.

*Communication from Governor*
*Communication from his Excellency the Governor, Covering the Report of the Jus-*

*tices of the Superior Court, on the Question of Granting New Trials.* n.i., [1819].

Concord Gazette

*Concord Gazette.* A weekly newspaper published in Concord, New Hampshire.

Concord Herald

*Concord Herald.* A weekly newspaper published in Concord, New Hampshire.

*Constitutionalist*

*The Constitutionalist and Weekly Magazine.* A weekly newspaper published in Exeter, New Hampshire.

*Controlling the Law*

John Phillip Reid. *Controlling the Law: Legal Politics in Early National New Hampshire.* DeKalb: Northern Illinois University Press, 2004.

Cooke, *Oration at Keene*

Phinehas Cooke. *An Oration, Delivered at Keene, N. H. Before the Washington Benevolent Society, on the 5th Day of July, 1813, Being the Anniversary of American Independence.* Keene, NH: John Prentiss, 1813.

Corning, "Highest Courts of Law"

Charles R. Corning. "The Highest Courts of Law in New Hampshire: Colonial, Provincial, and State." *Green Bag* 2 (1890): 469–89.

*Courier of New Hampshire*

*Courier of New Hampshire.* A weekly newspaper published in Concord, New Hampshire.

*Democratic Republican*

*Democratic Republican.* A weekly newspaper published in Walpole, New Hampshire.

Douglas, "Judicial Review"

Charles G. Douglas III. "Judicial Review and the Separation of Powers under the New Hampshire Constitutions of 1776 and 1784." *New Hampshire Bar Journal* 18 (1977): 250–64.

Egan, "Path to War"

Clifford L. Egan. "The Path to War in 1812 through the Eyes of a New Hampshire 'War Hawk.'" *Historical New Hampshire* 30 (Fall 1975): 147–77.

Eighth Plumer Letterbook

Letters to & from William Plumer Volume 8th. Beginning November 11. 1809, and Ending August 1. 1815. (Library of Congress, reel 3, container 8).

Evans, *Appeal to People*

Estwick Evans. *An Appeal to the People of New-Hampshire.* Exeter, NH: Henry A Ranlet, 1817.

*Farmer's Cabinet*

*The Farmer's Cabinet.* A weekly newspaper published in Amherst, New Hampshire.

*Farmer's Museum*

*Farmer's Museum, or Literary Gazette.* A weekly newspaper published in Walpole, New Hampshire.

First Plumer Letterbook

A Collection of Letters written to and by William Plumer, and transcribed for his Amusement & Instruction. Many to Jere[miah] Smith, MC. Volume 1. From January 18, 1781 to January 14, 1804. Contains 177 Letters, *Plumer Documents* (Library of Congress, reel 2, container 4).

Fourth Plumer Letterbook

Letters to & from William Plumer from January 25, 1804 to February 6th 1807. Volume 4th. *Plumer Documents* (Library of Congress, reel 3, container 7).

Fuess, *Daniel Webster*

Claude Moore Fuess. *Daniel Webster.* Volume 1 (1782–1830). Boston: Little, Brown, 1930.

Gannon, "Escaping Jefferson's Plan"

Kevin M. Gannon. "Escaping 'Mr. Jefferson's Plan of Destruction': New England Federalists and the Idea of a Northern Confederacy, 1803–1804." *Journal of the Early Republic* 21 (Fall 2001): 413–43.

Gates, *Oration at Bedford*

Isaac Gates. *An Oration Pronounced Publicly at Bedford, New-Hampshire. Before the Washington Benevolent Society in that Place, July 4th, 1814.* Concord, NH: George Hough, 1814.

General Regulations for Bar

*General Regulations for the Gentlemen of the Bar of New Hampshire.* Portsmouth, NH: J. Melcher, 1805.

Grafton Journal

*Grafton Journal.* A weekly newspaper published in Plymouth, New Hampshire.

Graham, *To Bring Law Home*

D. Kurt Graham. *To Bring Law Home: The Federal Judiciary in Early National Rhode Island.* DeKalb: Northern Illinois University Press, 2010.

Gray, "Jeremiah Mason"

John Chipman Gray. "Jeremiah Mason." In *Great American Lawyers: The Lives and Influence of Judges and Lawyers Who Have Acquired Permanent National Reputation, and Have Developed the Jurisprudence of the United States,* edited by William Draper Lewis, vol. 3: 3–36. Philadelphia: John C. Winston, 1908.

Gubernatorial Papers

Original Manuscript Acts Signed by William Plumer: Partial Representation of Original Acts found at New Hampshire State Archives. *Plumer Documents* (Reel 21, Frames 1 to 305).

Hesse, "Legislature, Court and Constitution"

Richard Hesse. "The Legislature, the Court and the Constitution." *New Hampshire Bar Journal* 41, no. 1 (March 2000): 38–45.

Historical Society Correspondence

Correspondence of William Plumer, New Hampshire Historical Society, *Plumer Documents* (Reel 8).

Holmes, "Address"

Nathaniel Holmes. "An Address Delivered at the 150th Anniversary of the town of Peterborough, N. H., October 24, 1889." In *Proceedings of the Susqui-Centennial Celebration Held at Peterborough, N. H. Thursday, Oct. 24, 1889*, pp. 16–56. "Peterboro," NH: Peterboro' Transcript Office, 1890.

Holmes, "Use of Law Schools"

Oliver Wendell Holmes. "The Use of Law Schools." In Oliver Wendell Holmes, *Collected Legal Papers*, 35–48. New York: Harcourt, Brace, 1920.

Horton, *James Kent*

John Theodore Horton. *James Kent: A Study in Conservatism, 1763–1847*. New York: D. Appleton-Century, 1939.

*House Journal* (June 1810)

*Journal of the House of Representatives of the State of New-Hampshire, at their Session Begun and Holden at Concord, on the First Wednesday of June, 1810*. Concord, NH: Isaac Hill, 1810.

*House Journal* (June 1812)

*Journal of the House of Representatives of the State of New Hampshire, at their Session Begun and Holden at Concord, on the First Wednesday of June, Anno Domini, 1812*. Concord, NH: Isaac and W. R. Hill, 1812.

*House Journal* (November 1812)

*Journal of the House of Representatives of the State of New-Hampshire, at their Session, Begun and Holden at Concord, on the third Wednesday of November, 1812*. Concord, NH, 1813.

*House Journal* (October 1813)

*Journal of the Proceedings of the House of Representatives of the State of New-Hampshire, at their Special Session, Begun and Holden at Concord, on Wednesday, October 27, 1813*. Concord, NH, 1813.

*House Journal* (June 1814)

*Journal of the House of Representatives of the State of New-Hampshire, at their Session, Holden at Concord, on the First Wednesday of June, 1814*. Concord, NH: George Hough, 1814.

*House Journal* (June 1818)

*Journal of the House of Representatives, of the State of New-Hampshire, at their Session Begun and Holden at Concord, on the First Wednesday of June, Anno Domini, 1818*. Concord, NH: Isaac Hill, 1818.

Ireland, *County Courts in Kentucky*

Robert M. Ireland. *The County Courts in Antebellum Kentucky*. Lexington, KY: University Press of Kentucky, 1972.

Johnson, "Dartmouth College Case"

Eldon L. Johnson. "The Dartmouth College Case: The Neglected Educational Meaning." *Journal of the Early Republic* 3 (Spring 1983): 45–67.

Judicial Act of 1813

"An Act Establishing a Supreme Judicial Court, and Circuit Court of

Commons Pleas." *The Public Laws of the State of New-Hampshire, Passed at a Session of the General Court, Begun and Holden at Concord on the First Wednesday of June, 1813*. Concord, NH: Published by Authority, 1813.

Kutler, *Charles River Bridge Case*

Stanley I. Kutler. *Privilege and Creative Destruction: The Charles River Bridge Case*. Philadelphia: J. B. Lippincott, 1971.

Lambert, *Ten Pound Act*

Richard M. Lambert. *The "Ten Pound Act" in Cases and the Origins of Judicial Review in New Hampshire* (master's thesis, University of New Hampshire, 1985).

Lawrie, "Interpretation and Authority"

Timothy A. Lawrie. "Interpretation and Authority: Separation of Powers and the Judiciary's Battle for Independence in New Hampshire, 1786–1818." *American Journal of Legal History* 39 (1995): 310–36.

Legislating the Courts

John Phillip Reid. *Legislating the Courts: Judicial Dependence in Early National New Hampshire*. DeKalb: Northern Illinois University Press, 2009.

Leidtker, *Political Development*

Frank L. Leidtker. *Political Development in New Hampshire from the Revolution to 1850* (master's thesis, University of New Hampshire, 1952).

Marietta and Rowe, *Troubled Experiment*

Jack D. Marietta and G. S. Rowe. *Troubled Experiment: Crime and Justice in Pennsylvania, 1682–1800*. Philadelphia: University of Pennsylvania Press, 2006.

Mayo, *John Langdon*

Laurence Shaw Mayo. *John Langdon of New Hampshire*. Port Washington, NY: Kennikat Press, 1970.

Mays, *Edmund Pendleton*

David John Mays. *Edmund Pendleton, 1721–1803: A Biography*. Volume 2. Cambridge, MA: Harvard University Press, 1952.

McNamara, "Separation of Powers"

Richard B. McNamara. "The Separation of Powers Principle and the Role of the Courts in New Hampshire." *New Hampshire Bar Journal* 42, no. 2 (June 2001): 66–87.

Melhorn, *Lest We Be Marshall'd*

Donald F. Melhorn, Jr. *Lest We Be Marshall'd: Judicial Powers and Politics in Ohio, 1806–1812*. Akron, OH: University of Akron Press, 2003.

Memoirs of Jeremiah Mason

*Memoirs of Jeremiah Mason: Reproduction of privately printed Edition of 1873 Illustrated and Annotated by G. J. Clark of Kansas City, Mo*. Boston: Boston Law Book, 1917.

Morison, *Life and Letters of Otis*

Samuel Eliot Morison. *The Life and Letters of Harrison Gray Otis, Federalist, 1765–1848*. 2 vols. Boston: Houghton Mifflin, 1913.

Morison, *Life of Smith*
John H. Morison. *Life of the Hon. Jeremiah Smith, LL.D.* Boston: Charles C. Little and James Brown, 1845.

Murphy and Van Oot, "Judicial Independence"
Walter L. Murphy and Mary Van Oot. "Please Be Careful with the Constitution: A Call for the Preservation of Judicial Independence." *New Hampshire Bar Journal* 42, no. 2 (June 2001): 11–15.

Nelson, *Americanization*
William E. Nelson. *The Americanization of the Common Law: The Impact of Legal Change on Massachusetts Society, 1760–1830.* Cambridge, MA: Harvard University Press, 1975.

Nelson, "Cases of the Judges"
Margaret V. Nelson. "The Cases of the Judges." *Virginia Law Review* 31 (December 1944): 243–55.

Nelson, *Common Law in Colonial America*
William Edward Nelson. *The Common Law in Colonial America: The Chesapeake and New England: 1607–1660.* New York: Oxford University Press, 2008.

New Hampshire Constitution
The New Hampshire Constitution 1784–1984: 200 Years of Constitutional Government. N.i., 1985.

*New Hampshire Gazette*
*The New Hampshire Gazette.* A newspaper published weekly in Portsmouth, New Hampshire.

*New-Hampshire Patriot*
*The New-Hampshire Patriot.* A weekly newspaper published in Concord, New Hampshire.

New Hampshire the State
*New Hampshire the State that Made Us a Nation: A Celebration of the Bicentennial of the United States Constitution.* Edited by William M. Gardner, Frank C. Mevers, Richard F. Upton. Portsmouth, NH: Peter E. Randall, 1989.

*Newhampshire Sentinel*
*Newhampshire Sentinel.* A weekly newspaper published in Keene, NH.

Ninth Plumer Letterbook
Letters to & from William Plumer, commencing July 22, 1817 and ending August 5, 1833. Vol. 9. *Plumer Documents* (Library of Congress, reel 4, container 9).

Opal, "Politics of Industry"
J. M. Opal. "The Politics of 'Industry': Federalism in Concord and Exeter, New Hampshire, 1790–1805." *Journal of the Early Republic* 20 (Winter 2000): 637–71.

*Opinions of Clagett and Evans*
*Opinions of the Hon. Clifton Clagett, and Hon. Richard Evans, Justices of the Superior Court of Judicature, on the Act of the Legislature of New-Hampshire,*

*Passed June 24, A.D. 1813, Entitled "An Act establishing a Supreme Judicial Court, and Circuit Courts of Common Pleas."* N.i., n.d.

Paludan, *Covenant with Death*

Phillip S. Paludan. *A Covenant with Death: The Constitution, Law, and Equality in the Civil War Era*. Urbana: University of Illinois Press, 1975.

*Papers of Marshall*

*The Papers of John Marshall: Volume 6, Correspondence, Papers, and Selected Judicial Opinions, November 1800–March 1807*. Edited by Charles F. Hobson. Chapel Hill: University of North Carolina Press, 1990.

Parker, *Charge to Grand Jury*

Joel Parker, *A Charge to the Grand Jury, upon the Importance of Maintaining the Supremacy of the Laws; with a Brief Sketch of William M. Richardson, Late Chief Justice of the Superior Court of New-Hampshire*. Concord, NH: Marsh, Capen and Lyon, 1838.

Parker, *Courts and Lawyers*

Herbert Parker. *Courts and Lawyers of New England*. 4 vols. New York: American Historical Society, 1934.

*People's Advocate*

*The People's Advocate*. A weekly newspaper, published in Portsmouth, New Hampshire.

[Plumer,] *Address to Electors*

[William Plumer.] *An Address to the Electors of New-Hampshire*. N.i., 1804.

Plumer, *Autobiography*

William Plumer. Memoirs of William Plumer With some Account of the Men, Measures, & Events of the Times in which he Lived. *Plumer Documents* (Library of Congress, reel 4, container 12).

Plumer, "Caleb Ellis"

William Plumer. "Caleb Ellis." *Plumer Documents* (Library of Congress, reel 12, vol. 5, frame 143).

Plumer, "Clifton Clagett"

William Plumer. "Clifton Clagett." *Plumer Documents* (Library of Congress, reel 12, vol. 5, frames 313–14, pp. 459–61).

*Plumer Documents*

Microfilm copies of the papers of William Plumer at the New Hampshire State Library and the Library of Congress. The first three reels contain letters in chronological order, and when cited those letters are not identified by reel.

Plumer, *Essays and Writings*

William Plumer. Proclamations, Political & Other Writings: A Collection of Essays and Writings. *Plumer Documents* (Library of Congress, reel 5, container 14).

Plumer, "John Langdon"

William Plumer. "John Langdon." *Plumer Documents* (Library of Congress, reel 12, vol. 5, frames 178–81, pp. 194–200).

Plumer, "Jonathan Steele,"
William Plumer. "Jonathan Steele." *Plumer Documents* (Library of Congress, reel 12, vol. 5, frames 244–47).

Plumer Letters to His Brother
Untitled Letterbook, Containing Letters from 7 December 1802 to 11 February 1807, from William Plumer to his Brother, Daniel Plumer. *Plumer Documents* (Library of Congress, reel 3, container 6).

Plumer, *Memorandum*
*William Plumer's Memorandum of Proceedings in the United States Senate, 1803–1807.* Edited by Everett Somerville Brown. New York: Macmillan, 1923.

[Plumer,] *Message from His Excellency*
[William Plumer.] *Message from His Excellency the Governor of New-Hampshire, to the Legislature, June 4, 1818.* N.i., n.d.

*Plumer Papers*
*Plumer Papers Correspondence* (mss. New Hampshire State Library).

Plumer, *Plumer*
William Plumer, Jr. *Life of William Plumer.* Boston: Phillips, Sampson, 1857.

Plumer, *Proclamations and Writings*
William Plumer, Proclamations, Political & Other Writings of William Plumer, Vol. 1. *Plumer Documents* (Library of Congress, reel 4, container 13).

Plumer, *Register I*
William Plumer, *Register Volume I (commencing May 2d 1805, & ending April 21, 1807), Plumer Documents* (Library of Congress, reel 1, containers 1 and 2).

Plumer, *Register II*
William Plumer, *The Register of Opinions & Events—his Rending of so, of William Plumer From May 1, 1807 to April 2, 1836. Plumer Documents* (Library of Congress, reel 1, container 3).

Plumer, Repository I
The Repository; Being a collection of Charges given to the Grand Juries; sentences pronounced against criminals; rules established by courts of law; and the regulations of the bar in the State of New Hampshire. Messages & Addresses from public bodies to the public & to & from public officers. Observations & Essays on various subjects. Volume 1. Collected by William Plumer for his own eye. *Plumer Documents* (Library of Congress, reel 13, frames 1–139).

Plumer, Repository II
The Repository being a Collection of Letters, Extracts from Records, Papers, Essays &c. Volume 2d (Library of Congress, reel 6, container 18).

Plumer, Repository V
Repository. A Collection of Facts Anecdotes, & observations. For private use by William Plumer. Volume 5. *Plumer Documents* (Library of Congress, reel 13, frames 491–713).

Plumer, "Richard Evans"

William Plumer. "Richard Evans." *Plumer Documents* (Library of Congress, biography vol. 5, reel 12, frames 132–33).

Plumer, *Speech on War*

William Plumer. *Speech of His Excellency William Plumer, November Session, 1812.* [Concord, NH: Isaac Hill, 1812].

*Portsmouth Journal*

*Portsmouth Journal of Literature & Politics.* A weekly newspaper published in Portsmouth, New Hampshire.

*Portsmouth Oracle*

*The Portsmouth Oracle.* Weekly newspaper published in Portsmouth, New Hampshire.

Pound, *Formative Era*

Roscoe Pound. *The Formative Era of American Law.* Boston: Little, Brown, 1938.

Preyer, "Federalist Policy"

Kathryn Preyer. "Federalist Policy and the Judiciary Act of 1801." In *Blackstone in America: Selected Essays of Kathryn Preyer*, edited by Mary Sarah Bilder, Maeva Marcus, and R. Kent Newmyer, 10–38. New York: Cambridge University Press, 2009.

Preyer, "Midnight Judges"

Kathryn Preyer. "The Midnight Judges." In *Blackstone in America: Selected Essays of Kathryn Preyer*, edited by Mary Sarah Bilder, Maeva Marcus, and R. Kent Newmyer, 59–91. New York: Cambridge University Press, 2009.

Proceedings of the Legislature

*Proceedings of the Legislature of New-Hampshire, on the Important Subjects Referred to in the Governor's Speech, at the Opening of the Special Session, October 27, 1813.* Concord, NH: George Hough, 1813.

*Public Laws June 1813*

*The Public Laws of the State of New Hampshire, Passed at a Session of the General Court, Begun and Holden at Concord, on the First Wednesday of June, 1813.* Concord, NH: George Hough, 1813.

*Public Laws 1813*

*The Public Laws of the State of New-Hampshire, Passed at a Session of the General Court, Begun and Holden at Concord, on Wednesday the Twenty-Seventh Day of October, 1813.* Concord, NH: 1813.

Publicola, *New Vade Mecum*

Publicola. *New Vade Mecum: Or a Pocket Companion for Lawyers, Deputy Sheriffs and Constables; Suggesting Many Grievous Abuses and Alarming Evils, which Attend the Present Mode of Administering the Laws of New Hampshire.* Concord, NH: Hews and Goss, and Isaac Hill, 1819.

Rantoul, *Eulogy on Woodbury*

Robert Rantoul, Jr. *Eulogy on the Hon. Levi Woodbury, Pronounced at Portsmouth, N. H. October 10, 1851, at the Request of the City Government.* Portsmouth, NH: C. W. Brewster & Son, 1852.

*Remains of Haven*

*The Remains of Nathaniel Appleton Haven. With a Memoir of his Life, by George Ticknor.* Cambridge, MA: Hilliard, Metcalf, 1827.

Report on Memorials
Report of Committee on Memorials, 5 November 1813. *House Journal* (October 1813): 71–85.

"Resolution of 29 November 1815"
Resolution of 29 November 1815, House of Representatives. *Acts of the General Assembly of the State of Georgia; Passed at Milledgeville; at an Annual Session, in November and December, 1815* (1815): 132–33.

Richardson, *Oration at Groton*
William Merchant Richardson. *An Oration Pronounced at Groton, July, 4, 1801; in Commemoration of the Anniversary of American Independence.* Amherst, NH: Samuel Preston, 1801.

Robinson, "Bartlett, Ichabod"
William Alexander Robinson. "Bartlett, Ichabod." In *Dictionary of American Biography*, 2: 5–6. New York: Charles Scribner's Sons, 1927.

Robinson, *Isaac Hill*
Francis E. Robinson. *Isaac Hill* (master's thesis, University of New Hampshire, 1933).

Robinson, "Perley, Ira"
William Alexander Robinson. "Perley, Ira." In *Dictionary of American Biography*, 7: 478. New York: Charles Scribner's Sons, 1934.

Roeber, *Faithful Magistrates and Republican Lawyers*
A. G. Roeber. *Faithful Magistrates and Republican Lawyers: Creators of Virginia Legal Culture, 1680–1810.* Chapel Hill: University of North Carolina Press, 1981.

Rowe, *Embattled Bench*
G. S. Rowe. *Embattled Bench: the Pennsylvania Supreme Court and the Forging of a Democratic Society, 1684–1809.* Newark: University of Delaware Press, 1994.

Rowe, *Thomas McKean*
G. S. Rowe. *Thomas McKean: The Shaping of an American Republicanism.* Boulder: Colorado Associated University Press, 1978.

*Rule of Law*
John Phillip Reid. *Rule of Law: The Jurisprudence of Liberty in the Seventeenth and Eighteenth Centuries.* DeKalb: Northern Illinois University Press, 2004.

*Senate Journal* (June 1809)
*Journal of the Honorable Senate of the State of New-Hampshire, at their Session, Holden at Concord, on the first Wednesday of June, 1809.* Concord, NH: 1809.

*Senate Journal* (June 1810)
*Journal of the Honorable Senate of the State of New-Hampshire, at their Session, Begun and Holden at Concord, on the first Wednesday of June, Anno Domini, 1810.* Concord, NH: Isaac Hill, 1810.

*Senate Journal* (June 1813)
*Journal of the Honorable Senate of the State of New-Hampshire, at their Session, Holden at Concord, on the First Wednesday of June, 1813.* Concord, NH: George Hough, 1813.

*Senate Journal* (October 1813)
*Journal of the Proceedings of the Honorable Senate of the State of New-Hampshire, at their Session, Begun and Holden at Concord, on Wednesday,*

*October 27, 1813*. Concord, NH: George Hough, 1813.

*Senate Journal* (November 1816)

*Journal of the Honorable Senate of the State of New-Hampshire, at their Session, Begun and Holden at Concord, on the third Wednesday of November, 1816*. Concord, NH: Isaac Hill, 1817.

*Senate Journal* (June 1856)

*Journal of the Honorable Senate of the State of New Hampshire, June Session, 1856*. Concord, NH: Amos Hadley, 1856.

Shirley, *Dartmouth College Causes*

John M. Shirley. *The Dartmouth College Causes and the Supreme Court of the United States*. St. Louis, MO: G. I. Jones, 1879.

Shirley, "Reporter's Note"

John Major Shirley. "Reporter's Note." 55 N.H. 6–8 (1876).

Smith, *Probate Law*

Jeremiah Smith. *Treatise on Probate Law* (mss), excerpts printed in *Smith's Reports*, 447–520.

Smith, *Sketch of Ellis*

Chief Justice [Jeremiah] Smith. *A Sketch of the Character of the Late Judge Ellis, as Delivered to the Grand Jury, after the usual Charge at the Opening of the Supreme Judicial Court, at Haverhill, on the 21st of May, 1816*. Portsmouth, NH: Charles Turell, 1816.

*Smith's Reports*

*Decisions of the Superior and Supreme Courts of New Hampshire From 1802 to 1809, and from 1813 to 1816. Selected from the Manuscript Reports of the Late Jeremiah Smith, Chief Justice of those Courts. With Extracts from Judge Smith's Manuscript Treatise on Probate Law, and from his other Legal Manuscripts*. Boston: Little, Brown, 1879.

*Speak for Yourself, Daniel*

*Speak for Yourself, Daniel: A Life of Webster in his Own Words*. Edited by Walker Lewis. Boston: Houghton Mifflin, 1969.

Stearns, "Livermore"

Ezra S. Stearns. "Hon. Arthur Livermore." *Proceedings of the Grafton and Coos County Bar Association* 9 (1892): 429–49.

Streichler, "Parker, Joel"

Stuart A. Streichler, "Parker, Joel," *American National Biography* 17 (1999): 31–32.

Sullivan, *Speech at Rockingham Convention*

George Sullivan. *Speech of the Hon. George Sullivan, at the Rockingham Convention, with the Memorial & Resolutions, and the Report of the Committee of Elections*. Concord, NH: George Hough, 1812.

Tachau, *Federal Courts*

Mary K. Bonsteel Tachau. *Federal Courts in the Early Republic: Kentucky, 1789–1816*. Princeton, NJ: Princeton University Press, 1978.

Taishoff, "State Politics"

Sue Taishoff. "New Hampshire State Politics and the Concept of a Party System, 1800–1840." *Historical New Hampshire* 31 (Spring-Summer 1976): 17–43.

Third Plumer Letterbook
Letters to & from William Plumer. Volume 3.5 (Library of Congress, reel 2, container 5).

Turner, "Jefferson Through Plumer"
Lynn W. Turner. "Thomas Jefferson Through the Eyes of a New Hampshire Politician." *Mississippi Valley Historical Review* 30 (September 1943): 205–14.

Turner, *Ninth State*
Lynn Warren Turner. *The Ninth State: New Hampshire's Formative Years.* Chapel Hill: University of North Carolina Press, 1983.

Turner, *Plumer*
Lynn W. Turner. *William Plumer of New Hampshire 1759–1850.* Chapel Hill: University of North Carolina Press, 1962.

Upton, "Independence of Judiciary"
Richard F. Upton. "The Independence of the Judiciary in New Hampshire." *New Hampshire Bar Journal* 1, no. 4 (July 1959): 28–39.

Wait, "William Plumer"
Albert S. Wait. "William Plumer." In *Proceedings of the New Hampshire Historical Society*, vol. 3, part 1: 119–42. Concord, NH: Printed for the Society, 1897.

[Webster,] *Appeal to Old Whigs*
[Daniel Webster.] *An Appeal to the Old Whigs of New-Hampshire.* N.i, 1805.

*Webster Legal Papers*
*The Papers of Daniel Webster: Legal Papers, Vol. 1: The New Hampshire Practice.* Edited by Alfred S. Konefsky and Andrew J. King. Hanover, NH: University Press of New England, 1982.

*Webster Papers*
*The Papers of Daniel Webster: Correspondence, Vol. 1: 1798–1824.* Edited by Charles M. Wiltse. Hanover, NH: University Press of New England, 1974.

White, *American Judicial Tradition*
G. Edward White. *The American Judicial Tradition: Profiles of Leading American Judges.* New York: Oxford University Press, 1976.

Woodbury, *Memoir of Woodbury*
Charles Levi Woodbury. *Memoir of Levi Woodbury*. Cambridge, MA: John Wilson and Son, 1881.

Worcester, *Fast Day Sermon at Salisbury*
Noah Worcester. *Abraham and Lot: A Sermon on the Way of Peace, and the Evils of War. Delivered at Salisbury, in New-Hampshire, on the Day of the National Fast, August 20, 1812.* Concord, NH: George Hough, 1812.

# Acknowledgments

Support for research was provided by the Filomen D'Agostino and Max E. Greenberg Faculty Research Fund at New York University School of Law and by Richard L. Revesz, dean of the School of Law. Research was made easier and convenient by the professional competence, help, and good cheer of the staff of the Huntington Library, in San Marino, California. Much of this book was written at the Huntington Library, where all activity is made pleasant by the encouragement of Alan Jutzi, Roy Ritchie, David Zeidberg, Susi Krasnoo, and Juan Gomez. The research was conducted chiefly in New York and New Hampshire. At New York University I owe special debts of gratitude to Calvin Hudson, who tracked many of the elusive and poorly indexed New Hampshire laws; to Kris Dalman, who obtained materials not readily available on Washington Square; and to Gretchen Feltes, Conservation Librarian at the School of Law, who with her computer found material I otherwise would not have discovered. Cite and substance checking was entrusted first to Barbara Wilcie Kern and later to Michelle Pinto. And finally, special heartfelt thanks are to be given to Annmarie Zell of the library of the School of Law who, when working on our companion volume, *Legislating the Courts*, spent hours tracking down the pictures of Jeremiah Smith, William Plumer, and Arthur Livermore and even more time obtaining reproductions suitable for publication. She also volunteered to complete this book by accepting on short notice the task of indexing when there was only one week to do the job.

In some inexplicable manner this study may have benefited from being read, discussed, and criticized by members of that distinguished gathering of American legal historians, the members of the New York University School of Law Colloquium in Legal History, led by William Edward Nelson and Daniel Hulsebosch, and including William P. LaPiana, Martin S. Flaherty, and especially Richard Bruce Bernstein, who fleshed out the sources for the introductory pages.

Finally special thanks are due to Douglas MacLennan, the well-known Franklin Pierce scholar. He prevented a serious error when, after reading chapter nine, he corrected Franklin Pierce's answer to Daniel Webster, who had criticized Pierce's father, the sheriff of Hillsborough County, for refusing to support Jeremiah Smith and Caleb Ellis when they attempted to use the courtroom in Amherst. MacLennan pointed out that Pierce did not say, as is reported in most New Hampshire histories, "When sheriff of Hillsborough County, my father refused to cooperate with Judge Smith because he believed the Judicial Act of 1813 was not only politically wrong, it was unconstitutional." Rather, Pierce explained, "My father was impressed with Richard Evans. Like Evans my father was not a lawyer. Smith and Ellis were lawyers. My father believed nonlawyers should be judges on the high court and felt Evans more qualified to be a judge than were Smith and Ellis. That's why he put Jeremiah Smith out of the courtroom at Amherst."

# Index

Lightning Source UK Ltd.
Milton Keynes UK
UKHW010336050719
345621UK00009B/511/P

9 780875 804514